NELSON'S ANNUAL

Youth Ministry Sourcebook

2005 EDITION

Nelson's Annual Youth Ministry Sourcebook

2005 EDITION

AMY JACOBER, EDITOR

NELSON REFERENCE & ELECTRONIC
A Division of Thomas Nelson Publishers
Since 1798

www.thomasnelson.com

Nelson's Annual Youth Ministry Sourcebook, 2005 Edition

Copyright © 2004 by Thomas Nelson, Inc.

Published in Nashville, Tennessee, by Thomas Nelson, Inc.

Book design and composition by Bob Bubnis, Booksetters, Inc., White House, Tennessee

Jacober, Amy Elizabeth (ed.)

Nelson's annual youth ministry sourcebook, 2005 edition

ISBN 0-7852-5206-1

Printed in the United States of America

1 2 3 4 5 6 7—08 07 06 05 04

CONTENTS

Feature Articles

So there I was, facing the student portion of my interview for my first church position. I figured that since I was a seminary graduate, I could hold my own with a bunch of junior high and high school students. Among the first questions asked was clearly from one of the leaders of the group. She raised her hand and before the din of whispers had ended she said, "We don't consider the Bible a valid document. What are you going to do now?" Coming from the West coast to the Bible belt, I never saw that one coming! And so my career in youth ministry began. It was a rough first 6 months (not to mention 12 months, 18 months, etc.), but we did get to a place of understanding. By the grace of God (and I mean that quite literally, not just as a convenient phrase), I walked alongside a group of cultural Christian students and witnessed them become a tight-knit, growing community seeking after Jesus.

I learned a lot in those first few years on staff. There are days when I think I need to track down every student I had in those days, to whom I am certain I taught something terribly wrong if not heretical. I had the heart, I even had the head knowledge, but to make it work in real life week after week—for that I wasn't so certain.

My struggles have shifted over the years. I no longer feel nauseous at the thought of preparing a lesson. I am much better at handling off-the-wall questions. Still, in the back of my head is the thought, can I really do this week after week? There are some weeks I feel better about what I have taught. You know those times when you just know you nailed it! Other weeks I simply wish I had a secret tunnel to my car so I could drive away in anonymous shame, knowing I nearly put them to sleep or ended up so off track that no one knew what the lesson was!

And then I remember. It's not about me. In fact, the more I worry and the focus is on me, the less my focus (and consequently that of my students) is on God. We all have bad days. We are all in danger of having a ministry that feeds our own egos instead of honoring God.

I have been picking up on a trend the last five years or so based on frequent comments I hear. I don't know if it has always been there and I am just now hearing it, but it is strong and clear. Comments like "Well, I'm probably the worst youth minister in the world anyway" or

"Too bad our students couldn't have a real minister. I'm just a volunteer." Again, this makes it about you and not about God!

Let's pretend for a minute that you indeed are *the worst youth minister in the world*! Congratulations! That is quite a title to engrave on your trophy. Whether you are the worst or not is irrelevant. If God has called you and God is in you, that is all you need. Do not be intimidated. That false sense of humility is nothing more than pride talking! And perhaps being let in on a little secret will help: Even those who speak and teach and write all of the time, in their most honest of moments, still wonder if they are doing it the right way. The more you shift the focus to God, the less the focus will be on you. All of this is to say: "You have been called by God to a special ministry!"

And now the connection to this book.

I am not certain whether it is easier to say what this book IS or IS NOT. It is not meant to be the easy way out. While there are many useful lessons, games, stories, songs, resources, and a whole bunch of helpful tips on everything from tending your own soul to the logistics of teaching, these are just tools. They are useless without your own heart, insight, and spirit behind them. Remember, just because it is written in ink on paper does not mean that you must do it that way. In fact, I encourage at least three things before every lesson.

(1) Pray that God will teach you so that as you lead, you may lead out of the overflow of your heart! Pray for your students as you wrestle with what it means to be a follower of Jesus.

(2) Read the Scripture in your own Bible before you read anything from this book. Let it speak to you and see what God is teaching you in those words.

(3) Pick up a pen or pencil before you read over the lesson. Mark it up, cross out what does not apply to your group, re-write it, add to it. Know that you do not have to do everything that is suggested!

The best teachers are not those who can follow the book, but those who know the Word, have taken the time to wrestle with it on their own, and can bring it to a group—not like a lesson to be memorized but out of the reality of their own lives. You will find very few stories or illustrations throughout this book. That is intentional. Use stories from your own life, from your own community.

God has called you (not us!) to work in your church. My hope is to be a support and an encouragement along the way, knowing that the

Holy Spirit will be working through you to minister to teenagers I will never meet. Know you have been prayed for by many fellow youth workers long before this book ever made it to print.

May this book be a springboard for your own creative self, to allow your students to experience the vitality not only of Scripture but of following Jesus in their lives.

CONTRIBUTORS

Dr. Cliff Anderson—A longtime youth worker and leader of youth workers, Cliff is the Vice President of Recruitment, Training, and Deployment for Young Life. While known and respected for his official work, he is often most appreciated for his natural giftedness as an encourager. Cliff makes his home in Colorado Springs, Colorado.

Anna Aven—After having worked the last few years as the junior high director at United Christian Church in Los Angeles, Anna is now pursuing a Ph.D. at King's College in London.

Dr. Chap Clark—A youth ministry veteran after years of staff and volunteer work with Young Life, Chap is a well-known speaker and writer and is currently Associate Professor of Youth, Family, and Culture at Fuller Theological Seminary.

Alicia Claxton—She has been actively involved in student ministry in various capacities for over 10 years. In addition to being a free-lance writer, she has worked in both the Christian music and Christian camping fields. Though she travels extensively, she considers Franklin, Tennessee, to be home.

Carrie Hildebrand—A senior in Seattle Pacific University, Carrie is active in her church and already a servant leader!

Dr. Amy Jacober—She has been both a volunteer and paid church staff youth worker. She has volunteered with Young Life and now is an Assistant Professor of Youth Ministry and Practical Theology at Azusa Pacific University. Raised in Phoenix, Arizona, she considers LA her second home.

John Losey—He has been teaching and leading people for 20 years and is currently director of Praxis Training Systems in Costa Mesa, California. His expertise is facilitating, program design, and staff development workshops. He speaks at conferences and has consulted for such organizations as Campus Life, Forest Home Christian Conference Center, Amor Ministries, and Center for Student Missions.

Debbie Karpinski-Novero—A designer by trade, Debbie has also worked as a volunteer leader at youth camps in both Bible study and in creative brainstorming workshops. She is from Ohio and now makes Los Angeles her home.

Sharon Koh—Her last few years have been spent as pastoral intern at United Christian Church, in Los Angeles. Sharon has just graduated from Fuller Theological Seminary with an M.Div.

Ric Lipsey—A fifteen-year youth ministry veteran, Ric has run the gamut from volunteer, to summer camps, to junior high minister and now to is the point person for the entire student ministry at First Baptist Church, Pasadena, Texas.

Amanda MacMillan—A Young Life volunteer and college student at Azusa Pacific University, Amanda brings energy and a desire to serve and learn to all she does.

Nathan Novero—An amazing blend of deep thought and remarkable talent, Nathan is a film editor in Hollywood, a camp pastor in the summers, and longtime youth group volunteer. A native of Arkansas, he now makes Los Angeles his home.

Tivis Ryan O'Quinn—His primary job is that of an actor. He also finds time for freelance writing, and his summers are filled with being a camp pastor and director in both the U.S. and Korea. Originally from Virginia, he now lives in Los Angeles.

Adam Robinson—He has spent the last seven years traveling as a speaker/evangelist for various camps, retreats, and churches. Currently he may be found as a teaching minister at The Church at Brook Hills, Birmingham, Alabama.

Dick Staub—He is host of a website on popular culture, speaker, writer, and longtime radio personality. He brings years of critical thought to topics related to the lives of adolescents. He currently calls Seattle, Washington, home.

Rick Steele—He is most often known as a professor of theology or a minister in the local church. His role for this writing… that of a father. His home is Seattle, Washington.

Sarah Ware—She is a theatre major in Seattle Pacific University and a Youth For Christ leader working with her local church. She brings both her heart and talent to the sketches she has offered.

West Coast Parents—I met this couple as if God ordained it. They are the parents of three children and offer their wisdom and insight of living the theology of keeping Christ at the center of their family. They reside outside Portland, Oregon.

January 1	New Year's Day
January 6	Epiphany
January 16	Sanctity of Human Life Sunday
January 17	Martin Luther King Jr. Day
January 20	Inauguration Day
February 1–28	Black History Month
February 1	National Freedom Day
February 2	Groundhog Day
February 6	Super Bowl Sunday
February 9	Ash Wednesday
February 9	Chinese New Year
February 12	Lincoln's Birthday
February 13	First Sunday of Lent
February 14	Valentine's Day
February 20	Second Sunday of Lent
February 21	Presidents' Day
February 22	Washington's Birthday
February 25–26	30-Hour Famine
February 27	Third Sunday of Lent
March 2	World Day of Prayer
March 6	Fourth Sunday of Lent
March 13	Fifth Sunday of Lent
March 17	St. Patrick's Day
March 20	Palm Sunday
	First Day of Spring
March 24	Maundy Thursday
March 25	Good Friday
March 27	Easter
April 3	Daylight savings time begins
April 17	National Youth Day
April 22	Earth Day
April 24	Passover
May 5	National Day of Prayer
	Cinco De Mayo
May 8	Mother's Day
May 15	Pentecost
May 21	Armed Forces Day

May 22	Trinity Sunday
May 30	Memorial Day
June 14	Flag Day
June 19	Father's Day
June 21	First Day of Summer
July 4	Independence Day
July 24	Parents' Day
August 1	Friendship Day
August 6	Transfiguration Day
September 5	Labor Day
September 11	Grandparents' Day
September 21	See You at the Pole Day
September 22	First Day of Autumn
October 1–31	Pastoral Appreciation Month
October 4	Rosh Hashanah Begins
October 10	Columbus Day
October 30	Reformation Sunday
	Daylight Savings Time Ends
October 31	Halloween
November 1	All Saints Day
November 2	All Souls Day
November 8	Election Day
November 11	Veterans Day
November 13	International Day of Prayer for the Persecuted Church
November 20	World Hunger Day
November 24	Thanksgiving Day
November 27	First Sunday of Advent
December 1	AIDS Awareness Day
December 4	Second Sunday of Advent
December 7	Pearl Harbor Remembrance Day
December 10	Human Rights Day
December 11	Third Sunday of Advent
December 18	Fourth Sunday of Advent

December 21	First Day of Winter
December 24	Christmas Eve
December 25	Christmas Day
December 26	Hanukkah Begins; Kwanzaa Begins
December 31	New Year's Eve

WEEKLY
WORSHIP SUGGESTIONS
FOR 52 WEEKS

JANUARY 2, 2005

Stargazing

By Amy Jacober

MEMORY VERSE:
And the light shines in the darkness, and the darkness did not comprehend it. —John 1:5 (NKJV)

SCRIPTURE: Matthew 2:1–12

LESSON IN A SENTENCE: Obedience comes in the journey following Christ; the reward for obedience is finding Him!

THE BIG PICTURE (OR WHAT YOU'RE TRYING TO GET ACROSS):

Each of us has a precious gift (some have many!) to carry and place before God. Just like the magi, most of the time we are not certain where this will take us. God does provide signs to guide us if we have the courage to follow. Once we have been with Jesus, we are changed and it is not safe to go back on the same path. The church learns this as the magi follow the star to arrive at the manger. Throughout history, this has come to be known as Epiphany. According to tradition, twelve days after the birth of Jesus the magi arrive, offering gifts and their worship.

Just like the magi, we too have a star to follow. God has a plan for each of us, a way to draw us closer to Him and to help us live our lives abundantly as He intended. This is easier said than done. Figuring out exactly where we are to go, what our gifts are, and then finding the courage to go may take a lifetime for some people. In our impatience we strain to see the path all at once. In reality God often reveals only one step of the path at a time. Epiphany is a reminder of the journey, a call to obedience in recognizing where God is leading and following even when we haven't a clue as to the destination.

IN THIS LESSON STUDENTS SHOULD:

- ○ Learn of the tradition of Epiphany in the church.
- ○ Be able to re-tell the story of the magi.
- ○ Recognize or at least be encouraged to look for the "star" God is asking them to follow.

STUFF YOU NEED:

- Stars cut from heavy paper (enough to give one to each person present)
- Or glow-in-the-dark stars (enough to give one to each person present)
- Copies of "Star Liturgy"
- Butcher paper
- Felt-tip markers

FOCUS

Choose either option 1, 2, or 3. Be certain to watch your time and not get carried away with this part of the lesson!

OPTION 1: HIGH SCHOOL

Tape butcher paper to the wall for a graffiti board. Have each student write at least one example of where they have seen a "star" in the last week. DO NOT clarify what you mean. Encourage them to be creative. They could mention anything from a star on a neighborhood sign to a singer on TV. Look over the list and read it together. Encourage them to keep their eyes open for stars in the coming week.

OPTION 2: JUNIOR HIGH

Have a star-drawing contest. Give each person a pen/pencil or marker and have him or her draw a five-point star. If this seems too easy, ask them to work on an eight-point star. Once both of these are done, have them pair up to be certain no cheating is going on and have them try to draw both the five-point and the eight-point star without looking. Decide as a group who has the best star drawn without looking.

OPTION 3: ACTIVE GROUP

This is very simply a harkening back to childhood. Play a game of hide-and-seek. Debrief at the end, pointing out that this was a game more about someone being willing to search, to seek than it was about those hiding. Today, just like in the game, we're going to look at some people willing to seek after something. God calls us to seek after Him with the same energy and enthusiasm that we use when playing this simple game.

DISCOVERY

Ask: Who can tell the story of the magi? Once you have a volunteer, before he or she tells the story, ask if anyone knows why you are asking about the magi so far after Christmas. If someone knows, let them explain Epiphany. If no one knows then you can explain (see Teacher's Note).

Go back to your volunteer and ask for the story of the magi.

Read Matthew 2:1–12

Ask: What was it the magi were following?

Did they know where the star was leading?

Would you ever follow something because you thought God put it there but didn't know where it was leading?

Think of a time when you followed God and had no idea how it would turn out. Share with your group a real story from your life. That is always better than anything you might read from a book! Don't be afraid to share or that it won't be as funny or pithy as ones you might read. Be certain the story ends with you finding Jesus after your obedience in following.

Ask: What would it mean for you to follow God where He is leading you right now?

(This is a difficult question for any group, but for junior high in particular. You may need to give some examples like "God is leading me to actually do my homework," "to not lie about how long I played games on the internet," "to respect my parents," etc.) Decide for your group whether this question would be better answered aloud or if you should offer a short time of silence for reflection. If you are meeting at night and it is possible to see the stars from where you are and not too distruptive, consider giving your students 10 minutes on their own to spend time in silence looking at the stars.

Teacher's Note: Epiphany is a transliteration of the Greek word *epiphaneia* meaning disclosure or unveiling. This word is used in two ways in the Christian church. The first is for any occasion in which God incarnate was revealed to people. The second, by tradition, is twelve days after Christmas when the magi arrived to present the Christ child with gold, frankincense, and myrrh. In some cultures Twelfth Night or Epiphany is the time to exchange gifts, while Christmas is solely for celebrating the birth of Christ. (If you have not already pointed this out to your group, the Bible never mentions three wise men; rather we assume three wise men because of the three gifts.)

LIFE APPLICATION: Have groups of no more than ten sit in a circle. Explain to them what it means to be reverent, and ask them to move into these groups quietly. You may want to consider playing a very quiet worship CD to set the tone. Pass out the "Star Liturgy" and have them follow the directions.

Star Liturgy

Please go around the circle, taking turns reading each sentence out loud.

Creator God, give to me eyes able to see the star You have flung out for me and the courage to leave where I am comfortable to follow it.

Give me the guts to start the journey, even when the road seems too hard.

Give me the guts to stick to it when I'm tired or feel attacked and I want to go back where it is warm and comfortable.

Give me eyes to be able to recognize the dream-stealers who try to discourage me on the way and keep me from going where You have called.

Guard my ears from the voices that tell me I am foolish, until they fade beneath Your call.

Give me a heart like Yours so I can help my friends to follow their star.

All: Jesus, do this for us.

When my heart becomes discouraged and I think only a lucky few get anything good in life, lift my eyes to the starry heavens and remind me of the star You have in place for me filled with Your generosity.

When my school is hostile and my home in chaos, help me to live in peace, hope, and encouragement.

All: Jesus, do this for us.

When the world seems against me, when I try really hard and get only criticism, remind me that You understand me and have placed a star for me to follow.

All: Jesus, do this for us. Jesus, thank You for being our guide, and remind us when we forget.

MAKING IT PERSONAL: Stars are all around us. Remind the students of your opening activity.

If you followed option one: Remind the students of the list of all the stars they had seen in the past week. Encourage them to have a new way of seeing these stars. Invite your students to use each star sighting as a reminder of the star God flung into the sky for the magi to follow in order to see the baby Jesus.

If you followed option two: Remind the students of the stars they tried to draw at the beginning of your time together. Ask if it was easier to draw the stars when they could look or when they couldn't. Why? Trying to draw a star without looking is no easier than trying to follow one without really looking. God places signs for us to follow all around us. It makes a difference whether we are open to seeing them or not.

If you followed option three: Remind the students of playing hide-and-seek at the beginning of the time together. Ask if it was hard to look for each other and why. Ask if it is hard to look for what God wants from us. Why does it seem more difficult to seek and follow God?

MEMORY VERSE ACTIVITY

Ask: What would make it easier for us to recognize and follow the "stars" God has put in our lives?

Give each student a cut-out star to take home. Have them write the memory verse on the back. Encourage them to put the star somewhere in their room or as a bookmark in a place where they will see it often. Close in prayer, asking God to use these stars to remind each person that God does have somewhere they are to be and is longing for their obedience to follow where He leads.

SONGS: "You Already Take Me There," Switchfoot

CONNECTIONS: Stars are used throughout Scripture in various ways. They are references to: creation (Genesis 1:16–18; Psalm 136:9); images of glory (1 Corinthians 15:41); wandering (Jude 13); symbolic of people (Daniel 12:3; Philippians 2:15); mystery (Revelation 1:16; 2:1); and Christ Himself (Revelation 22:16).

EXTRA! EXTRA!: I was well into adulthood and a graduate from seminary before I learned Epiphany was a part of the greater church calendar. I love my tradition and am thankful for all I hold dear because of it, but I felt a bit cheated! My first encounter with this as a holiday was at Westminster Abbey. I was blown away by the history and tradition of which I had never heard! It is never too late to learn.

QUOTABLE QUOTES:

I think that, regardless of our culture, age, or even personal handicaps, we can still strive for something exceptional. Why not expand our sights instead of restricting our lives and accepting the lowest common denominator of a dormant existence? Faith, either in God or ourselves, will permit us to take a chance on a new path, perhaps different from the one we now follow. It may be surprising where it leads.

—Jimmy Carter (1924–)

Stargazing —Midweek

MEMORY VERSE:
And the light shines in the darkness, and the darkness did not comprehend it.—John 1:5 (NKJV)

SCRIPTURE: Colossians 3:22–25, focus on v. 23

LESSON IN A SENTENCE: Obedience comes in the journey following Christ; the reward for obedience is finding Him!

FOCUS

Ideally have two people who have rehearsed this prior to your time of meeting. If this is not possible, this is short enough and simple enough to photocopy and give to two readers.

Reader's Theatre

R 1:   And God said, "Let there be light."

R 2:   Your light shall break forth like the dawn.

R 1:   The Jews had light and gladness and joy and honor.

R 2:   Your word is a lamp unto my feet and a light unto my path.

R 1:   The people who walked in darkness have seen a great light.

R 2:   On those living in the shadow of death

R1 & R2: a light has dawned.

R 1:   Giving thanks to the Father who has qualified you to share in the inheritance of the saints in the kingdom of light.

R 2:   He has rescued us from the dominion of darkness and into the kingdom of the Son He loves, in whom we have redemption, the forgiveness of sins.

R 1:   Light has come into the world, but men loved darkness instead of light because their deeds were evil. Everyone who does evil hates the light, and will not come into the light for fear that his deeds will be exposed.

R 2:   (start at the end of the first sentence above) Light has come into the world, but men loved darkness instead of light because their deeds were evil. Everyone who does evil hates the light, and will not come into the light for fear that his deeds will be exposed.

R 1:   Let your light so shine before men

R 2:   that they may see your good works
R1 & R2: and give glory to your Father who is in Heaven.

While most of us say that we would prefer to live in the light, many of us spend a great deal of time in the dark. We follow after the things of the world and stumble in the dark trying to figure out where God wants for us to be.

DISCOVERY

In pairs, read through Colossians 3:22–25 and answer the following three questions:

What is this asking you to do?
What happens if you obey?
What happens if you do not obey?

Re-read verse 23. What does it mean to do everything heartily as to the Lord?

APPLICATION: Think through all of the things you do in a typical week. Pick three of those things. How could you do them "as to the Lord"? (Your students may need help. What would it look like if homework was done as a service to God and not just because it was an assignment? What would it look like to clean your room, do the dishes, or any other chore as to the Lord?)

This week is the week of Epiphany. On Sunday we looked at exactly what that means. The magi followed the star to find Christ. They followed the light that pierced the darkness. Regardless of what anyone thought and in spite of their not knowing exactly what it was that they were to do or to find, they followed and presented the gifts they had. They did what they did "as to the Lord and not to men."

We all have something to offer to God. He has already set a light that pierced the darkness as He stepped out of heaven Himself as the incarnation. We can be constantly in the light if we do all that we do as to the Lord. Follow the star He has flung before us and we will always find Christ as we lay down our gifts.

CONNECTIONS: Light and dark have a long-standing relationship all through Scripture. Among these are Genesis 1:4; Genesis 1:16; Job 12:25; Matthew 5:15; Matthew 6:22–23; and John 9:4. There are literally hundreds of references that could be listed here. In thinking through what it means to be in the light and out of darkness, these references can only help to further your group's understanding of being a follower of Christ.

SPEAKING IS ONE THING,

IN FRONT OF OTHERS IS ANOTHER

By Adam Robinson
EVANGELIST/ASSOCIATE MINISTER

It always used to frustrate me that when I would teach a Bible study for students or preach on a Wednesday night I couldn't seem to keep their attention. I guess I had this mental image of me teaching a group of students on the edge of their seats in rapt anticipation as I explained the Word of God. This, however, never really happened. As I looked out on the 10 or so kids gathered I always got the same thing. Shift. Fidget. Doodle. No eye contact. In my mind this translated into "Please stop talking, you're boring me."

How frustrating! I had prepared all week for this, and apparently they could care less! On a particular night this exasperation got the best of me. One of the students, one of only five I might add, had been doodling the entire time—right in front of me. It looked as if he was creating a major piece of art, and this was infinitely more interesting than my talk. It was time to call him out, I thought, to show him and everybody he wasn't listening. I asked him a very pointed question, a question he could only answer if he had been listening the whole time. As he stopped doodling I prepared myself for sweet vindication. He then calmly looked up at me and proceeded to review my entire talk up to that point. And then he went back to doodling. Shift. Fidget. No eye contact.

Point to remember: Things are not always what they seem. It may not look like it, but they really are listening.

Speaking to youth is a tricky deal. There's no magic formula, and every group is different. You have to gauge generally where everyone is and what they will respond to best. And I have never found anyone who could tell me how to do that. Sound hopeless? It can feel that way sometimes. I think teenagers actually relish the idea of being aloof and incomprehensible. And acting interested doesn't seem to come natural to them. But they are listening. More than that, they crave someone to love them with the Truth. And that's where we come in. Even though we feel inadequate most of the time, our seemingly fumbling efforts can have profound and lasting impact on the spiritual lives of students. It takes time, and trial and error, and lots of trust in the Lord and His giftings. But it can be done. In walking this road as a fellow teacher, here are some of the lessons I've learned so far.

Be real. The fallacy in speaking to students today is that if you're not fun, cool, hip, can tell lots of funny stories, and talk about the latest pop song, students won't be interested in what you say. The problem? That isn't us. Personally, I'm not cool, I don't want to dress like them, and I don't properly appreciate pop music. Fortunately, there is something that students crave more than all the outward glitz: they just want to know you're real. I don't know about you, but I never feel comfortable around people who are trying too hard to be something they aren't, who are putting up an obviously fake front. Students are no different. Their lives are filled with such people. What they don't have, and desperately desire, are just some people who will be honest, real, and tell them the Truth. And that you can do. You'll be surprised how much this works.

For the past six years I've been teaching a small group of five students, and looking back I can see how drastically my style has changed. In the early days I spent a lot of time trying to find the perfect illustration, or game, or anything that would get my point across. Most of the time these things flopped. But I also started hanging out with them a lot. I would arrive early, talk about what interested them, tried some of the things they enjoyed, got to know them. These days they come to my house hours before Bible study just to hang out and then have dinner. Then we study the Bible. I don't have a lot of illustrations, or games, or funny stories, but they're completely focused. I had to become the illustration, to be vulnerable and real and show them that I was a real person telling them things that I dealt with too. Once I became a real person to them, they had no problems listening to me teach. I had earned the right to be heard just by being real. Always pass on a canned story or illustration about someone else when you can be personal and real instead.

In some situations you don't have the luxury of time to build relationships, but the same principle still applies. However or wherever you teach, be yourself instead of "a teacher." The most consistent compliment I get from junior high students as I travel and speak at camps and events is "You talk about things in a way I understand." The funny thing is, I don't do a lot of translating between how I think and what I say. I just try to talk to students like I would want someone to talk to me—like a real person dealing with real problems. And it works. If they know you struggle, and that you treat them like real people, they can trust you to give them advice on how to handle their struggles. So "speaking their language" turns out to be less about knowing the lingo and more about being honest and genuine.

Question everything. A preaching professor once told his students to imagine him sitting at the back of every church they preached in, saying "So what?" This is a valuable lesson. It is also a reality for anyone speaking to youth, who will not have to imagine this situation—many youth will gladly ask you this to your face. But it is not an unreasonable question. Anyone being preached to has the right to ask why this is important to them, why they should listen. As speakers and teachers we cannot abuse the privilege we have to teach the Word of God. We may be called to teach, but others may not be called to listen! So when we teach we need to make sure that we tie our teaching into the lives of students by making the application clear.

Some would say that we should just teach the Word, no matter if it is applicable or not, and ultimately this is true. But until you help a student understand who they are in Christ, how they can personally walk with the Lord, and how He wants to teach them, they will never understand this concept. It all goes back to answering the question: So what? Why should I do this, learn this, change my life?

One way I try to incorporate this into my teaching is to be honest about my own questions. While preparing I often have questions myself, and most times I find that these are the same questions other people have. Often I will say "Now at this point you're probably wondering. . ." or "When I read this I asked myself. . . ." This accomplishes two things. First, you are being real by showing that you struggle to understand Scripture too. This puts them on your level. Second, if they have the same question, it takes them right into the heart of what you are talking about. Now you are not just talking *about* some passage, you are showing them that they are *in* the passage, right there with you in the journey of interpretation. This is the difference between talking *with* people instead of *at* people. The older we get the more we will have to work at this, since the distance between our life stages prevents us from assuming that my questions are their questions. But spending time with the age group you are teaching will quickly give you a sense of what they are interested in and concerned about.

Materialism

By Alicia Claxton

MEMORY VERSE:

"Do not store up for yourselves treasures on earth, where moth and rust destroy and where thieves break in and steal. But store up for yourselves treasures in heaven, where moth and rust do not destroy, and where thieves do not break in and steal. For where your treasure is, there your heart will be also." —Matthew 6:19–21 (NIV)

MEMORY VERSE ACTIVITY

Because this is a long memory verse (but well worth the extra effort), it might be best to introduce it with a hands-on activity. Take several children's puzzles (20–25 pieces) and put them together beforehand. Write the memory verse with marker on the back of each puzzle, then take them apart and put back into their individual boxes. Divide the group into teams and give each team a puzzle. Tell them that the first team to find the memory verse and say it wins. They will figure out where the answer is found once they get started.

SCRIPTURE: 1 Timothy 6:6–12, 17–19

LESSON IN A SENTENCE: The stuff of this world can easily distract us from the real treasure in life—knowing Christ!

THE BIG PICTURE:

Cars, houses, DVD players, laptops, big toys, little toys, electronic toys—we live in a world full of "stuff." And we're told that stuff will make us happier, healthier, more popular, and more successful. The truth is that material wealth brings only temporary happiness and always leaves us wanting more. Before long we become bored with what we have and want something new. We keep collecting more stuff in our search to find satisfaction. The only true treasure that can satisfy us from now to eternity is a relationship with our Creator through Jesus Christ His Son!

IN THIS LESSON STUDENTS SHOULD:

- ○ Be able to identify the signs of materialism.
- ○ Recognize the danger and effects of materialism.
- ○ Be willing to deal with their own attitudes towards material wealth and allow God's truth to change their hearts.

STUFF YOU NEED:

○ Pens/several sheets of paper/one sheet of butcher paper
○ Small paper bags (for white elephant game)
○ White elephant gifts (one for each student–explanation found in Focus–Option 1)
○ Magazine advertisements (explanation found in Focus–Option 2)
○ Candy or small prizes for winners of Focus–Option 2
Optional Supplies:
○ Several small puzzles (for Scripture memory activity)

FOCUS

Depending on group size, choose option 1 or option 2. Be sure to watch your time and not get too carried away with this part of the lesson.

OPTION 1: SMALL GROUP ACTIVITY

Organize a White Elephant Gift party (you can ask students to bring a cheap item from around their house OR you can provide a random assortment of items). For those who are not familiar with the White Elephant Gift concept, the "gifts" are usually things you find lying around the house or office and range from pencil sharpeners to candy. Items should be put in paper sacks at the beginning so students cannot see what each "gift" is. Place paper bags in the center of a circle of chairs and have the first player choose a "gift" and open it. From that point on, students can choose a gift from the center or steal a gift that has already been opened. Once an item has been stolen twice, it cannot be stolen again. Once everyone has had a chance to go, the first player gets one last opportunity to steal a gift from around the circle. Take a few minutes to discuss what happened throughout this game. Are there any lessons to be learned? Transition to lesson by saying, "This game was a fun way to illustrate the signs and effects of materialism at work. Even with cheap and goofy stuff we find ourselves wanting what we don't have."

OPTION 2: LARGE GROUP ACTIVITY

Before the session, find advertisements for popular products (magazine or newspaper ads or for the more high-tech groups tape some popular commercials off the television). Display a portion of each ad or slogan on sheets of paper, making sure that the brand name of the product cannot be seen. This activity is to be played like a game show. Divide students into teams of 3–4 people and have each team send a different representative to the front for each round. Begin the game by holding up a piece of paper with an ad on it (or show a segment of the commercial) and having players "buzz in" when they know the brand name of the item being advertised. Give points to teams for each correct answer. Continue playing until everyone has had a chance to guess.

NOTE: You can either provide a "buzzer" like a bell or have teams make up their own "buzz in" sounds. After the game is finished, hand out a prize to the winning team. Transition to lesson by saying, "This was a fun way to illustrate how easily the 'stuff of this world' can get into our heads."

DISCOVERY

As you begin the Bible study, ask for a volunteer to say (or read) the memory verses introduced earlier in the session—Matthew 6:19–21. Ask students to briefly explain the principles taught in those verses and give examples of treasures on earth and treasures in heaven.

Split students into groups of 3–4 people and give each group a blank sheet of paper. Have them write down the Scripture passage (1 Timothy 6:6–12, 17–19) and the following questions:

1. What does Paul say is the formula for success in this life (v. 6)?
2. What is the definition of contentment, in your own words?
3. What is the enemy of contentment and the root of all kinds of evil (vv. 9–10)?
4. Is it a sin to be wealthy? List proof for your answer from this passage.
5. How can we honor God with our material possessions and resources (vv. 17–19)?

Give students 5–8 minutes to work through these questions. Once groups are done, have them share some of their answers.

LIFE APPLICATION: Ask students to define the difference between our wants and our needs. Using a sheet of butcher paper, make a list of things we commonly want and things we really need.

Ask: Why is our list of wants always bigger than our list of needs? (Answer: because we are selfish by nature.) What is our greatest need and the only source of true contentment in this life? (Answer: a relationship with God.) Why is it necessary for us as believers to flee from materialism or the love of things? (Answer: because the love of money can cause us to fall into temptation and turn our attention away from Christ.)

MAKING IT PERSONAL: Think about the last three things you spent money on or asked someone to give you. Did those things fill a need or a want in your life? Would they end up as treasures stored up on earth or in heaven? Knowing now what the greatest treasure is, would you be willing to focus less on the stuff of this world and more on the things of God? Challenge students to spend a few minutes thinking about their answers to these questions and praying for God's help in overcoming materialism.

Close in prayer.

CONNECTIONS: If you have extra time at the end of this session or have students who want to study more about this topic, instruct them to read other passages that deal with material wealth such as Matthew 19:16–30 (Jesus speaks to the Rich Young Man), Luke 16:13 (You cannot serve God and money), and Ecclesiastes 5:10–11, 18–19 (Riches are meaningless).

SONGS: "Is It Any Wonder" by Nichole Nordeman (from the album *Wide Eyed*)

Materialism —Midweek

MEMORY VERSE:
"Do not store up for yourselves treasures on earth, where moth and rust destroy and where thieves break in and steal. But store up for yourselves treasures in heaven, where moth and rust do not destroy, and where thieves do not break in and steal. For where your treasure is, there your heart will be also." —Matthew 6:19–21 (NIV)

SCRIPTURE: Matthew 19:16–30

LESSON IN A SENTENCE: The stuff of this world can easily distract us from the real treasure in life—knowing Christ!

FOCUS

Use this activity to help prepare your students for the Bible study. Keep an eye on the time as you play this game.

Play a couple rounds of *"Who Doesn't Want to Be a Millionaire?"* Game. Before the class make up a variety of multiple-choice questions (some good suggestions for topics are sports, pop culture, fun facts about your youth minister, etc.). Before getting started, ask if everyone is familiar with the game "Who Wants to Be a Millionaire?" Summarize some basic rules such as they stay in the game and earn more money each time they answer a question correctly; they are out of the game as soon as they answer incorrectly. For the sake of time, they only get one lifeline ("phone-a-teammate" which allows them to get help from their team) and money is earned as follows: Question #1 = $1000 / Question #2 = $25,000 / Question #3 = $100,000 / Question #4 = $500,000 /Question #5 = $1,000,000. They can choose to walk away at any time with the "money" they have earned, but if they miss an answer they lose everything. Divide your students into 4 or 5 groups and have each group nominate a captain. The captain will represent the group and try to win them a million dollars. To make the game more fun, let them turn in their team winnings at the end for prizes (the more money they earned, the better the prize).

DISCOVERY

Start the study by debriefing the game in a lighthearted way. Ask the teams that lost everything how they felt watching others win. Ask team members how hard it was to let their captain make decisions that affected all of them. Ask the team that won why, though given the opportunity to walk away with some money, they were willing to risk everything for the chance to win more. We all struggle with the desire to "store up" things here on earth. It becomes a dangerous problem when we let our earthly stuff robs us of our love for eternal treasures.

Ask a student to read Matthew 19:16–30.

In this passage, Jesus meets a rich young man who wants to know how he can get eternal life. Notice the way in which he asks, "Teacher, what good thing must I do to get eternal life?"He is respectful of Christ but doesn't seem to recognize Him as the Son of God. He is motivated by a desire to get something rather than have a relationship with the One who could offer him what he sought.

Ask students the following questions:

1. What is Jesus' first response to the man's question?

2. Who is Jesus referring to when He says, "There is only One who is good"?

3. What is the Lord's final answer to the man's question in verse 21?

4. Why do you think Jesus requires the man to go and sell his possessions BEFORE he can come and follow Him?

5. In the end, what did the rich young man choose?

6. Why do you think it's so hard for "a rich man to enter the kingdom of heaven" (v. 23)?

7. What does Jesus say will be the reward for those who choose to follow Him (vv. 28–30)?

We see by the young man's decision just how dangerous the "love" of money can be. Being rich is not a sin (1 Timothy 6:17–19) but when we hold more affection for the things of this world than for the things of God, wealth becomes destructive. There is a reason why Jesus says we cannot serve both God and money (Matthew 6:24). We must submit to one or the other. Either we will serve money and spend our lives focused on earthly treasures, or we will serve God and pour our lives (talents, resources, affection) into eternal treasures.

LIFE APPLICATION: On a sheet of butcher paper, list some ways we can use our earthly resources for eternal purposes. Encourage students to come up with specific ministry opportunities that they could invest time and resources into.

PERSONAL APPLICATION: One of the best ways to avoid falling into the temptation of materialism is to follow God's instruction on how to handle money. The Lord requires that we tithe 10 percent of everything we earn and we are encouraged to give an offering beyond that in thankfulness for all we've been given. Ask students to spend a few minutes thinking about the following questions:

1. Do you tithe?
2. Do you give an offering beyond your tithe?
3. Do you give reluctantly or cheerfully?
4. What changes do you need to make in how you view material wealth based on our study?

Once students have had a few minutes to reflect on these questions, close in prayer.

JANUARY 16, 2005

Precious in His Sight

By Amy Jacober

MEMORY VERSE:
For God so loved the world that He gave His only begotten Son, that whoever believes in Him should not perish, but have everlasting life. —John 3:16 (NKJV)

SCRIPTURE: Genesis 1:26–31

LESSON IN A SENTENCE: God views each and every human life as precious and in His image.

THE BIG PICTURE (OR WHAT YOU'RE TRYING TO GET ACROSS):

Somewhere on the journey from childhood to adulthood we all move from seeing everyone as a playmate to seeing everyone through our own broken and sinful lenses. In this process, subtle as it may be, we begin to judge others as worthy or unworthy of our time, our kindness, and even our respect. Ironically, as we are becoming such expert judges we too are being judged by those around us. The weight of this often bears down and we adopt the unworthy perspective from others into our own identity. This can pass when we have healthy others in key roles during our adolescence. We all need to hear that we are created, just as we are, in the image of God. Adolescents in particular need to hear this and be reminded that just as they are, God finds them to be precious and valuable.

Scripture offers valuable insight into these lessons. I am amazed, even in the last month, in working with both high school and college-aged students, to find a resignation that while they believe God loves us all by His grace, boys/men are seen as more valuable. These comments are not said in frustration or even with lament. Rather it is with a matter of fact presentation and acceptance that they believe they not only have differing roles but the role of a woman is less important. I am equally amazed that many of my students (most often male) do not hold as strongly to this belief but often do not feel the need to try to offer their alternative opinion as it does not concern them. As youth ministers, we need to be a voice reminding each of our students of the preciousness of their lives, male and female. That life is sacred, and the very breath they hold in their lungs is nothing short of a miracle.

Regardless of where you are on this issue, the consequences are great. In this lesson the scripture chosen is most clear on issues of gender. Depending on the needs of your group, you may wish to extend the discussion beyond the sanctity of life and being created in the image of God and consider issues of disabilities (both physical and mental), race, class, education, etc.

IN THIS LESSON STUDENTS SHOULD:

○ Be able to explain what it means for God to love all people regardless of gender, race, health, age, ability, class, education, and any other distinguisher.
○ Begin to deal with their rightful position as being one of God's creations and therefore one God loves.
○ Identify God's statement of "good" with regard to His creation and connect this to His love for the world.
○ Be able to talk about the phrase "sanctity of life."

STUFF YOU NEED:

○ Create and copy enough game sheets for each person present
○ Pens/pencils or markers
○ Worther's toffee candies (enough to give one to each person)

FOCUS

OPTION 1: ACTIVE GROUP

Create a sheet with the following directions and list:

This is a race to see who can do the greatest number of these activities in 5 minutes. After completing each one, have the person initial beside the line of the activity.

1. Give one dollar to someone.

2. Give a 30-second back rub.

3. Tell someone their hair looks good today.

4. Tell a funny joke to someone.

5. Shake the hand of someone you don't know well and say "Nice to meet ya!"

6. Look someone in the eye and tell them "God loves you."

7. Sing "Jesus Loves Me" with two other people.

8. Find someone walking around and tell them how impressed you are that their feet work so well.

9. Find the person in the room with the closest birthday to yours.

10. Learn the middle names of at least three other people.

11. Find someone who can tell you what "sanctity of life" means.

At the end of 5 minutes call time. Ask who has completed the greatest number of activities. Feel free to go over each activity for which the person has initials. Once confirmed, let them know they have won the privilege of getting to offer a piece of Worther's candy to each person present.

As the Worther's are being passed out, ask youth to eat the candy but to hold the wrapper in their hands for a moment. Explain that these candies are a great reminder to us of the love of God. They are named Worther's, which can remind us that we are worthy before God. The wrappers are gold on the outside and silver on the inside. These are precious metals and quite expensive. We are precious and have great value before the Lord. Finally, hold the wrapper up and look to a light. The wrappers are actually see-through. As much as we may try to present a certain image on the outside, God sees straight through and sees us for our true selves, made in His image.

(If you group is neither active nor mature, use the Worther's candy object lesson to bring focus to your group. You may want to begin by asking what they find to have value or worth. After a few minutes of discussion, pass out the candies and debrief as above.)

OPTION 2: MATURE GROUP

If your group is small enough, do this activity all together. If you are larger, split into 2 or more groups, ideally to have no more than 8–10 per group, with an adult volunteer leader in each group. Sit in a circle and have the adult begin with the person to his or her right. Explain that each of you are going to go around the circle and say something positive or encouraging to this person. If you don't know them well, say the best you can. As the adult, set the tone—something like "I have seen you consistently greet newcomers and make them feel welcome" or "You have an amazing voice for singing" etc. Try, as best as you can, to encourage your students to not just offer superficial comments. As you finish with the last person, make a space and say this is the space for Jesus. If you could, what would be one positive thing you would like to say to Him about what you know of Him or have seen Him do?

At the end of this read Genesis 1:27. While we are not God, we have been created in His image. All of the compliments and positive things you have just said to Jesus, apply to each of you as well. You are His image here on earth.

DISCOVERY

In your same circle groups, read Genesis 1:26–31.

Ask: What stands out to you?

This is most likely a passage (even if you have not grown up in church) that has some familiarity.

In pairs, ask them to answer the following three questions.

1. What is the image of God?

2. What is our role according to these scriptures?

3. What does it mean to you to know that you are the image of God?

Share the responses with the whole group.

Teacher's Note: It is difficult to tell in English, but verse 26 actually sets the tone for the equal value and worth of males and females. The Hebrew word for man is transliterated (as opposed to translated, transliterated means what it sounds like in Hebrew put into English sounds) as 'adam. The Hebrew translation for 'adam is "humankind." God is saying, right from the beginning, Let Us make humankind in Our image. Most often we focus on females being created from males and forget that females too are in the image of God. This Hebrew word is to be understood as humankind in Genesis 1:27; 2:5, 7, 8, 15, 16, 18, and 25. In Genesis 2:19, it refers to the proper name Adam.

LIFE APPLICATION: Ask if they have ever noticed anyone being treated as less than human? Who in our world falls into these cate-gories? (Encourage them to be open and honest. Remind them that you are not asking for their personal stories of not treating others well but of the big picture. Examples may include the homeless, people with AIDS, the poor, different races, women, etc.) How should we as Christians respond to these mistreatments of people all over the world?

What does this scripture say about the humankind that God cre-ated? If they are stuck, ask someone to re-read verse 31. God said "It was very good." Interestingly, God declared "It was good" at the end of each day of creation. The only exception was on the day He created humankind. On this day alone, He declared "It was very good." What does this declaration mean for each of us today?

(If you have a group you know struggles with negative self-concepts or if circumstances in life have led them to feel less than valuable, this is an excellent time to reiterate how precious each person is to God and how much you value them being present. They may believe everyone else is valuable to God except them. Talk through this and re-read the scripture.)

MAKING IT PERSONAL: If you have not yet given a Worther's candy, do so now.

Find your wrapper from the Worther's candy. Encourage them to tuck it in their Bible or take it home and tape it to the mirror. As much as this wrapper is meant as a reminder to you that you are worthy, that you have value for who you are on the inside and as the created image of God, allow it also to remind you of the worth of others. Think right now (don't say it out loud!) of who gets on your nerves, who you don't like and find no value in. Ask God to help you see them with His eyes, beyond what they present on the outside.

CONNECTIONS: The memory verse is intentionally taken from the New Testament. This lesson has been about the sanctity of life. God has valued us from the beginning at creation to His incarnation and declaration that He so loved the world! John 3:16 is such a familiar verse that we often overlook the power and truth behind those words. God loved the world. He didn't love anyone more or less than others. This is the gospel, the good news for all! In times when we feel superior to anyone else for any reason, God sees us *all* as precious and valuable. In times when we feel inferior and worthless, God again sees us *all* as precious and valuable, even when we do not or cannot believe that about ourselves.

Connect to Midweek:

Type up a list of trail mix ingredients. Be certain to make enough copies to hand one to each student. Tell students that if they are going to come on Wednesday that you need for them to each bring at least one item on the list you created. Feel free to create a list with whatever ingredients you like, but a few suggestions would be: peanuts, chocolate chips, cashews, raisins, pretzels, etc.

SONGS: "Your Pretty Baby" 77s
     "Everybody's Beautiful" Waterdeep

QUOTABLE   QUOTES :

When the day comes, the fears of insecurity and the doubts clouding our future will be transformed into radiant confidence . . . where the brotherhood of man will be undergirded by a secure and expanding prosperity for all. Yes, this will be the day when all God's children, black men and white men, Jews and Gentiles, Protestants and Catholics, will be able to join hands all over this nation and sing the words of the Negro spiritual: "Free at last, free at last. Thank God Almighty, we are free at last."

—Martin Luther King Jr. (1929–1968)

Precious in His Sight —Midweek

MEMORY VERSE:
For God so loved the world that He gave His only begotten Son, that whoever believes in Him should not perish, but have everlasting life. —John 3:16 (NKJV)

SCRIPTURE: Matthew 6:25–27; 10:30–31

LESSON IN A SENTENCE: God views each and every human life as precious and in His image.

FOCUS

Have a large bowl (or more if you need!) to mix all of the trail mix ingredients. You may want to have a few extra bags of nuts or chocolate chips on hand. Collect all of the ingredients on one table.

As one of your volunteers is putting together the trail mix, ask your students to gather on the floor for a story. Very much like a grade school after recess time, you will read and show the pictures. Use the story *Stone Soup*. (Many if not most of your students will have read this when they were much younger. Really ham it up as you read the story to keep their interest and to allow them to hear it fresh.)

At the end of the story, ask how the town was able to make soup from just a stone? Who was able to eat the soup? Were there any restrictions? Can you think of any ways this story might remind us of God?

DISCOVERY

While the groups are looking up their Scriptures and answering the questions, pass out the trail mix. Point out the parallel that just like in the story, when each person contributes just a little, something better is created and there is enough for everyone!

Split your students into at least two groups.

Have group 1 read Matthew 6:25–27.
Is it realistic to not worry about your life?
What do we need (not want) beyond food and clothes?
Do you believe God values you enough to provide for your needs?

Have group 2 read Matthew 10:30–31.
What does it mean or what does it matter that the very hairs of your head are numbered?

What does it mean to be more valuable than many sparrows?

Both passages declare that we are valuable to God. Both also say in one way or another that we shouldn't worry, that God will provide exactly what we need. Do you believe this? How do you think God provides for us?

APPLICATION: Both groups have read passages that talk about how valuable each individual is. We have looked at this in several ways over the past week.

Who are the people in life who are seen as less valuable?

Have you ever felt like you didn't fit in or were less valuable than others around you?

Have you ever wondered why God provides great things for others but seems to forget you?

How does this fit with what these Scriptures say?

Remind them that at the beginning of your time you read *Stone Soup*. In this story, the soup was made only when each person gave what he or she had. There was no measure of whose contribution was the greatest or who deserved the most once it was put together. God does provide for us, often through others. One of our greatest difficulties is in recognizing the ways in which God provides. He works through others and gives what we need, which is not always (in fact is often a far cry from) what we want.

Look back at the memory verse. Many of us know this verse by heart. God so loved the world. He finds the world valuable. He loves old and young, rich and poor, male and female, all colors, education levels, able-bodied and not! He is madly, passionately in love with us. He not only finds us to be valuable, but He wants to provide for our every need. He alone knew of and exclusively could provide for our greatest need, the need for salvation. Regardless of where we were born, how we were raised, or what we have learned along the way, God loves us and demonstrates this through His death and resurrection.

JANUARY 23, 2005

Poverty

By Amy Jacober

MEMORY VERSE:

"He judged the cause of the poor and needy; then it was well. Was not this knowing Me?"says the LORD.—Jeremiah 22:16 (NKJV)

ALTERNATIVE:

"He pled the cause of the afflicted and needy; then it was well. Is not that what it means to know Me?" declares the LORD.—Jeremiah 22:16 (NASB)

SCRIPTURE: Jeremiah 22:13–19

LESSON IN A SENTENCE: Knowing God will lead to caring for the troubled and needy.

THE BIG PICTURE (OR WHAT YOU'RE TRYING TO GET ACROSS):

In a country and culture that says "more is better," at every turn most of us have difficulty just trying to keep up. And then there are those who are not keeping up, in fact they are struggling to have essentials. We talked just a few weeks ago about the sanctity of life. This lesson is a good reminder in that every life, even those in poverty, is precious to God. As Christians it is not just our right to help others but it is our responsibility. In a fallen and broken world, it is easy to find the cause and place blame for others in bad situations. Often, programs (and sadly even we as Christians at times) divide people into the worthy and unworthy poor. We assign, through our criteria, who ought to deserve help and who ought not, forgetting that poverty is not a choice. For those of us who know God, it is clear we are to care for those in need.

It's pretty easy to become jaded with so many people who do take advantage of others trying to help. We give a dollar to someone on the corner and wonder if we've just helped them buy dinner or a bottle. We give money only to find out it is being spent on new carpeting at a corporate office. We volunteer our time only to learn how much bigger the problem really is and we feel worse than ever. While it may be easier to ignore the issue or blame others, that is not what we are to do. The first step was learning to see others with the eyes of Christ, as valuable, worthy, made in His image. The next step comes in following God's lead in what to do.

IN THIS LESSON STUDENTS SHOULD:

○ Recognize they are much wealthier than they originally assumed.
○ Be able to list and discuss key qualities God expects of His people.
○ Begin to shift from an inward focus to an outward focus, looking for those in need not to judge or put down but to become aware and discover ways to make a difference.

STUFF YOU NEED:

○ Sheets of paper
○ Pens/pencils or markers
○ A trip to the grocery and/or chamber of commerce for prices
○ If you choose, a guest speaker

FOCUS

JUNIOR HIGH OPTION:

Split into groups of 3 or 4. Have each group make a list of everything they consider to be a necessity in life. Encourage them to leave nothing out. You may have to work to help your students understand the difference between a need and a want. For some a skateboard is just behind air to breathe and before food!

Give each group a second sheet of paper and remind them that Christmas was just one month ago. Have them make a list of everything they can remember that they received for Christmas. Tape the two lists up next to each other in your room.

SENIOR HIGH OPTION:

This one is going to take some preparation and investigation ahead of time on your part! It is well worth it to shed some light on these often elusive issues. You will need to find the actual prices of these items in your community. Prices vary greatly across the country, making the impact of this exercise much greater if taken from your own stores and communities. For much of this information you can get in touch with your local chamber of commerce. Feel free to use the suggested items and services, but be as creative as you like to gear this to your community!

○ Create a list of essentials in your community, i.e. milk, bread, transportation (bus/subway/train fare), average rent, prescriptions, clothing (check out costs for a pair of jeans, shirt, and shoes at a store where you know your students shop), can of soup, cost of a gallon of gas, etc.

○ Create a list of non-essentials but not frivolous, i.e. a visit to the doctor, a visit to the dentist, a visit to the eye doctor, typical electric bill, water bill, gas bill, etc.

○ Look up the most current reporting of the national household income considered to be poverty. This can easily be found on the internet at www.census.gov. (Look for statistical abstracts.) Have this amount written in bold numbers before you begin.

There are many ways to approach this exercise. Decide which would be best for your group. You may create a worksheet and have each person guess the prices. You may also create a game show to help them guess the actual cost for each item. Regardless of the format you choose, by the end as a group you should have filled in the costs for the essentials and non-essentials. In the end, total the cost of essentials and non-essentials. Write the totals in bold numbers and tape those at the front of the room. Finally, bring in the national average for household incomes in poverty. Not only is the amount not enough to cover the costs, the numbers of households falling into this category are increasing.

DISCOVERY

We've looked at wants and needs, at poverty from a worldly perspective. What do you think God has to say about this?

Have your students read Jeremiah 22:13–19 in small groups. Ask each group to list the characteristics that God condemns (the one's where He says "woe to him who . . .") and the characteristics that God desires.

Invite a guest to come share how they have pled the cause for the afflicted and needy. (The guest can be a Christian from a shelter, a food pantry, HUD, a social worker, a nurse or doctor from the county hospital, or anyone you may know who is living this out in their daily life. Look around your church—chances are you have some great resources right there and people who may have never thought they had anything to contribute to youth ministry! Ask the guest to simply share their story. Let him or her know what scriptures you will studying and that you are looking at poverty and the response God calls us to have.)

Teacher's Note: Jeremiah is a prophet in the southern kingdom of Judah. His call came in the days of King Jehoiakim. Jehoiakim had already moved Judah far from the days of obedience to God under his father's leadership. The reference in Jeremiah 22:18 to Josiah is in relation to the father-son relationship between Josiah and Jehoiakim but also the relationship between Judah when following God and not following God. Jeremiah was not the most popular guy in town with the people of Jerusalem, as he was telling them what was going to happen, that they were on the path to destruction. In fact, he was so unpopular, in just a few short chapters he is arrested. He was trying to call all of the people back to following God, which included pleading the cause for the afflicted and the needy. While most of us won't be thrown into jail for standing up for others or trying to right wrongs, there are costs.

LIFE APPLICATION: Ask if they have ever had a time when they were actually in need of something they were afraid they might not get. What was it and what did they do? Did anyone help them? If yes, was it easier with help? If no, would you have wanted help?

Call attention to verse 16. The one who is said to know God is the one who pled the cause for the afflicted and needy. Ask who they would consider to be afflicted or needy in their schools, in their neighborhoods.

What would it mean to plead their cause?

Is that something they could do? Why or why not?

MAKING IT PERSONAL: In thinking about poverty both here in this country and around the world where do you see yourself fitting in?

Have you ever heard the proverb "There but for the grace of God go I"? Ask what they think this means.

Funny wording to remind us that none of us are exempt from the possibility of poverty completely changing our lives. If you knew you were going to be in poverty in 15 years, is there anything you would do differently now?

Have each person present choose one characteristic God desires as listed from the Scriptures. Invite each person to share this characteristic with one other for accountability. Over the next week, look for ways to put this characteristic into practice.

SERVICE OPTIONS: If your group is more mature, consider looking into a service project. There are many good ways to become involved in your own community. At the end of the lesson, brainstorm ways you may serve as a group in a way to work against poverty or to understand those in poverty with compassion.

Another option would be to partner with one or more of the Christian organizations working around the world such as Compassion

International, World Vision/30 hour Famine, One Life Revolution or check with your denomination for additional programs. Several of these will include videos with real life stories and current statistics regarding poverty. Some have short-term projects, others encourage the sponsorship of a boy or girl in need. Each publishes their budgetary information and is approved as a responsible charitable organization. Contact information is available for each of the national organizations in the back of this book.

SONGS: "Kamikaze" Five Iron Frenzy

SPIRITUAL DISCIPLINE CONNECTION: Poverty is not the same as simplicity. When looking at economics, there is always a voice stating that wealth is not of God and only those in poverty are truly faithful Christians. Dallas Willard offers great insight into this issue in his chapter on poverty in *The Spirit of the Disciplines: Understanding How God Changes Lives*, HarperSanFrancisco, 1988.

QUOTABLE QUOTES:

The poor of the United States and of the world are your brothers and sisters. . . . You must never be content to leave them just the crumbs from the feast. You must take of your substance, and not just from your abundance, in order to help them. And you must treat them like guests at your family table.
—Pope John Paul II (1920–)

The test of our progress is not whether we add more to the abundance of those who have much; it is whether we provide enough for those who have too little.
—Franklin D. Roosevelt (1882–1945)

Poverty —Midweek

MEMORY VERSE:
"He judged the cause of the poor and needy; then it was well. Was not this knowing Me?" says the LORD.—Jeremiah 22:16 (NKJV)

ALTERNATIVE:
"He pled the cause of the afflicted and needy; then it was well. Is not that what it means to know Me?" declares the LORD.—Jeremiah 22:16 (NASB)

SCRIPTURE: Psalm 63:1

LESSON IN A SENTENCE: Knowing God will lead to caring for the troubled and needy.

FOCUS

Choose a story that clearly reflects the relationship between poverty and struggle from DC Talk's *Jesus Freaks*. (If you are unfamiliar with this book, it is a collection of historical and current martyrs. The stories are short and poignant. If you are unable to get a copy of this there are a number of resources on the internet offering specifics regarding believers living in poverty.) Before reading the story, ask your group to consider whether it is worse to be in spiritual poverty or material poverty?

Did their answer change after hearing the story at all?

None of us wants to be in poverty. There are many wonderful things in the world to have, use, play, or own. TV shows, movies, and even the news are infatuated with the wealthy, with the often hidden lifestyles of the rich. It is always portrayed as glamorous and exciting! Just off the tops of your heads . . . who are the wealthy people you know about and what are the things they are doing or buying? (It shouldn't take long to think through what current movie star, athlete, or musician has been in the news and some recent purchase or trip to define their wealth and position.)

While we can't all dash off on a trip to Barbados or buy $2,000 sneakers, there are things for which we work or dream to get. As a group, make a list of all the things that we seek after in this world.

DISCOVERY

Read Psalm 63:1 together out loud.

Does this psalm say anything about seeking after stuff? Longing for trips? Thirsting for popularity or prestige?

David was in the wilderness when this psalm was written. When all else is removed, it is God who captivates His attention not a longing to be back in position or for wealth.

Ask again, would it be worse to be in poverty spiritually or materially? Would you be willing to give up your relationship with God in order to gain the world?

APPLICATION: Next to the list of things we seek after in this world, make a list of all that you think God may want for us to seek after. How do these two lists compare? Knowing that we do live in a world where we need to eat and wear clothes and the seemingly mixed messages that God wants for us to live an abundant life, how do we figure out how these two relate?

SPIRITUAL DISCIPLINE CONNECTION: Simplicity is not the same as poverty. While simplicity may never eliminate poverty, it can certainly make an impact. If in no other way, it helps to prevent spiritual poverty in the lives of those who practice it. We touched on this concept on Sunday. While this is true, they are certainly related. There are many excellent ancient writings regarding lives of simplicity. For an excellent introduction, including questions and exercises, *Spiritual Classics: Readings for Individuals and Groups on the Twelve Spiritual Disciplines*, edited by Richard Foster and Emilie Griffin, HarperSanFrancisco, 2000, is an excellent resource.

Consider choosing one way in which you as a group may simplify. Talk through the spiritual benefits of not being consumed by material goods and refocusing as you seek after God and not things.

What's Mine Is . . . God's!

By Amy Jacober

MEMORY VERSE:

Remove falsehood and lies far from me; give me neither poverty nor riches—feed me with the food allotted to me.—Proverbs 30:8 (NKJV)

ALTERNATE VERSION:

Keep deception and lies far from me, give me neither poverty nor riches; feed me with the food that is my portion—Proverbs 30:8 (NASB)

SCRIPTURE: 1 Chronicles 29:10–15; Psalm 24; Proverbs 30:8–9; 1 Peter 4:10

LESSON IN A SENTENCE: We have a responsibility to be wise stewards of everything in this world and all we have, as it really belongs to God.

THE BIG PICTURE (OR WHAT YOU'RE TRYING TO GET ACROSS):

We live in a temporary throw-away world. Fast food comes in sizes many of us cannot finish and then we throw away the cups and wrappers. We only have two feet and yet it's hard to find many people who own only one pair of shoes. While it may seem like our resources are endless, they are not. Stuff can also become a burden! Taking care of things, keeping track of it all, and always being consumed with getting more can be a full-time job! God wants us to use what we have, enjoy abundance in life, but to be consumed by His love not our stuff. Our charge is neither to horde nor to waste what God has given to us. We are to be wise stewards.

- Know that everything we have in this world comes from God.
- Brainstorm ways to be generous with what they have, since it belongs to God anyway.
- Consider how to be truly content with what has been given to them.
- Learn that God wants us to neither horde nor waste what we have.

STUFF YOU NEED:

- Pillowcase
- Loaf of bread
- Marshmallows
- Spam
- Play-Doh®
- Spackle
- Prize (silly certificates or candy)
- 3 x 5 card with scripture written on it
- "Puzzles" that you make from the memory verse ahead of time

FOCUS

If you eat before your meeting, pay attention to whether your students took more than they could eat or not. Make mention that you noticed much went to waste. (Don't embarrass anyone by pointing them out in particular.) If you don't eat just before, ask what they have wasted in the past week—how many lunches not finished, drinks thrown away, papers not recycled, scraps not composted, etc. Even the most conscientious person wastes some each week.

OPTION 1:

This is all about making the most with what you've got! Divide your group into at least 4 teams. In a pillowcase place four items: a large can of Spam, at least a 3–pack of Play-doh®, a loaf of bread, marshmallows, and spackle. Have one person from each group draw an item from the pillowcase. Once each group has their item, let them know they are to make the best sculpture possible, given the item they chose. Give a time limit and remind them of the value of creativity! Invite a few adults from the church to be the judges! Give the winning team a prize.

OPTION 2:

Don't wear a watch for your time together. Ask if there is someone there from whom you can borrow a watch or cell phone (to use the clock on the phone). If more than one person offers, take them all. Thank them and put a few watches on, put the other watches or phones in your pockets. Then make a big deal thanking them for being so generous and sharing what they have. Let them know you will put all of their things to good use.

Teacher's Note: Depending on the part of the country where you live, recycling is either a very normal way of life or seen as a new age practice. Stewardship is a biblical concept. This includes stewardship of talents, of time, of money, of material provisions (the stuff we have) and yes, even of the world around us. Stewardship of our world includes recycling. If your group has never thought about recycling, this may be a good time to begin, even in the smallest of ways. If this is already a part of the culture where you are, explore options beyond recycling soda cans and newspapers.

DISCOVERY

Already split into groups from their teams, hand each group a 3 x 5 card with a Scripture passage and questions written on it.

Group 1 / 1 Chronicles 29:10–15

Who actually owns all things in heaven and earth?
Put verse 14 into your own words in one sentence.

Group 2 / Psalm 24

According to this psalm, who is the Lord?
Put verse into your own words in one sentence.

Group 3 / Proverbs 30:8–9

Put verse 8 into your own words in one sentence.
What are the consequences of either being in poverty?
Of being too rich?

Group 4 / 1 Peter 4:9–10

What do you think it means to be hospitable?
Put verse 10 into your own words in one sentence.

Have each group share their one sentence. Listening to these four sentences, ask how they think they relate. (All four of these Scriptures are related to all things belonging to and coming from God and our role in managing them, our role in stewardship.)

LIFE APPLICATION: Let's assume we not only believe the Scriptures when they say that all things in heaven and earth belong to and come from God but that we are going to try to live by this. The last group had the word "stewardship" in it.

What does stewardship mean?

How would we change if we really believed that we were overseers or managers of things that do not belong to us? What if we were to manage an offer from a Master who would never run out?

The point you are getting at is whether what we have is really ours or simply ours to manage and use as we borrow from God for our short time on earth.

FOR THE MORE MATURE GROUP:

While we most often talk of stewardship with regards to possessions in this culture, the Bible is clear that this is not where it stops; in fact it is probably not even the main focus.

Why do we so often begin looking at possessions?

Over what other things could we have stewardship?

Begin thinking through creation (Genesis 1—3) when all but God were put under the rule of humanity. By the time we reach the New Testament, stewardship has a lot more to do with the gifts of God and the gospel. Check out 1 Corinthians 4:1–2; 9:17; Ephesians 3:2; Colossians 1:25; Titus 1:7 for explicit examples.

What would it mean for us to take seriously this kind of stewardship?

MAKING IT PERSONAL: Wisely using what you have has been the theme for this lesson. We began with some lovely sculptures sure to make any art school green . . . with envy, of course! Even with less than perfect materials, you were able to be creative and offer some great work. You managed what you had been given and pooled your resources to make something amazing!

God is very clear that He gives us all that we need. Our culture is constantly sending the message that not only do you not have enough but what you do have is inadequate. God does not see it that way. In fact, He calls us to share, manage and use what He has given better.

Every single one of us has something to which we cling tightly. Many of us are not even aware of what that is. It is always easy to think of more things we want and hope to be getting in the near future. Many of us shop when we are bored, as a hobby, to relieve stress or feelings of depression. We consume huge amounts and waste huge amounts of paper, clothing, food, the list goes on and on. Think of one way you are going to choose to be a better steward. It may be walking to school so you are not using extra gas, taking only what you can eat or vowing to not buy new shoes until they are actually needed. Share these with your group and pray that God helps you to remember this commitment and that you will be able to keep it.

CONNECTIONS: Probably the most commonly thought of passage for looking at stewardship is that of the parable of the talents (Matthew 25:14–30). If you haven't looked at this one in awhile, it is a great way to explain a difficult concept! As this is the more common one, after you have looked at the scriptures for this lesson, ask your students if it reminds them of any other parable they may know. If they don't think of this one direct them to read the passage in Matthew. Compare and contrast this parable from Jesus with the other Old and New Testament scriptures. This concept is a running theme throughout the Bible!

MEMORY VERSE ACTIVITY

On brightly colored construction paper write out the memory verse but not the Scripture reference so that it takes up the entire page. Make enough of these to have one for every 4–6 people in your group. Cut the paper into puzzle pieces and either put in an envelope or paper-clip together so the "puzzles" don't get mixed up. Give each group a puzzle to put together. (This won't take long unless you are a really skilled puzzle maker!) Once they have the puzzle put together, ask what they think of it. What do "lies and deception" have to do with poverty or riches? What does it mean to have food that is "my portion" and not something else? If you were going to re-write this, what would it say?

QUOTABLE QUOTES:

It is high time that the ideal of success should be replaced by the ideal of service.
—Albert Einstein (1879–1955)

Let us not be satisfied with just giving money. Money is not enough, money can be got, but they need your hearts to love them. So, spread love everywhere you go: first of all in your own home. Give love to your children, to your wife or husband, to a next-door neighbor.
—Mother Teresa of Calcutta (1910–1997)

February 2, 2005

What's Mine Is . . . God's! —Midweek

MEMORY VERSE:
Remove falsehood and lies far from me; give me neither poverty nor riches—feed me with the food allotted to me—Proverbs 30:8 (NKJV)

ALTERNATE VERSION
Keep deception and lies far from me, give me neither poverty nor riches; feed me with the food that is my portion—Proverbs 30:8 (NASB)

SCRIPTURE: Ephesians 3:20-21; Philippians 4:19–20

LESSON IN A SENTENCE: We have a responsibility to be wise stewards of everything in this world and all we have, as it really belongs to God.

FOCUS

This game is a bit counterintuitive! Think of it as similar to a tag game where everyone is It. Give each person at least 3–5 clothespins. The object of this game is to give your clothespins away by clipping them on others. For each round, time and play for 10 minutes. The person with the *most* clips at the end of 10 minutes, loses. Play 2–3 more rounds. Debrief this game, pointing out that they were working hard to give things away!

TIP: (Be certain to quit while they are still wanting to play! It is always better to end with them wanting more than to drag a game on after they have lost interest.)

DISCOVERY

Read Ephesians 3:20-21 together.
This is a hard verse to read, as we can all think of things we were hoping to get, and yet what we really received fell short of our expectations. What does this mean?
What does this verse say about God? Do we believe it?
What does our belief (or unbelief) in this Scripture say about us?
(Be certain to not move through these questions too quickly. These are tough questions and some silence is to be expected!)

Read Philippians 4:19–20 together.
Does this verse shed any light on what we just read in Ephesians?

Teacher's Note: Paul is sending a message back to the church in Philippi. They have given generously to him. As he acknowledges this, he is also reminding them that God will also provide for them just as they have allowed God to provide for others through their generosity.

APPLICATION: The Scriptures both from today and last Sunday make it clear that God wants to provide for us beyond what we ever dreamed (though perhaps not always in the ways we have dreamed!)

What do you think of the phrase "You cannot outgive God"?

Do you think it is possible to be too generous for God to keep up? What have we learned about stewardship to support this?

It really is a cultural paradigm shift to think of praying not to be poor but also not to be rich. The memory verse this week teaches us to not look for more than our portion. Jesus teaches on money more than any other topic. God's provision and how we view it is of great importance.

Close your time together with an exercise in praying Proverbs 30:8 together. Offer time and space for personal reflection and meditation.

(If you are unfamiliar with the discipline of praying Scripture, check out *Read, Think, Pray, Live: A guide to reading the Bible in a new way* by Tony Jones, NavPress, 2003.)

What Do You Want?

By Amy Jacober

MEMORY VERSE:
Praying always with all prayer and supplication in the Spirit, being watchful to this end with all perseverance and supplication for all the saints.—Ephesians 6:18 (NKJV)

SCRIPTURE: Matthew 20:29–34

LESSON IN A SENTENCE: God's compassion is enough for all our needs.

THE BIG PICTURE (OR WHAT YOU'RE TRYING TO GET ACROSS):

The last couple of weeks we have spent time looking at those who are in poverty and what our response should be and then learning to be wise stewards of what God has given to us. This week we turn from material things to the needs of our hearts. We all have needs that lie within us. When we seek God and request these needs to be met in order to be closer to Him, His compassion is greatly moved. Our students are still often in the place of asking God for things (both materially and otherwise) for their own benefit. They may have a hard time accepting, let alone whole heartedly believing, that God can be moved to have compassion on them when all they see is a world full of darkness and sin and in their own lives fights with friends, struggles with teachers, and wondering why they can't have as many nice things as their friends. Even the most grounded adolescent has places which need to be turned over to God—places where they need help if only they would ask. God's compassion is sufficient. Our role in their lives is first to model what it is to be open before God and secondly to teach them of this wonderful benefit in a relationship with the Creator of the universe.

IN THIS LESSON STUDENTS SHOULD:

- ○ Hear that it is OK to want God to do something for them.
- ○ Learn of God's compassion toward our needs.
- ○ Feel free to be open and vulnerable before God and ideally others.

STUFF YOU NEED:

○ "would you rather . . ." list

FOCUS

Have a list of "would you rather . . ." questions ready before your students arrive. They can be totally silly and pointless or serious. If you have never created any of these, they go something like this!

Would you rather always be able to tell when others are lying or to be unable to lie yourself?

Would you rather travel the world vacationing for a year and then never be able to travel again or travel the world for the rest of your life serving others?

Would you rather use mustard or ketchup on everything?

Would you rather never worry about money and have no friends or never worry about having friends and have no money?

Would you rather have to cut your hair every day or have no hair at all?

End with . . .

Would you rather make a fool of yourself to get what you need or remain silent, having others think you are fine, but never asking for what you need?

Today we are going to look at two men who made a clear choice and didn't care who heard them.

DISCOVERY

Read Matthew 20:29–34 together.

Explain that you are going to read this again in small groups but that the group is going to assume one of three roles.

For the first group, ask them to read this passage and to assume the perspective of the two blind men. What was this experience like for them? Were they nervous to ask for help? How did they know to ask Jesus? What was it like to be healed?

For the second group, ask them to assume the perspective of the multitude, the crowd. What was the experience like for them? Why did they tell the blind men to be quiet?

For the third group, ask them to assume the perspective of Jesus. What was the experience like for Him? Do you think He was annoyed to be stopped by people He had never met? What do you think was going through His mind with regard to the difference in the way the blind men behaved and the way the crowd behaved?

Teacher's Note: There are many things that get in our way of taking our needs to God. Not the least of these are the times when we believe that the creator of the universe could not possible be interested in our particular situation. Nothing could be further from the truth. Not only is the story of Jesus having compassion on the blind men encouraging in it's own right, but when placed in context its poignancy is nothing short of miraculous. Jesus and His followers were leaving Jericho on their way to Jerusalem. What Jesus knew and His followers did not yet realize was that He was on His way to the cross. Jesus not only took time to check on those along the way but He, in the midst of what had to have been the most difficult journey of His life, had compassion on others. In our limited ability confined in a sinful world, it is almost impossible to comprehend. And yet, it is true. God always has time for us and compassion sufficient for the smallest and greatest of our requests. Whatever is troubling our hearts, God wants to know what He can do for us.

LIFE APPLICATION: We have now heard the same story from three very different perspectives.

Ask: How does this relate to the Christian church today?

Make a list of the needs all people have. Keep this where it can be seen easily.

Is it easier to think of material needs or spiritual/emotional? Why?

Do you think everyone gets to have these needs met?

What, if anything, should the Christian church do to help in these areas?

Is God's compassion enough for the needs of everyone?

MAKING IT PERSONAL: In many Christian settings, voicing needs is encouraged on one level but the social pressures to be perfect and not to express any real needs is strong. This is the opposite of what Jesus desires. He has more to give than any of us could ever imagine. Most teenagers in the U.S. are not truly concerned with whether they will have shoes to wear to school or not. There is a great concern for whether they will have friends, whether they will be able to do their homework with, whether their family likes them let alone loves them. The pressure to look perfect, to be polite, to not offend, or to always be happy can weigh you down.

On His way to the crucifixion, Jesus slows down to ask of beggars, "What do you want for Me to do for you?" The beggars were seen as valuable and precious in His sight. Jesus sees you as just as valuable and is able to provide beyond what you ever dreamed.

Jesus asks, "What do you want for Me to do for you?" Jesus is concerned not only with our material needs but with our spiritual and emotional needs. Close with a time inviting your students to picture themselves sitting with Jesus as He asks this question. This can be an intensely emotional and difficult time if they are able to be gut-level honest in their prayer. Even if they are unable to do this as you are present in the group, invite them to find a time to get alone with Jesus this week and wrestle with that question and how they would respond.

CONNECTIONS: Both Mark (Mark 10:46–47) and Luke (Luke 18:35) tell this story mentioning only one blind man with the name Bartimaeus. While there is no definite conclusion, one theory suggests that there were two beggars but that Bartimaeus was the better known of the two and consequently his name was used in the other Gospels.

There is a clear understanding by the blind men of who Jesus is. Along with all of the stories that were surely being told in the towns, His actual position and role were accepted and proclaimed by the blind men. In Matthew 20:30, the phrase "Son of David" is used. This is a messianic phrase. See Isaiah 9:6–7; Matthew 1:1; 12:23; 15:22; 21:9; Mark 10:48; 12:35; John 7:42; Romans 1:2, 3; Titus 2:8; Revelation 5:5.

February 9, 2005

What Do You Want? —Midweek

This lesson, while loosely tied to Sunday's, is more of a focus on Ash Wednesday. Many traditions do not observe this formally, though many do. This lesson is intended to honor the tradition of Ash Wednesday within the church calendar without requiring a liturgical background.

MEMORY VERSE:
Praying always with all prayer and supplication in the Spirit, being watchful to this end with all perseverance and supplication for all the saints. —Ephesians 6:18 (NKJV)

SCRIPTURE: Genesis 3:19

LESSON IN A SENTENCE: God's compassion is enough for all our needs.

FOCUS

Enlist students to be readers before your time together. If you have a drama team, invite them to really make this their own and present as the opening focus!

Sketch:

One student sits in a chair in the front of the room

One by one students enter the stage area and offer reminders of weekly activities. They begin slowly with at least the first three coming in one at a time. As the time passes, the students begin coming in more rapidly and overlapping their conversations and reminders.

ST1	Don't forget youth group Wednesday at 7:30.
ST2	Hey! See you at FCA Tuesday morning.
ST3	Are you still organizing the before-school weekly prayers?
ST4	Thanks so much for being willing to tutor me before church!
ST5	I've got the music copied for youth band. Can you pick me up for practice?
ST1	Are you coming to discipleship group?
ST2	I saw that you signed up for the mission team. How many times do we have to meet before we go?
ST3	Are you still going to spend the night to make posters for the fundraiser?

ST4   Do you want to rehearse?

ST5   Have you memorized your verses?

ST1   Don't forget, payment is due for camp!

ST2   I'm volunteering at the shelter. Where have you been going?

ST3   My mom says idle hands are the devil's workshop.

ST4   It's your turn to bring snacks.

ST5   How's your prayer life? (said sarcastically.)

Youth Minister   (Ask person in the chair) So did you get all of that?

Chair   Sure! Bring music snacks to the mission shelter at the devil's workshop.

Youth Minister   And how exactly does that help you to know God?

Segue from the sketch:

Ask: Have you ever known someone who seems to be trying to earn the favor of God?

What does this look like?

Think back to Sunday. We learned that Jesus wants to know what He can do for us. His compassion is great enough to cover our needs. While many people become busy and involved in serving in response to the blessings God has given in their lives, many others work hard to try to earn His favor or to stay so busy that they never actually acknowledge or deal with their own needs. While it may look good for awhile on the outside, it does not bring us any closer to God.

Let your students know that the tone for this time together may be a little more serious than usual. While we have the joy of living this side of the resurrection, a reminder of the need for the cross is healthy.

DISCOVERY

Today is Ash Wednesday. Ask them to take their best guess at what this means.

Traditionally it is from the custom of putting ashes on your forehead as a sign of penitence. (Penitence is the same as repentance—a recognition of sin in one's life, sorrow as you really understand what this sin means, and turning from that sin 180 degrees to lead a new life.)

Read Genesis 3:19.

Today's lesson is a rather somber one. Ask what they understand simply from this verse. In your own words, explain why ashes are used on this day.

Ashes are associated traditionally for another reason. They are a symbol of repentance and the cost of sin but also the purity that is brought through fire—of the cleansing that transforms a sinful human to one properly postured humbly before God.

Teacher's Note: The wage of sin is death. In death, we are returned to the ground, dust to dust. While we most often focus on the free gift of eternal life (Romans 6:23), today is the day to remember that while the gift was free for us, it came at a dear cost. Ashes are used throughout the Scripture in association with repentance and mourning (Job 30:19; 42:6; Daniel 9:3–5; John 3:6; Matthew 11:21; and Luke 10:13). It is our reminder that we deserve to be sent back to dust.

APPLICATION: All over the world, Christians are focusing this night on their sin and their need for Christ. Ash Wednesday is traditionally the beginning of Lent. Lent is a 40-day period leading up to the passion of Christ.

On this night, think over the verse Genesis 3:19. If it were not for the death, burial, and resurrection of Jesus, we would all be returning to dust. By grace the way has been opened for forgiveness of sin and a reconciled relationship with God. Think through what in your life is in need of being burned and transformed to a new way that glorifies God. What needs to be cast back to ashes in repentance? Take this and offer it in prayer to God.

ALTERNATIVE: If you are of a tradition that observes Lent, allow this to be an evening in which you declare what you will give up for Lent. By tradition, many give up something, a fast, in preparation for Easter. This is a way to focus on repentance and the upcoming passion. If you are looking for more information on fasting, see *Spiritual Classics: Selected Readings for Individuals and Groups on the Twelve Spiritual Disciplines*, edited by Richard Foster and Emilie Griffin, HarperSanFrancisco, 2000.

FEBRUARY 13, 2005

Choices . . . Love, the World and God!

By Amy Jacober

MEMORY VERSE:

We love, because He first loved us.—1 John 4:19 (NASB)

SCRIPTURE: Luke 7:36–50

LESSON IN A SENTENCE: It is our choice what we do with the love God gives freely.

THE BIG PICTURE (OR WHAT YOU'RE TRYING TO GET ACROSS):

Valentine's is either one of the greatest days of the year or an evil conspiracy promoted by Hallmark! For many of your students it is a painful reminder of just how unlovable they feel. Looking to Scripture at first glance can be confusing. We are to love the world as God loves the world but we are to love God and not the world. The variations can be dizzying. Many choose to love the world hoping to be loved in return, and they miss the blessing of the One who already loves them. Others choose to hate the world and live in anger and bitterness out of not realizing how much they are loved. Regardless of the path chosen, both lead to disappointment and frustration. This lesson needn't necessarily be blatantly about Valentine's Day as much as a strong reminder for everyone that God loves us and we in turn are capable of loving others in response.

Serving is one way to show this response. Serving, however, is not meant to replace a relationship with God. Many students see the rewards of helping at church and are seen as great Christians when what they are seeking is the approval of the adult leaders and not seeking to honor God. Adult leaders reinforce this as we look to them, offer special accolades and promote them as the "good Christians" and "strong leaders" in our groups. What we offer ought to come from the overflow of what God is doing in our hearts!

IN THIS LESSON STUDENTS SHOULD:

- ○ Look at their own hearts in relationship to God.
- ○ Make connections between being loved and being able to love.
- ○ See that what we give in service is not a competition.

STUFF YOU NEED:

- ○ Glue/gluesticks
- ○ Scissors
- ○ Colored paper
- ○ Glitter or any other crafty supplies if you choose option 1
- ○ Pencils/pens
- ○ Index cards (Don't forget to write the scripture and questions on them!)

FOCUS

OPTION 1:

Break into pairs and tell them they will have about 10 minutes to make their own Valentine's Day creation. Give everyone a piece of blank construction paper and a glue/gluestick. Give half of the pairs extra paper, scissors, etc. with no instructions to share or not to share. (Or you can give some paper, some glue, some scissors etc.)

At the end of the time ask each group to share their creation and a brief explanation of what it symbolizes. Did any pairs share their materials? Remind them that in the big picture of things, this little activity does not matter. Sharing what they have been given does!

OPTION 2:

Shout Out Elimination. This is a fast-paced game where each group has to come up with an example from the category without pausing. (Yes, this is pretty arbitrary. Name one of the adult volunteers as the official judge to be certain they are not taking too much time!) You as the leader will name the category, offer one minute for brainstorming and then move from group to group until there is a pause and one group is eliminated. Keep playing until only one group remains. The rest join back in with each new category.

Break into at least four groups. Ask each group to come up with two categories and let you as the leader know. Categories can include types of cereal, cars, countries, or candy bars—anything they wish. After you as the leader have gathered the categories, play may begin!

After several rounds, you as the leader will end the game with your own category: love songs.

DISCOVERY

We all know tomorrow is Valentine's Day. While we may not all be experiencing what these love songs are talking about (and thank goodness for that, considering some of the lyrics!) there is plenty of love to go around. God gives to us! We are able to give love just as He has first loved us!

Ask: Do you ever feel like you don't have anything to offer in this world? Is there anyone who would be willing to share a time when they knew they were in over their head and had nothing to contribute either to a class project, a musical at church, whatever?

Say: All of us feel at times that we have nothing to offer. That simply is not true. What is needed is an adjustment of what you see of value and what others may want or need.

Break into 3 groups. Give group 1 Luke 7:36–39, group 2 Luke 7:40–43, and group 3 Luke 7:44–50. Each group will have a thought and question to work through. When they are done let them present their section and open up to the rest of the group for discussion.

FOR GROUP 1—LUKE 7:36–39

The woman who offered what she had not only gave a valuable possession but was known to be a sinner. What would this look like today if the characters were a teenager we know, coming before Jesus?

FOR GROUP 2—LUKE 7:40-43

The parable says the one who owed more and was forgiven will recognize God's love more. Do you agree or disagree? What would this parable look like if it were being told about a teenager today?

FOR GROUP 3—LUKE 7:44–50

This woman gave out of what she had. It was not the customary oil with which a king ought to be anointed, but was merely perfume. She not only gave out of the overflow of what she had but sacrificed to give her best (even if it was not the best in the land).

What could a teenager offer today that would be sacrificial and mean as much?

LIFE APPLICATION: Ask: Do you think most people give out of an overflow in their life or do we give trying to earn acceptance and recognition? Why?

Make a list as a group of how a Christian is supposed to behave. (It will include things like waiting until married to have sex, don't get drunk, don't cheat, don't steal, etc.)

Look back over your list and ask why these things made the list. These are good actions. Actions are empty, however, if they are not out of the overflow of what God is doing in your life. Some of the busiest Christians (teenagers included) are the furthest from God. Adults are always telling you what to do and how to act, but they rarely remind you God doesn't want a perfect little robot but wants someone who sincerely wrestles with hard issues, seeks His face, and is willing to change from the inside out. He is looking for the follower who will share what they have, not those who work to get something better and withhold what is currently within reach because it's not good enough. Life is not a competition with other believers. There will always be someone better than and someone worse than you. When you take your focus off you and those around you and place it on the loving face of God, you no longer care if what you have to offer is appropriate or not. You simply want to be in His presence.

MAKING IT PERSONAL: As a group, choose one thing to do for the church as an act of service—not for recognition, but simply because you are able. (This may be folding bulletins, vacuuming the sanctuary, writing notes of encouragement to the pastors/ministers on staff, or whatever creative thing you can think of!) Remember, this is not a competition, it is from the overflow of what God is doing in you. No act is too small if done with the right attitude.

SONGS: "With All My Heart" ZOEGirl
"Everything" Stacie Orrico

QUOTABLE QUOTES:

God cannot give us a happiness and peace apart from Himself, because it is not there. There is no such thing.
—C. S. Lewis (1898–1963)

Choices . . . Love, the World and God! —Midweek

MEMORY VERSE:
We love, because He first loved us.—1 John 4:19 (NASB)

SCRIPTURE: 1 John 4:4–11

LESSON IN A SENTENCE: It is our choice what we do with the love God gives freely.

FOCUS

Give each student five strips of paper. Ask each person to think of their top five most valuable possessions and write one on each strip. Now ask them to set them in front of them in rank order. Go around the group and let each person tell their items and why for the most important of all. When they are done, ask each person for the strip of paper with their top choice and let them keep the other four. Make a chain with the top choices.

Ask: What would be worth giving up this item to you?

Can you think of other things you have that would be no big deal to get rid of? What makes the things different?

DISCOVERY

There is a whole lotta love going on in these verses! So much so that they can seem confusing.

Go through each verse word for word and decipher what the sentence means. (By the way this is broken down into verses, full sentences are included in only one verse.) Re-write each verse as you best understand it. Look for common themes. While it seems confusing, it's not that different from many song lyrics today where the same thing is said over and over in slightly different ways.

Teacher's Note: Ultimately, the end result of your study and wrestling with this passage can be summarized in the memory verse. Christians show love because God loves us. We are able to offer love as a result of what we have experienced. The test of our loving God is in direct proportion to our knowing God. It is only by knowing the love of God that we are truly able to love others and love this world as God would love the world. However you want to say it, love and God are inseparable!

APPLICATION: Refer back to the chain.

Say: What you have written here may or may not be something you are unwilling to offer to God. Chances are you did not write down what you hold closest to your heart. Those are the things we dare not even mention out loud. What can you offer from the overflow of who you are?

MEMORY VERSE ACTIVITY

Take the chain apart and hand each link back to the original owner. Write 1 John 4:19 on this link. This is a stark reminder that there are things we struggle to offer to God. Realistically, this should be an easy decision when we remember that all we have is a result of His love for us. Make this a bookmark or a reminder taped to your mirror. Find a place to set this so that you memorize this verse if you have not already.

FEBRUARY 20, 2005

God Forgives

By Amy Jacober

MEMORY VERSE:
Jesus answered them, "Most assuredly, I say to you, whoever commits sin is a slave of sin." "Therefore if the Son makes you free, you shall be free indeed." —John 8:34, 36 (NKJV)

ALTERNATE VERSION:
Jesus answered them, "Truly, truly, I say to you, everyone who commits sin is the slave of sin." "If therefore the Son shall make you free, you shall be free indeed." —John 8:34, 36 (NASB)

SCRIPTURE: John 4:7–29, 39–42; Romans 3:23; 5:8; 6:23; 10:9–10

LESSON IN A SENTENCE: God wants to forgive you regardless of your past.

THE BIG PICTURE (OR WHAT YOU'RE TRYING TO GET ACROSS):
This is a great day to look at questions and issues surrounding salvation and struggles. Last week you talked about being loved. While this may sound like great news (and it is!), there are many teenagers who simply do not think God can love them because of what they already carry from their past. The idea of God being able not only to forgive them but to genuinely love them just as they are seems absurd. While we know this is not true, for a teenager, this is their reality until shown something else.

The story is of the woman at the well. Focus on the issue of forgiveness and the woman entering into a relationship with Jesus that changed her more than the details of the story or issues of prejudice. Your group will determine the real focus of this day. You can focus on salvation for non-Christians and/or focus on struggles that keep us prisoners for the Christians in your group.

You will also be covering a handful of verses in Romans. Be certain to get across that everyone has sinned, that no sin is too great for God, that forgiveness must be accepted, He will not force it. Finally, that it takes more than being a good church attender and knowing the answers. Romans 10:9–10 makes it clear that you not only have to be able to say it but you have to believe it.

IN THIS LESSON STUDENTS SHOULD:

○ Be able to explain forgiveness.
○ Connect forgiveness of sin with salvation.
○ Identify sins in their own life they consider unforgivable.
○ Walk through the plan of salvation.

STUFF YOU NEED:

○ Pens/pencils/markers
○ Butcher paper
○ 3 x 5 cards with scripture written on them
○ Chain from yesterday
○ Coffee can or something similar
○ Matches
○ Water (to put out the fire)
○ 1–2 pieces of posterboard or butcher paper for movie poster
○ writing paper for movie review

FOCUS

OPTION 1: EVERYONE

Have a piece of paper in the center of the floor. Ask one person to act as a scribe and have everyone else call out descriptive words of a prisoner. In other words, how can you tell if someone is a prisoner? Keep the list in sight.

OPTION 2: EVERYONE

Swamp Crossing—Form groups of 10–15 (if you get over 15 go back to two groups of 7–8). Give each group two pieces of construction paper. Create a playing area at least 20 feet across. Tell them they are going to cross the "swamp" with the entire team. They may not step in the swamp, as there are alligators in the water. If they touch even with a toe they will lose that leg, if they touch with an arm they will lose the arm, etc. The group must work together to get the entire group across. Debrief by talking about having to use other people in order to accomplish certain tasks. You could not get your whole team across if you did not work together, just like there are things in life that you cannot accomplish without God.

DISCOVERY

Break into three groups. Have each group read John 4:7–29. Tell them to think of this as a script for a movie

Would it make for a good plot? Setting? What kind of actors would they need?

Group 1 is to re-enact the events either in biblical times or modern day.

Group 2 is going to make a movie poster about this story.

Group 3 is going to write a movie review of this story.

Have each group present their piece.

Ask: What theme did all three presentations have in common?

Can anyone give a one-sentence summary of the entire story?

Write the best summary on a piece of butcher paper and place it where it will be seen.

LIFE APPLICATION:

Have 3 x 5 cards prepared:

Group 1—Romans 3:23 and Romans 5:8

Group 2—Romans 6:23 and Romans 10:9–10

Group 3—John 3:16 and Ephesians 2:8–9

Have each group read the scripture and tell how it ties back to the story of the woman at the well. Have them present their findings.

Say: We've looked at a story today of a woman who was considered unforgivable. She couldn't even go to the well at the same time as the other women because of her reputation. And yet Jesus approached her, had a conversation with her, and changed her life.

Ask: What things today are considered unforgivable? Is there anything that is truly unforgivable? In light of the scriptures in Romans that we've just read, how would you respond to someone who is still in sin?

MAKING IT PERSONAL:

Read John 4:39–42.

Say: According to these few verses this woman was changed as a result of Jesus' forgiveness. True forgiveness brings change—so much so that she couldn't keep it to herself. As a result of the overflow of her heart the Bible says many people (Samaritans in particular) believed in God.

Think of a time when something amazing happened to you that you just couldn't keep to yourself.

Ask: What made this so easy to talk about?

Could you honestly share out of the overflow of what you are experiencing with God right now?

Close with these two questions in a guided prayer. What in your life do you consider to be unforgivable? What makes you so unique that you are unable to accept the forgiveness of God when He has stated that He wants to forgive all?

End with an invitation to take what seems unforgivable to us and to lay it at the feet of Jesus.

Teacher's Note: Samaritans in general were considered a lower class and not to be associated with by the Jews. In addition, this was a woman, and women had little to no status in this culture. Finally, this was a woman known to be an adulterer and openly living in sin. Whether to avoid the certain namecalling and shunning she would have received had she gone to the well during the morning hours or if she was actually forbidden to associate with other women is not known. In John 4:6 it says it was the sixth hour. By Roman chronicling this would have been high noon, the least favorable time to fetch water. Jesus ignored all of the taboos and approached this unclean, sinful woman with dignity and compassion in broad daylight.

CONNECTIONS: The Psalms are full of verses along this theme. A few worth noting are Psalm 103:3 and Psalm 130:4. In the New Testament, Acts 13:38 offers a very clear declaration of the forgiveness that so often seems unbelievable.

SONGS: "Shackles" Mary Mary

Q U O T A B L E   Q U O T E S :

Forgiveness is integral to letting go. We are bound to people we cannot forgive. Holding even a small grudge takes up space in the soul and captures the energy needed for moving on. To bless the people who are our oppressors is the only way to heal the wounds they have inflicted and to break the chains that bind us to them.

—Elizabeth O'Connor (1921–1998)

God Forgives —Midweek

MEMORY VERSE:
Jesus answered them, "Most assuredly, I say to you, whoever commits sin is a slave of sin." "Therefore if the Son makes you free, you shall be free indeed." —John 8:34, 36 (NKJV)

ALTERNATE VERSION:
Jesus answered them, "Truly, truly, I say to you, everyone who commits sin is the slave of sin." "If therefore the Son shall make you free, you shall be free indeed." —John 8:34, 36 (NASB)

SCRIPTURE: 1 John 1:8–10

LESSON IN A SENTENCE: God wants to forgive you regardless of your past.

FOCUS

Bring a few dictionaries to the group tonight. You will also need many strips of paper, a sheet of paper/person, and pencils. Divide into groups of 6–8. (If you have a large group have several games going at once.) Each person will choose a word from the dictionary. That person writes down the actual definition of the word. He or she shares the word with the rest of the group. Each person writes down what they think the definition of the word might be. Place all the strips of paper facedown in the middle of the table and mix them up. Once they are all there and mixed up, flip each one over. Read each definition aloud and each person writes on their own sheet of paper which definition they think is the actual definition. Once each person has written their guess, reveal the actual answer. For each incorrect guess, the person who chose the word gets a point. For each definition that was chosen, the person who created the definition also gets a point. If the actual definition is guessed, the person who guessed it gets a point and the person who chose the word loses a point. A new person now chooses a word. Play until each person who wants to choose has a turn.

Just like in this game, many of us try to present who we are to be different than (often better than) we really are! Definitions were made up for words and the whole point of the game was to try and trick each other into not knowing the real definition. While we may not do this on purpose all of the time, our Christian culture says that we must put our best self forward. Scripture tells us that God already knows our hearts and that each of us is sinful. It is only when we are able to be honest with those around us, and more importantly with ourselves, that God is able to really enter into our lives.

DISCOVERY

First John 1:9 is a well-known verse. It is known as the Christian bar of soap! (A rather silly phrase but it will stick with you!) While we tend to know this one, the two verses on either side are often ignored.

Read 1 John 1:8–10 together.

Have the following questions ready for discussion. Hand each one out and then give at least 7 minutes for the group to wrestle with the answer. These are questions that can be answered easily on the surface level, but try to encourage thoughtful reflection and discussion.

1 John 1:8—Is this referring to never having committed a sin or to not having a nature able to sin? Are either of these possible?

1 John 1:9—Why is confession a key component to forgiveness?

1 John 1:10—Why would God have to be a liar if we have no sin?

Everyone has sin. Romans 3:23 says that "all have sinned and fall short of the glory of God." While this is all very easy to say, to get our minds wrapped around it is difficult. This is even more so for a teenager moving from concrete to abstract thinking. They have been told their whole lives that there is good and bad. By the time they are reaching high school many have had the chance to have behaved in ways that would seem irreparable and certainly that would disgust God. All the while, they carry the mask of being well put together and the model Christian. Being reminded that all have sinned is a welcome relief. They don't need to keep up the act. You may not know the details of what they have done but you do know they are sinners. You also know the beautiful blessing of the gospel that Jesus wants to forgive them. He does not care how awful of a past they think they have. He cares for their future and wants to walk that journey with them, openly and honestly.

APPLICATION: Warts and all . . . think of your closest friends or family members. Think only of the ones you really consider the closest to you. Without saying who they are, share two or three of their characteristics that you love about them. There may be several people, so feel free to share as many of the characteristics as you like.

Now, think of those same people and think of their worst traits. What are the things about them that you know are awful or frustrating, but you love them anyway. Again, without saying who they are, share some of those characteristics.

If there are people you can truly know, the good and the bad, and still love them, what would ever make you think God couldn't do the same for you?

First John 1:9 says that He is faithful and just to forgive our sins if we would only confess them. Take a few moments to confess your sins before God, asking Him to help you repent and cleanse you from the unrighteousness they bring.

FEBRUARY 27, 2005

Justice

By Amy Jacober

MEMORY VERSE:
But let justice run down like water, and righteousness like a mighty stream.—Amos 5:24 (NKJV)

SCRIPTURE: Matthew 23:23–28

LESSON IN A SENTENCE: Jesus calls us to more than behavior that makes us look good; He calls us to behavior that makes a difference.

THE BIG PICTURE (OR WHAT YOU'RE TRYING TO GET ACROSS):
    The underdog always cries out for justice, but the top dog has a little different take on things. So where does God stand on the matter? Throughout the pages of Hebrew history we hear God speaking through His prophets. He demands full respect for every person, a lifestyle that works to put an end to abuse and neglect. Teens may already have been on both ends of the stick. Now they need to hear Christ's challenge to become advocates for "the least of these."

- Be able to define justice both from their experience and in looking at Scripture.
- Identify real-life issues where one's definition of justice is having an impact.
- Learn how Jesus views those who follow the bare minimum of the law attempting to look good.
- Consider how we may truly follow Christ in His understanding of justice.

STUFF YOU NEED:

- Newspapers from at least a week (enough for at least 3 for every 6 students)
- Headlines gathered and written on strips of paper
- Scissors
- Tape
- Copies of the Reader's Theatre

FOCUS

BEFORE THEY ARRIVE:

Find a large wall space that can be a central focus for the room. Tape up two strips of paper with "most just" and "least just" written in them. This will become the place where the students tape the stories they find to the wall.

Gather headlines from the past week. Listen for those first stories on the news, check the internet, look at the front pages of several different newspapers. Write these in bold letters on strips of paper (about the size of cutting a large piece of construction paper in half lengthwise) and tape them on the walls around the room. Don't draw any particular attention to them. You will be using this later.

ONCE THEY HAVE ARRIVED:

Have students gather in groups of no more than 6. Hand each group at least 3 days' worth of newspapers. This is a hunt! Ask them to look for the story that is the "most just" and the "least just." Don't offer much explanation. Allow them to determine what they would consider as justice being served. Once they have found their top story for each, have them cut it out and tape it to the wall under the category where it fits. Allow each group to share the story they chose and why. (Depending on your group, they may find other stories that they just find interesting, silly, or that caught their eye. Feel free to let them share these as well, but don't let this consume too much time or get you off track from looking at justice.)

Ask, from their perspective and world, are there stories that didn't make the paper that are important to them? Does it matter what kind of paper they read? (If you already know what your students read, try picking up a few copies of their favorite papers and magazines: *Spin*, *NewTimes*, *Rolling Stone*, *Vibe*, *Seventeen*, etc. See if there are any stories in these you can use.)

Looking at our stories and thinking through how you decided which ones made it, how would you define justice? (If they can't give a definition in a sentence or two, ask them to talk about it. What concepts have to be present for justice to happen?)

What do you think God has to say about justice?

Reader's Theatre

Enlist a few very strong readers to present this. While it is always preferable to involve students as much as possible, this is better done by adult volunteers if you don't have any students who can carry it well. The reading needs to be done in very loud but controlled, intense voices. Instruct the reader's to begin from the back of the room as soon as you ask "What do you think God has to say about justice?"

R1:   Woe to you, scribes and Pharisees, hypocrites!

R2:   Woe to you church goers and perfect-looking Christians!

R1:   You pay tithe of mint and cumin.

R2:   You pay with what is easy and cheap for you, no sacrifice or value here!

R1:   You have neglected the weightier matters of the law; justice and mercy and faith.

R2:   You are preoccupied with petty little rules, with legalisms that make you look good and let you judge others' actions, knowing nothing of their hearts; you have forgotten justice is inseparable from mercy. One cannot exist without the other.

R1:   Blind guides

R2:   Blinded by your own self-righteousness

R1:   Blind guides who strain out a gnat and swallow a camel

R2:   Do you even have a clue how ridiculous you are?

R1:   Woe to you, scribes and Pharisees, hypocrites!

R2:   Hypocrites, even as you sit and hear this, you still don't know we are talking about you.

R1:   You cleanse the outside of the cup and dish so it looks good for all those you think are looking.

R2:   There are not nearly as many looking as you have imagined in your head.

R1:   Blind Pharisee

R2:   Blinded by your own wants and needs

R1:   Blind Pharisee, wash the inside of the cup and dish. The only one who matters looks to the inside. When this is clean, so goes the outside.

R2:   It must be in this order. Take care of what is on the inside; the outside will be as clear glass for the dirt or cleanliness of the inside.

R1:   Woe to you, scribes and Pharisees, hypocrites!

R2:   Surely we don't need to point you out or say your name!

R1:   You are like a whitewashed tomb.

R2:   A tomb is a tomb, whether it looks good on the outside or not. If you are in a tomb, you are decaying, filled with brittle bones and death.

R1:   Even so, you appear righteous to everyone around.

R2:   You say the right things, do the right things, you recycle, sign the letter for Amnesty International, and even volunteer at the homeless shelter once a year to get service credit for school.

R1:   You look perfect.

R2:   You look perfect.

R1:   You look perfect to all but the one who can really see you.

This is taken from Matthew 23:23–28. Still gathered in small groups around the newspapers, have each group read the scripture for themselves.

Does this sound like the loving, gentle language we usually associate with Jesus?

How can this be a part of the Jesus we have always known and seek to follow?

LIFE APPLICATION: Jesus has some very strong words regarding justice. Particularly look at Matthew 23:23. Jesus calls us to not get tripped up with the petty legalistic offerings that are of little to no consequence anyway. His focus is on justice, mercy, and faith.

Look at the headlines taped around the room.

Choose one or two of the stories you know well. Would they meet the criteria Jesus has set for what is important? Are the issues of justice, mercy, and faith being considered as decisions are being made?

What would it look like if everyone worked for a just world that Jesus intended and not just to look good on the outside?

Issues of right and wrong are in the news every day. We often use the language of what is just without really knowing what this means. Considering the scriptures, what definition for justice could you now offer?

MAKING IT PERSONAL: We've looked at headlines and the way justice is being handled in the big events of our community and world.

What is one thing you could consider doing right now to be working toward a more just world? This can be as simple as sticking up for someone at school who gets picked on or as huge as learning about and fighting drunk driving.

CONNECTIONS: The possibilities are numerous. God is quite clear that His desire is for justice, and in the way He views it best. We are to help the helpless and those less fortunate. We are not to take advantage of others. Our commitment is to be more than superficial, as it is a reflection of our faith. Among the references: Deuteronomy 16:20; 24:17; Psalm 82:3; Proverbs 21:3; Colossians 4:1.

Q U O T A B L E   Q U O T E S :

Justice is not a case of the "haves" giving to the "have nots." That is far too unworthy and shallow an interpretation of God's intent for us. We must recognize that all people are our brothers and sisters . . . we are all members of God's family. We would want the best for our family. . . . It is our responsibility as part of being God's children to actively try to make God's Kingdom come on earth.

—Desmond Tutu (1931–)

Mercy is only to the undeserving.
But such we all are made in the sight of God. . . .
Nothing can make injustice just but mercy.

—Robert Frost (1874–1963)

Justice —Midweek

MEMORY VERSE:
But let justice run down like water, and righteousness like a mighty stream.—Amos 5:24 (NKJV)

SCRIPTURE: Amos 5:21–24

LESSON IN A SENTENCE: Jesus calls us to more than behavior that makes us look good; He calls us to behavior that makes a difference.

DISCOVERY

Monopoly is one of the best-loved family games of our time. When the rules are switched and not everyone knows them, it's not nearly as much fun for those without the power. A game already based on greed and acquisition becomes a cutthroat example of the haves seeking even more! The have-nots have no hope of getting ahead. Welcome to the world of Amos.

Read Amos 5:21–24 together.

Before you continue, it will help to spend a little time giving the background of the Book of Amos to your students. Without background, these verses are very difficult to understand. Use a commentary or Bible handbook for a full explanation. See the Teacher's Note for a brief introduction.

Ask students to pair up and answer the following questions.

Amos 5:21—Why would God hate the feasts and sacred assemblies of Israel?

Amos 5:22—Why would God not accept any of the offerings, neither grain nor burnt?

Amos 5:23—The offering is from the talents of the people themselves and are still rejected. Why is this so?

Amos 5:24—Justice and righteousness are to flow. The people have been offering all of the right things according to the letter of the law and they have been rejected. What would need to change in order for justice and righteousness to come?

Teacher's Note: Amos was a prophet in a time of extreme wealth and indulgence for Israel. As a man who understood God's desire for all, he was offended morally. He saw the corruption in a society that looked brilliant on the outside, powerful and wealthy. He was not impressed with Israel equating their success as being in favor with God. He saw past the façade, and the continued presence of the rich oppressing the poor was a constant heartache for Amos. He was concerned for the spiritual life of the northern kingdom. His concern moved beyond that of a human concern; his prophetic message also was an expression of the biblical covenant requiring social justice. It is under this umbrella that the Book of Amos was written.

APPLICATION: In what ways are we currently living in a world just like the one in which Amos was prophesying?

Should we as Christians do anything about this? If yes, what?

What do you think Amos would say about our world? About this country? About your role or responsibility?

God's people have always been intended as those set apart. We are to be the defender's of the oppressed near and far. Living in this sinful and broken world, injustice will always be present. While this can be discouraging, it does not change what we have been called to do.

As a Christian in this country, we are aware of needs in the community and world, but it is easy to forget that the ability to meet and worship safely is a blessing not all Christians share. A group in the world desperately in need of our prayer is that of the persecuted and suffering church. While we have responsibilities in many areas to fight oppression and not give in to the lure of luxuries and self-indulgence, we also have responsibilities to our fellow believers. You can find many resources on the internet to keep you posted in the condition of Christians and churches around the world. www.barnabasfund.org is one such web site where you can learn and be updated.

Close in prayer for those struggling and oppressed in this world. You may want to offer an open time for a popcorn prayer where your students call out different groups in need of justice in the world.

MARCH 6, 2005

Reality? What Is It?

By Ric Lipsey

MEMORY VERSE:
This is real love. It is not that we loved God, but that he loved us and sent his Son as a sacrifice to take away our sins.—1 John 4:10 (NLT)

SCRIPTURE: Genesis 1:26; Deuteronomy 8:3; Psalm 139; Isaiah 43:1; Jeremiah 29:11; John 1:12; 15:15; Romans 3:23; 6:23; 12:1; 1 Corinthians 6:19–20; 13:4–8; Ephesians 1:3–4; 2:8–10; 2:19; Philippians 4:19; 1 John 4:8–10

LESSON IN A SENTENCE: This lesson will help students come to an understanding that the love of God is what makes them complete.

THE BIG PICTURE (OR WHAT YOU'RE TRYING TO GET ACROSS):
   We are continually bombarded with images of who we should become or what we should achieve. If we pursue what the world views as important we will become shallow people who only follow the latest fashion or trend. We try hard to "keep up with the Joneses" and all too often find our worth in our status or our possessions. Eventually we find out that nothing the world has to offer us satisfies for any length of time. To be truly satisfied we must find our contentment in the love of God.

IN THIS LESSON STUDENTS SHOULD:

- Be able to distinguish between real and false perceptions of who they are in Christ.
- Be able to understand their self-worth comes from being a child of God.
- Confirm their own relationship with God as Heavenly Father.

STUFF YOU NEED:

- Magazines
- Poster boards/butcher paper
- Glue sticks
- 3 x 5 cards

○ Pens/pencils/markers
○ A copy of the book or video *The Velveteen Rabbit*

FOCUS

Ask students to define REALITY in their own words and discuss their answers.

Reality: the actual state of things, the state of being real.

Divide students into teams of two or three. Distribute magazines, posterboard, and glue to the groups. Have them tear out ads or stories about things that make the people in the magazines feel good about themselves and paste them on the posterboard. You could even have the teams develop a storyline about the "Pursuit of Happiness" with their findings. Have each team present their work to the entire group. Discuss with group what the magazines communicate about how to achieve happiness.

(For further research: perform an internet search of "Marketing to Teens" and you will be amazed at how the advertising industry seeks out teen dollars and brand loyalty.)

On 3 x 5 cards: have students list 3 things about the *real* them that no one in the group knows. Ask students to share one or more of these if they feel comfortable.

Ask: What makes you feel good about yourself? Material things, getting asked to the right parties, the perfect date, the family you're born into, your looks?

What do these things do for your self-esteem?

Are the above things the real you?

Is there anybody that knows the real you?

Give the students the following definition of the word real.

Real: authentic, genuine, not artificial or counterfeit, actually existing.

In light of this definition ask the question again: Is there anybody that knows the real you?

DISCOVERY

The answer to that question is a resounding "Yes." There is one who knows the real you. It is the God of the universe. The one and true God knows you. He knows every thing about you. He knows your thoughts, desires, strengths, weaknesses, successes, and failures. He knows it all because He created you.

Read: Psalm 139

Real life comes from the giver of life Himself.

Read 1 John 4:10

If real life comes from God, how do we become real?

What actually makes us real?

Read *The Velveteen Rabbit* to the group. If time does not allow, read the conversation from the book between the Skin Horse and the Velveteen Rabbit concerning how toys become real.

Ask: Did you catch it? What is it that makes a toy become real in the story?

Say: The answer is love. Not a passing infatuation but a love that is committed.

We hear the word love used in so many contexts that it has lost its importance. We talk about how we love a television show, a restaurant, a pair of shoes, or our favorite sports team. Then we use the same word to express our feelings to our family and even to God. We have somehow lost the true definition of the word love.

Let's go to the Bible to see how God defines love.

Read: 1 Corinthians 13:4–8

Have students come up with a brief and modern definition of love based on the above scripture.

Like the love of the little boy made the Velveteen Rabbit real, the love of God makes us real.

Ask: How does the love of God truly make us real? The best answer can be found in 1 John 4:7–10.

All of the stuff in the magazines or that the world has to offer will never make us real. Once we obtain what is being sold we will find that there will always be something bigger and better. The computers and cars will only get faster. The fashions will eventually go out of style. What now?

LIFE APPLICATION: When we feel the desire to give in to the trappings of this world, how do we respond? When we want to feed the greed that consumes all of those around us; what should we do? When we begin to base our worth on our looks, status, or possessions, where do we go?

We go the same place that Jesus did, and that is to the Word of God.

Read: Deuteronomy 8:3

This is what Jesus quoted when tempted in the wilderness.

So if we are to live by the Word of God, what does it say about the real us? What should we base our self-esteem on? There will always be someone prettier, faster, smarter, or stronger than us. But is that what we should we dwell on?

Prior to the lesson write the following verses on 3 x 5 cards and assign them to students to read out loud to the group:

Psalm 139:4; Genesis 1:26; Isaiah 43:1
Ephesians 1:3–4; Jeremiah 29:11; John 1:12
John 1:12; Ephesians 2:8–10; John 15:15
Philippians 4:19; Romans 12:1; Ephesians 2:19

Let the group discuss how knowing the above things can help us in our everyday lives.

MAKING IT PERSONAL: Isn't it incredible that God has said all of these wonderful things about each one of us? How does it make you feel to know that the Lord knows you so personally?

However, there is one more thing that must be said. God only says these things to His children. The fact is that not all of the billions of people on this planet are God's children. Yes, we are all created in His image, but our sinful nature has separated us from our Heavenly Father.

Yes, it is true, we cannot escape the reality of sin in our lives (Romans 3:23).

But the good news is we can be restored to God's family by putting our faith in His Son Jesus Christ to save us from our sin.

This is how much God really loved us (Romans 6:23; 1 Corinthians 6:19–20).

If there has never been a time in your life when you have placed your faith in Christ to save you and make you real, there is no better time than right now.

If you have been made real by the love of God through Jesus Christ, share with someone else how they too can become real.

Helping Others Become Real — Midweek

MEMORY VERSE:
We love Him because He first loved us.—1 John 4:19 (NKJV)

SCRIPTURE: Mathew 28:18; John 6:1–14; Mark 5:1–20; 5:22–24, 35–43; 5:25–34; Luke 5:17–26; 5:12–15; 6:6–11; Matthew 20:29–34; 8:5–13; Mark 8:22–26; Luke 7:11–16; 13:10–17; 17:11–19; John 4:46–54; 6:1–14; 9:1–7; 11:1–45; Matthew 5:13–14; Galatians 3:28; 1 Peter 3:15; 1 Corinthians 9:19–23; Philippians 2:1–3; Hebrews 10:24.

LESSON IN A SENTENCE: Students learned in the previous lesson that it is the love of God that makes us real; now they will be taught the need of evangelism, servanthood, and missions.

STUFF YOU NEED:

- Copy of *The Message*
- Verse references to be read
- Note pads and pens
- Copy of Dr. Seuss' *Horton Hears a Who* book or video (Optional)
- Copy of the movie *First Knight* (Optional)

FOCUS

In our last lesson we discovered that it is the love of God through a relationship with Jesus Christ that makes us real. In this lesson we will answer the question:

Why should we want to help other people to become real?

First John 4:19 tells us why.

Do you remember the Dr. Seuss story *Horton Hears a Who*?

It is a delightful tale about an elephant named Horton, who hears the voice of a tiny person called a Who, (in fact a whole city named Whoville) living on a dust speck. Without the benefit of Horton's elephantine ears, no one else can hear anything coming from the dust speck, so the other inhabitants of the jungle come to suspect that Horton is crazy because he is trying to save those on the dust speck from all kinds of peril. As Horton makes his way through the jungle he keeps repeating "I just have to save them. Because, after all, a person is a person, no matter how small."

That little phrase is what the business world would call Horton's MISSION STATEMENT.

DISCOVERY

All major corporations have a mission statement. (If you want to have some examples of this, most have them listed on their corporate websites, i.e., Coca Cola, Mc Donald's, etc.) Mission statements help businesses keep them on track. They make sure that they do not lose focus of why they are in existence. If companies did not have a clear direction they would get confused and what would the result be? Federal Express would be delivering pizzas and Domino's would be bringing you overnight packages.

Ask: How do we as the church stay on track with what God has designed us to do? Do we have a mission statement as Christians? What would it be?

Read: Mathew 28:18 (The Message gives a great interpretation of this verse)
1 John 4:21

Let's look at Jesus on mission: (pass out the following stories to either individuals or divide into small discussion groups)

Legion: Mark 5:1–20
Jarius' daughter: Mark 5:22–24, 35–43
Diseased woman: Mark 5:25–34
Paralyzed man: Luke 5:17–26
Leper: Luke 5:12–15
Withered hand: Luke 6:6–11
Bartimaeus: Matthew 20:29–34
Servant: Matthew 8:5–13
Blind man at Bathesda: Mark 8:22–26
Widow's son: Luke 7:11–16
Handicapped woman: Luke 13:10–17
Ten lepers: Luke 17:11–19
Nobleman's son: John 4:46–54
Man born blind: John 9:1–7
Lazarus: John 11:1– 45
Five thousand fed: 1 John 4:21

Have individuals/groups briefly report what they read with the whole group. (You may want to have them do the reporting in the form of a newscast with each group picking a representative to be their "reporter.")

Ask: What can we learn from Jesus' mission?

Possible Answers:

Jesus helped every class of people.

All sexes and ages

Believers and unbelievers

He met them on a physical level before a spiritual one.

Other's people's faith played a part.

Helped when others did not like it

He used a variety of methods.

Things are not too different today. We come in contact with people every minute of every day who are in need of the touch of Jesus.

Ask: Who needs healing? Can we say that everyone needs some sort of healing? (spiritual, emotional, physical, relational, etc.)

What does Jesus say we are to be to these people?

Read: Matthew 5:13–14 (The Message).

We are not to *be* salt and light but in all actuality we *are* salt and light—it's up to us as to how flavorful and illuminating we are. We need to be the extreme butter-flavored microwave popcorn instead of the light, low-sodium variety when it comes to showing those around us the love of God. We need to be a strong and steady beacon of hope, not a flashy inconsistent strobe light, so our friends can make it through this journey of life without stumbling.

LIFE APPLICATION: Jesus spent much time with outcasts.

Who are the outcasts of today?

(Nerds, poor, homeless, minorities, handicapped people, drug heads, teen moms, AIDS patients)

How are we to respond to these people?

Galatians 3:28—with no partiality to gender, status, or skin color

1 Peter 3:15—with gentleness and respect

Just as Christ loved us when we were outcasts

1 Corinthians 9:19–23 (*The Message*)

MAKING IT PERSONAL: In the movie *First Knight* starring Sean Connery as King Arthur this phrase is engraved around the mythical "Round Table":

"In serving each other we become free."

Read Philippians 2:1–3 and Hebrews 10:24.

How do these verses relate to the message on King Arthur's "Round Table?"

Jesus came to earth to serve and to save. We should adopt this mindset into all we do as those who bear His name as Christians.

Make it a personal goal to serve someone this week.

You Want Me To Do What? (following God in His will)

By Amy Jacober

MEMORY VERSE:
I can do all things through Christ who strengthens me. —Philippians 4:13 (NKJV)

SCRIPTURE: Nehemiah 2:9–20

LESSON IN A SENTENCE: Following God may seem impossible by the world's standards, but what is really impossible is trying to live excluding Him from your plans.

THE BIG PICTURE (OR WHAT YOU'RE TRYING TO GET ACROSS):
Walking into the wind, the deck stacked against you, an uphill battle . . . there are many ways to say what it feels like when we are called to what seems to be the impossible by God. It would be nice if obedience to God came with a guarantee of ease and peace. He never says this, however. What He does say is that He will be with us, that we can do anything through His strength, that what He calls us to He will prosper in His time. It is true that for most of us as leaders, we don't know what it is like to be in junior high or high school in an age of open discussion of terrorism, in an age where the very concept of truth is up for grabs, where what is billed as "reality TV" is actually carefully edited renditions of a false environment. God is calling us as adults to be His instruments in the lives of teenagers. As adults, if we're really honest, this is a rather daunting task, if not downright scary. For our students, he is calling them to Himself. This is equally as daunting and scary. God wants us to do what He asks. Fortunately He has not abandoned us; He offers His guidance and strength on the journey.

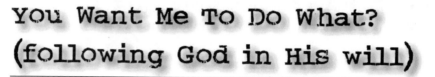

IN THIS LESSON STUDENTS SHOULD:

- Be able to identify God as the ultimate authority.
- Learn that what they once thought was impossible becomes possible through the power of Christ.
- Gain confidence for daily living, knowing God is with them.

FOCUS

OPTION 1:

Begin with a game of Simon Says. For this age it works much better if you go very fast, with no pause between directions. Allow the winner to lead the next round. Play this 2–3 times.

Switch the rules a bit to play Silent Simon Says. Create a gesture that must precede each action to show they are to do the action. Play Silent Simon Says for at least 2–3 rounds. This should be considerably more difficult than the first few rounds.

After the novelty has worn off, ask what would it be like to go into a movie theatre and just begin playing Silent Simon Says? What about in the middle of church on Sunday?

Being able to do this would require a few easy but significant things. You have to be able to follow, to know who to follow, and what to look for to be able to follow where the leader intended. You also have to be able to care only about what the leader says and thinks. Most of us are able to follow others as long as it makes sense. If someone were to begin Silent Simon Says in a movie theatre, most of us would not follow. We would laugh, try to ignore that we knew the person, or simply join the others sure to question or mock that person.

Following Jesus can be very much like this.

OPTION 2:

Play a mind game such as Black Magic. Black Magic requires at least two people who know how to play. One of you will take the lead and let the group know the two of you are able to communicate telepathically. Have the other person leave the room. While he or she is gone, invite someone there to choose an item in the room. Invite your partner back and they are to tell you if the item you have named is the one chosen or not. For example, let's assume a beach ball is chosen. You will go around the room and suggest items. Ask was it the coke can in the corner? No. Was it the dry erase board? No. Was it the stereo? No. Was it the beach ball? Yes. Your partner will know to say yes to whichever item comes directly after the "black" item. The stereo was black, therefore the very next item needs to be the one chosen.

This game is a lot of fun, particularly for those in the know. It can be exceedingly frustrating if not seem impossible for those who do not know the rules to follow.

Following Jesus, in particular following His will, can seem impossible, especially when the world's standards confuse matters.

DISCOVERY

Read Nehemiah 2:9–16.

In brief, ask for a summary of what Nehemiah was doing.

Without Nehemiah revealing to anyone else, he went to scout out the territory. He went in the night, keeping secret his plan and permission he carried from the king, not to mention the direction from God.

Read Nehemiah 2:17–18.

Nehemiah is talking to the priests, nobles, and officials here. What exactly does he tell them?

Jerusalem has been in ruins for more than 100 years. Imagine their surprise when Nehemiah comes to town declaring his intentions to rebuild!

Read Nehemiah 2:19–20.

Verse 19 has some of the officials trying to cause trouble. They are aware that no building may take place apart from permission of the king. How does Nehemiah respond to these officials?

It is curious that Nehemiah, who did receive permission from the king and earlier stated so, chooses to remain silent on this point at this time. When the officials asked, it would have been easier for Nehemiah to lean on his permission from the king. By their worldly standards, the king was the ultimate authority. Nehemiah, however, chose to rely on what he recognized as a higher authority. He made no mention of the permission King Artaxerxes had given, instead giving full honor to God.

Teacher's Note: Nehemiah was a prophet in the reign of King Artaxerxes. One day while serving, the troubles of his heart were apparent on his face. This was an offense that carried stiff punishment. A servant was not to trouble royalty with their own worries. The king looked with favor on him and asked what was the trouble. Nehemiah told the king of his desire, and King Artaxerxes granted him permission to head to Jerusalem. All of this can be found in Nehemiah 2:1–8.

LIFE APPLICATION: It seems so easy to read the story of Nehemiah going to Jerusalem to rebuild the walls. Think about this for a moment. A city that has been in ruins for over 100 years, a servant who has no position of authority or nobility heads out, traveling over 900 miles to do the impossible. All of the odds were against Nehemiah, and yet he knew the impossible was possible by the power of God.

Ask your students to write up the major pattern of this story.

It should go something like this. (You may need to help get them started.)

Feel called to do something
Ask permission from the earthly authority set over you
Plan and prepare

Share your vision
Have the world question what you are doing
Remain obedient
Rely on God and give Him the honor
How practical is this pattern for life today?

What are times you have heard of or know God called people to do something that didn't seem to make sense?

Can you think of a time when you were asked to do something that you knew would make you look foolish? Did you find a way to pass the blame? A good excuse why this really wasn't *your* idea but that you were just following orders? Oddly enough, for the world in which we live, many who are choosing to do the right things will be the ones questioned. It is easier to cheat, lie, drink, or a host of other things and fit into society. Choosing to follow Christ will feel impossible on some days. Fortunately, we have a God who specializes in impossibilities!

MAKING IT PERSONAL: What is God calling you to right now?

Can you be obedient to the calling of God or do you need a person to have authority over you?

Being a follower of Christ can be confusing. The greatest blessings come in our relationship with Jesus. Some of our greatest sorrows can also come from the misunderstandings of others with regard to our relationship with Jesus.

There are times when what God is calling us to seems impossible. Dig deep! What impossible thing is God calling you to?

MEMORY VERSE ACTIVITY

Philippians 4:13 tends to be a favorite verse. It is a good one to keep on the tip of our tongues in an unpredictable world. I have yet to meet the person who would say that memorizing scripture is bad. And while most of us would give some acceptable reason for why it is good, many of us don't practice this very well. Let this be a time to not only work on memorizing scripture but to work on how we may be blessed by that memorization.

Ask your students to think of the impossible thing they believe God has placed in their life. Invite them to pray Philippians 4:13, replacing "I can do all things . . ." with "I can get along with my dad through Christ who strengthens me" or "I can make it through this illness through Christ who strengthens me."

SONGS: "The Calling" Benjamin Gate
          "Do That" KJ-52

Q U O T A B L E   Q U O T E S :

Give us grace, O God, to dare to do the deed which we well know cries to be done. Let us not hesitate because of ease, or the words of men's mouths, or our own lives. Mighty causes are calling us . . . But they call with voices that mean work and sacrifice and death. Mercifully grant us, O God, the Spirit of Esther, that we say: I will go unto the king and if I perish, I perish.

—W. E. B. DuBois (1868–1963)

You Want Me To Do What? (following God in His will) —Midweek

MEMORY VERSE:
I can do all things through Christ who strengthens me. —Philippians 4:13 (NKJV)

SCRIPTURE: Acts 5:17–32

LESSON IN A SENTENCE: Following God may seem impossible by the world's standards, but what is really impossible is trying to live excluding Him from your plans.

FOCUS
Foreign exchange

Have everyone in the group get in pairs. Ask each group to come up with a list of ten things they would pack in a suitcase if they were going to be foreign exchange student in another country for a year. Collect the lists and read through the lists and see if the group can guess who made each list. It's amazing how little we can get along with when we have to. If they included the Bible, commend them for remembering an important item. If they did not include the Bible, ask them where they are getting their priorities for what is important.

How important is it to include God in your plans?

If it is so important, can you honestly say that you consistently include God in your plans?

DISCOVERY

Have the group number off as 1's and 2's.

After they have split into two groups, have each read their scripture and then summarize what is happening.

Have all of the 1's look at Acts 5:17–25.

Have any of you ever been in prison?

What would you imagine it would be like to have an angel free you from prison and then to go teach in a very public place?

Peter and the apostles had been thrown in prison. This was a seemingly impossible situation. Locked doors, guards—the future was looking bleak.

Have all of the 2's look at Acts 5:26–32
For what did the captain scold the apostles?
How did Peter respond?
What does it mean to obey God rather than men?

APPLICATION: Let's take that last question. What does it mean to obey God rather than men?

Following God's will can be tough when it doesn't seem to make sense. He has promised, however, that He will not fail us nor lead us astray. His heart is for us, His will that of a parent wanting nothing less than the best for His children.

Peter was in prison, freed and facing the anger of a captain and the priest again. Yet he did not waiver. He declared boldly that they would obey God not men.

Ask your students: Where is God calling you to obey Him rather than the ways of this world? Through what impossible task must you walk by the strength of Christ?

Your Will Be Done (Palm Sunday)

By Amy Jacober

MEMORY VERSE:
Father, if it is Your will, take this cup away from Me; nevertheless not My will, but Yours, be done.—Luke 22:42 (NKJV)

SCRIPTURE: Matthew 26:36–46

LESSON IN A SENTENCE: God's will, in the short term, may seem confusing or unbearable and yet, that is still what we are called to follow.

THE BIG PICTURE (OR WHAT YOU'RE TRYING TO GET ACROSS):
We all face points in our lives where what is occurring is not what we had hoped for or planned. We walk difficult paths that no one can smooth over, take our place, or change. Jesus was no exception. When God stepped out of heaven and manifested Himself in the incarnation, He knew exactly what He was getting into. Choosing to walk through this did not make the actual act of the crucifixion any less painful or humane. Jesus truly does understand what it is to be abandoned, abused, humiliated, and gasping for the breath of life. He chose to enter Jerusalem amid all of the waving of branches and cheers tossed His way, knowing that in a few short days these fans would turn to foes. He chose to live what He prayed earlier with His followers, teaching them on the mountain (Matthew 6:10). We can take encouragement and strength from this example. At times, we too are called to live through things that are very different from what we would choose for ourselves. While difficult, these are not impossible, as we are called to seek God's will above our own.

IN THIS LESSON STUDENTS SHOULD:
- Learn that even Jesus struggled with circumstances in life.
- Be encouraged by the example of Jesus to submit His will.
- Begin or continue the discipline of seeking God's will and not their own.

STUFF YOU NEED:

○ Paper
○ Pens/pencils
○ Palm fronds
○ Permanent marker
****for the Midweek lesson this week, if you do not have
    a video depicting the crucifixion, you will want to
    rent one ahead of time!

FOCUS

OPTION 1:

Imitation is the sincerest form of flattery, or so they say! Choose 3–4 students at least a few days prior to your time together. Ask each of these to imitate one of your adult leaders. (Remind them to do this in a spirit of fun and not critically. They may need your help drawing out characteristics that are distinct.) Have each of them offer their imitation without saying who they are imitating. Have the remainder of the group guess who is being imitated. Another option is to imitate a few of your students. If you choose to do this, be certain you are doing this in a spirit of fun and choose students who are able to take that kind of attention well. After all of the laughing has stopped, ask the following:

How did you know what person they were imitating?

Is this all there is to the person?

What else could they have done to let you know who they were imitating?

While a perfect imitation is hard unless you've really studied someone, there are certain things that stick out about everyone—the way a hat is worn sideways, glasses always being lost, certain phrases people use. Hang out with someone long enough and you'll find we all have these little identifying characteristics.

OPTION 2:

Give each person a paper and pen or pencil. Ask them to think back through times when they wanted to do something and they knew they were supposed to do something else. As they think of times they submitted their will to God, draw this on a timeline. In hindsight, can they see where their choices or will may not have been the best for them? (This can be a tricky exercise because a person may also see a pattern of never doing what they feel would be best and only doing what others wish—a student with an overbearing parent or one who has a people-pleasing attitude. Submitting our will to God is not the same as being a person with no backbone.)

Ask, was it always easy to follow God's will?
If you had to do it over, would you?

God's will does not often lead us out of the fire; it often has us walk right through. When we submit however, we are no longer walking on our own strength but in His.

DISCOVERY

I can think of nothing more intense than knowing you could escape a horrible situation and yet choosing to remain. That is exactly what Jesus did in the garden of Gethsemane. (Prepare to read Matthew 26:36–46 from a red letter edition of the Bible.)

The first time you go through this passage, ask your students to be silent, perhaps close their eyes. They are not going to read along, rather have them listen to what was happening. Have one person read as the narrator (words in back) and a second person read as Jesus (words in red).

What did they hear in this story? What words stood out to them?
(You may want to do this a second time.)

ANCIENT PRACTICE: This is a great time for a *lectio devina*. Even if your group has never done one, this passage lends itself well to this and could be a great time for teaching a new discipline. The passage as a whole is rather long but you could begin with the entire passage and narrow down to just Matthew 26:39. If you are unfamiliar with *lectio devina*, check out *Soul Shaper: Exploring spirituality and contemplative practices in youth ministry* by Tony Jones, YS/Zondervan, 2003.

In small groups have them read the passage for themselves.
What did the mood of Jesus seem to be?
Look at Matthew 26:39 in particular. What do you think was really going on?

Teacher's Note: In our society when we talk of submitting to any authority our own red flags go up, but this is still what we as Christians are called to do. This is no pathetic giving up of the spirit. It is not a command to roll over and allow life to just happen to you. Submitting to the will of God is actively cooperating with Him, with His revealed purpose. Another lesson for another time but think of what we know we are to do: The Great Commission, to act justly, love mercy, and walk humbly with God. These are not small matters. Submitting to the will of God is one of the most intentional, active things we can do.

LIFE APPLICATION: Try to think apart from the scripture we have just read. What comes to mind with the phrase "not my will but yours"? If you are like most people, this position does not compute. We are all about being certain our rights as an individual are not touched. Submitting to any authority is seen as a threat to our very existence.

Ask your students to name a recent event in the news where someone was showing an example of refusing to follow anyone's will but their own.

Teacher's Note: You may want to bring in a recent story of a child actor who is suing a parent, a musician suing an agent, or an athlete who trashed a hotel room on a traveling game. Bring a story that will connect with the interests of your students. Sadly, you only have to look as far as the newspaper to find one.

How was Jesus different from the examples we just mentioned?

Jesus was facing His own death. He knew it was coming, and regardless of how He may have wanted to change the process, He had to walk through the experience.

If you chose option 1 at the beginning:

At the beginning of our time, we saw some great imitations. You also told me a few ways that you were able to tell who was being imitated. The only way to know those kinds of things is to be around that person.

If you chose option 2 at the beginning:

You each created a timeline of times you submitted your will to God.

Ask: How many of you know what your parents are going to say when you ask them how late you can stay out? What about if you ask their favorite flavor of ice cream? If they like to sleep in on Saturday or not? How do you know these things?

How can you know what is your will and what is God's? Just like being able to give someone's answer to a question you have asked, it comes from being around that person a lot. It comes from building a relationship with them, being open and honest.

How else can you know the will of God for your life?

MAKING IT PERSONAL: If it were perfectly clear exactly what God wanted for you to do, would you? God says He will be with us in the most difficult of situations, but it is still our choice.

We all have places that are strongholds in our lives. These are the places where we are able to say we know God will take care of us but we insist on wrestling and living from our own strength just in case He is busy.

"Not my will but Yours."

These words are powerful and considerably more serious than most of what we talk about on any given day. Take a few moments to ponder these in silence. After 1–2 minutes, close in prayer.

MEMORY VERSE ACTIVITY

As this is Palm Sunday, if you have palm fronds available bring them to your time together. Either write the memory verse on the palm frond with a permanent marker beforehand or have your students do so. (Sharpie's work well!) Just before the closing prayer, remind your students that today was the day Jesus entered Jerusalem and it was a party! He entered on a donkey to cheering crowds. Even in the midst of the crowds and the cool breeze being created by waving palms, He was there not for His will but for that of His Father.

CONNECTIONS: While many of us know the Lord's Prayer by heart, its connections are often overlooked. This was not simply a beautiful piece of prose. This is the model by which Jesus was teaching us to pray. He models this again in the Garden of Gethsemane in Matthew 26:42, recalling the words of Matthew 6:10: "Your kingdom come, Your will be done on earth as it is in heaven." We are to be seeking God's will at all times, even when we don't understand it. Ask your students, can they say honestly that they seek God's will over their own? Why is this so hard?

SONGS: "King of Glory" Third Day

QUOTABLE   QUOTES:

God was executed by people painfully like us, in a society very similar to our own . . . by a corrupt church, a timid politician, and a fickle proletariat led by professional agitators.

—Dorothy Sayers (1893–1957)

Your Will Be Done (Maundy Thursday) —Midweek

MEMORY VERSE:
Father, if it is Your will, take this cup away from Me; nevertheles not My will, but Yours, be done.—Luke 22:42 (NKJV)

SCRIPTURE: John 13:34

LESSON IN A SENTENCE: God's will, in the short term, may seem confusing or unbearable, and yet that is still what we are called to follow.

Holiday!

If your students are unfamiliar with some of the language surrounding the Passion, this is a great time to have a low-key time to talk and explain some key concepts taught across Christianity.

This is passion week. If you asked your students what passion meant, would they know it was the suffering of Christ?

As this is commonly considered the most holy of weeks for Christians, it is only fitting that this time together be a little different to set it apart.

It is a holiday but not in the commercialized sense of the word. It is a *holy*day. This week is filled with days to remember. Nearly 40 days ago we touched briefly on the meaning of Ash Wednesday and Lent. That period is coming to a close. Tomorrow is known as Maundy Thursday. Not every tradition follows or acknowledges Maundy Thursday. Whether you do formally or not, it is a part of passion week.

Maundy Thursday is known as the Thursday of commandments. It is named from the Latin word *mandatum*, a mandate, a commandment.

Look up John 13:34.

What did Jesus just command?

Where are Jesus and the disciples when this command is given?

How are we to take this command today?

The night before He was taken and crucified, Jesus was still taking care of others. He knew exactly what was coming up, and yet His words and actions reflected His desire to care for those He loved and to be certain when He could not be with them physically that they would care for and love one another.

Tomorrow is Maundy Thursday. Most often, if your tradition celebrates this event it is with the Lord's Supper. The following day is

Good Friday. Ask your students what happens on Good Friday? Why do we call it "good"?

Obtain a copy of the *Jesus Film* or any other orthodox version showing the crucifixion. You will want to have reviewed this and have it cued before your students arrive. Once you have finished looking at John 13:34 and have discussed the commandment, introduce the clip as a picture of Good Friday. You may want to turn the sound down and allow the pictures to speak for themselves. Another option is to play Third Day's *King of Glory* while the crucifixion scene runs. (You will want to cue this beforehand as well.)

Show the video with little set up. Be certain to stop at the end of the crucifixion scene before any hint of the resurrection.

This is a powerful way to consider exactly what Jesus went through. Allow the gravity of this scene to sit with you. You may need some time to debrief and answer questions with your group. Offer plenty of time for silence before jumping into a discussion.

Close in prayer as we consider the commandment Jesus left with us and the events coming up in a few short days.

MAINTAINING YOUR MINISTRY HEADING

By Chap Clark
PROFESSOR/YOUTH WORKER

One of my favorite loves is being on a boat, any boat, so long as it is on some open water. While in graduate school I owned a small ocean ski boat. I had the chance to take it about thirty miles across the open ocean from Los Angeles to Santa Catalina Island a few times. One pristine morning my roommate and I left harbor, feeling confident that we were prepared for the short trip across the ocean. As we rounded the breakwater, we set our course according to the compass and opened the throttle.

Because we were having such a good time, and because we could see the island far off in the distance, neither of us paid much attention to our heading. We figured that we knew what we were doing and were more or less on target. Suddenly, out of nowhere, we were enveloped in the thickest fog bank either of us had ever seen. Knowing we were right in the middle of a busy shipping lane, we slowed to a crawl and began to focus on trying to make our way through the fog and the danger.

About an hour later, as the fog lifted, we quickly realized what a near-deadly mistake we had made both when we had first set out and in the midst of the fog. In our initial excitement and subsequent anxiety, we had failed to maintain a careful eye on our compass heading. We had figured that since the island was within sight, and we felt like we were staying more or less true to our heading (whenever we had checked, at least), we would be fine. In the wildness of the fog bank, we literally focused on the urgent need before us to the detriment of the vital responsibilities of the journey.

We discovered, however, that even a small divergence from our original heading over time had caused us to be miles off course when the fog lifted. When we could finally see the island, we were so far south that we could easily have run out of gas miles from shore, not having any idea where we were. A few degrees may seem to make no difference when the seas are flat and the visibility is clear, but that morning we found out firsthand that to count on conditions always being calm and stable is to court disaster.

I have learned, usually the hard way, that this is true of ministry leadership as well. When we lose sight of our heading, as when we allow ourselves to relax our focus and direction because things seem to be working well, we can find ourselves to have slipped over time quite a distance from where we intended to go. Or, when the unexpected slips in, we may become overly consumed with the immediate. Under those circumstances it is all too easy to allow our heading to slip—perhaps only a few degrees—but when we are finally able to look up from the tempest, our neglect has taken us far off course.

When we disregard the basic task of leadership—navigating those we lead on a straight course—we cannot hope to fulfill our call. Sometimes this lack of focus on what is the most important can lead to unforeseen and devastating consequences. Anyone in ministry leadership is called to stay the course God has called us to travel as we represent Him toward those we serve. To do this, among the most important "compass headings" that must be carefully attended to is a commitment to people over program.

Leadership Compass Heading—A Commitment to People over Program

Most leadership experts affirm that people need to be encouraged and nurtured to be productive and effective participants in reaching the goals of the group. But for those that seek to honor God in how they lead, people are not a means to an end; they are an essential focus of our ministry. One of the most seductive traps that few in Christian leadership can avoid is the temptation to make what we do more important than who we are. We may blithely assume that because we are doing "the Lord's work," how we treat one another is secondary at best. This perspective, however, denies the essential teaching of Jesus and the Bible regarding the kind of leadership God calls us to—how we love, nurture, and encourage one another *is* our ministry calling, regardless of the tasks we are attempting to accomplish.

When I was around thirty years old, I was in charge of the program for a large weekend outreach conference. The intricacies of the schedule, the vast numbers of details that needed to align, and the dozens of people playing various parts provided an exhilarating opportunity for me. I loved seeing how the many things my team and I had worked on for months were able to create the environment where the musicians, speaker, and counselors could connect with their students. Throughout the weekend, the machine was humming, and I was on top of the world.

On Saturday night, however, the wheels began to fall off. The speaker had gone on too long, and those responsible for the entertainment that night were not as prepared as I had hoped. I decided, on the spot, to cut one of the longer acts—the band was scheduled to sing two fun songs, and without processing with anyone, I simply told them when the lights went out that they were cut from the program. The decision may have been right, but the process was not—I was curt, authoritative, and final. They had worked hard to prepare, they were excited, and I treated them like pawns on a chessboard. While single-mindedly focused on producing the "most effective environment for ministry to kids," I had devalued and hurt those who were there to serve God with me. The worst part of this story? I walked away being absolutely convinced I was right.

That next week I met with my intern, Donn, to debrief how much he had learned from getting to spend the weekend as my assistant. The gentlest of souls, Donn began our time being uncharacteristically blunt. "You did a great job, Chap, but you were a jerk all weekend." If anyone else had said this to me, especially while I was still enveloped in the euphoria of the experience, I would have been mad and defensive. But Donn is such a wonderful, tender guy that he got my attention. As we talked, he helped me to see how far I had drifted from what I knew to be true, both about me and about ministry. I had allowed my own distorted understanding of the importance of "excellence" and "programmatic effectiveness" to violate a far more insistent and obvious call of ministry as reflected in the words of Jesus: "This is how everyone will recognize that you are my disciples—when they see the love you have for each other."[1]

Staying the Course

For followers of Jesus Christ, and especially those called into ministry leadership, our heading is set from the outset—to live a life "worthy of the calling" we have received (Eph. 4:1). God's call provides both the motivation for how we treat others as we lead, as well as the Spirit-driven power that enables us to love as we lead. Leadership theorists agree that "principled leadership"[2] is a necessary ingredient to productive leadership. The apostle Paul puts it more pointedly: "the only thing that counts is faith expressing itself through love," and "the entire law can be summed up in a single command: love your neighbor as yourself" (Gal. 5:6, 14). Love and care for people is *always* our primary ministry, no matter what the job description states. The direction of our calling is clear, and we must be careful to pay attention to that compass heading when things are going well and when we face an unexpected crisis. How we treat people is the central calling of any follower of Jesus Christ. Loving people *always* matters more than anything we will ever do in God's name.

Maintain your heading. Love, nurture, and show tender care to those God puts in your path, both those you work with and those you serve. This is your calling. Stay the course.

---

[1] John 13:35, *The Message*

[2] See as an example *Teamwork: What Must Go Right, What Can Go Wrong*, Carl Larson and Frank LaFasto, Sage, 1989.

MARCH 27, 2005

Easter

By Amy Jacober

MEMORY VERSE:
For I delivered to you first of all that which I also received: that Christ died for our sins according to the Scriptures, and that He was buried, and that He rose again the third day according to the Scriptures.—1 Corinthians 15:3–4 (NKJV)

SCRIPTURE: 1 Corinthians 15:1–20

LESSON IN A SENTENCE: Jesus is the Christ, dead, buried, *and* resurrected.

THE BIG PICTURE (OR WHAT YOU'RE TRYING TO GET ACROSS):

Easter is a time for celebration! It is the very crux around which we as Christians have placed our faith. Perhaps even more than Christmas, Easter is slipping into a mythical holiday that has lost its meaning for many in our society. It is not considered polite to point out that Jesus was killed and certainly not that this He is *the* only way to a reconciled relationship with God. This ultimate celebration, while a time to honor God, is more of a reminder to ourselves of just how great a love Jesus has for us.

Struggles with the concept of the resurrection are nothing new. There were some in Corinth as well who denied the possibility of the resurrection of the dead. If this were impossible, though, so too would the resurrection of Jesus be impossible. The implications for this are great. Like Paul, we must declare that Jesus was raised from the dead and is with us today!

IN THIS LESSON STUDENTS SHOULD:

- Be reminded of the full and true meaning of Easter.
- Hear the story of Jesus being seen not by one or two but hundreds!
- Know in full confidence that the resurrection did actually happen.

STUFF YOU NEED:
○ Videotape from previous Wednesday

FOCUS

Begin your time with two truths and a lie. Have a few pre-selected volunteers to get the ball rolling. Each person is to think of two things that are true about themselves and one lie. For example: I was born in California, I am an avid surfer, and literature was my favorite subject in school. Now the group guesses which is the lie. (In case you were wondering, I am not an avid surfer. I have tried and, well, I'm rather pathetic, but it is fun!) This is a pretty easy activity and you can involve many students as the turns move quickly.

Ask: How do we know when the person is telling the truth?

(Answers may include that a sibling or friend knows, someone saw it, they trust them or have faith that they are not lying when they say they are not.)

Can we apply these same principles to the resurrection?

Keep these principles visible and refer back to them as you go through 1 Corinthians 15:1–20.

DISCOVERY

Split into four groups. Give each group a scripture and a question that they are going to share with the rest of the group.

1 Corinthians 15:1–2
What does Paul mean with the phrase "believed in vain"?

1 Corinthians 15:3–4
How did Paul know what he preached?

1 Corinthians 15:5–7
Why is it so important to list all of the people who saw Jesus after the resurrection?

1 Corinthians 15:8–10
How does Paul describe himself?

After looking at these scriptures and having each group share their response, have each group look at and discuss the following.

1 Corinthians 15:11–20
What does it matter if Jesus was really dead or had only fainted?

Assuming Jesus was indeed dead, what does Paul say is the consequence if there is no resurrection?

What would this mean for us today?

LIFE APPLICATION: The resurrection is true.

How did the resurrection of Christ impact the society in Jerusalem and the surrounding areas?

How does the resurrection impact us today?

References to God are all through media. Take a few minutes to brainstorm movie lines, TV shows, songs, sports, etc. where God has been mentioned.

Why do you think these themes are still so present when so many reports say that God is no longer a fundamental part of our culture?

Say: While each of these may not exactly be lifting up the name of Jesus, what happened on the cross and through the resurrection has left an imprint on our world that is clearly visible 2,000 years later.

MAKING IT PERSONAL: Think through what the truth of the crucifixion and resurrection means for you. Do you live daily allowing the resurrection to impact your life?

On Wednesday you watched only the crucifixion. Today, cue the tape to begin with the crucifixion but run it through to the resurrection.

Ask: For those of you who were here Wednesday, what was it like to have left and had the video end at the crucifixion?

How long does it take for news to travel around your school? Your family?

Think of major events in our country. Does it take long for everyone to know?

Can you imagine what joy must have spread through the town and the energy when the story on everyone's lips was the resurrection of Jesus?

You have amazing news. The resurrection is true. How will you allow this news to impact your life?

Close in prayer celebrating with God the overcoming of death, the resurrection, and the blessing of being able to be reconciled and in relationship with Him.

CONNECTIONS: For the account in the Gospels of the resurrection, see Matthew 28; Mark 16; Luke 24; and John 20.

The Result of the Truth of the Resurrection —Midweek

MEMORY VERSE:
For I delivered to you first of all that which I also received: that Christ died for our sins according to the Scriptures, and that He was buried, and that He rose again the third day according to the Scriptures—1 Corinthians 15:3–4 (NKJV)

SCRIPTURE: John 20:11–22

LESSON IN A SENTENCE: Jesus is the Christ, dead, buried, *and* resurrected.

FOCUS

OPTION 1:
If you have a digital camera and the capability to project a power point or mediashout presentation for your group, this is the way to go. Take at least 10 pictures of very common everyday items, but be certain that they are extreme close-ups. Examples might be someone's eye, the keyhole on a door, the curb of a street—have fun looking for everyday items! Once you have the pictures taken, create a slide show.

ALTERNATE OPTION
If you have some extra time and access, visit the homes of your students and allow their belongings to be the items you choose. When you go through the slide show a second time, show the broader picture with the item in context!

Give each person present a sheet of paper and a pencil. Have them number their paper to ten and guess what each item is beside its corresponding number. Go back over the slides and give the actual answers. Give a small prize for the one who had the most correct guesses.

OPTION 2:
Bring one rope or webbing at least 20 feet long for every 8 people. If you have blindfolds, have each person place a blindfold on their eyes. Have one person as a spotter to be certain no one is peeking! The spotter may not offer help to the group. Tie the rope in a circle and have each person grab hold of the rope. Once each person is in place, ask the group to make a circle. Give a minute or so and then tell them they may

look. Eyes closed again, make a square. After a minute have them stop and see how close they are. Repeat for a few more shapes.

Say: These are elementary shapes. How easy or hard was this without being able to see what you were doing?

Why is it that very familiar things become hard to recognize when they are taken out of context?

DISCOVERY

Jesus appeared to many people after his resurrection. There were a few with whom He spent more time than others. Mary Magdalene was the first to see Jesus and almost missed Him! The disciples John and Peter came next. Both were equally as shocked!

Say: We read on Sunday that Paul had heard the story of the resurrection from those who were there and saw Jesus. The stories were spreading like wildfire. You are going to look at two stories. Try to think like a reporter. Your assignment is to report what you are reading for the viewing audience. Think of interview questions and any missing pieces you may want to ask. (If you have a larger group, split into at least 4 smaller groups, two that can do TV reports and two that can work on a newspaper article.)

Group 1 will have John 20:11–18

Pay particular attention to the moment when Mary was talking directly with Jesus and didn't even realize it was Him.

Group 2 will have John 20:19–22

Pay particular attention to the order of events that led to the disciples saying they were glad to see the Lord.

How do both of these interactions fit with knowing that both Mary and the disciples had been told that Jesus would die and that He would raise from the dead?

APPLICATION: Sometimes God shows up when we least expect Him. We know He has promised to be with us and to provide. Just like Mary and the disciples we can become so overwhelmed with grief and our own heartache that we miss Jesus. There are some things that seem fairly obvious, but when taken out of context we miss their presence.

Where in your life can you look back and see times when God was at work but only in hindsight can you recognize it?

Where do you currently need to have your eyes open for what God would want for you to see as He provides for you?

QUOTABLE   QUOTES :

The way of Love is the way of the Cross, and it is only through the cross that we come to the Resurrection.
—Malcolm Muggeridge (1903–1990)

What Can You Know?

By Amy Jacober

MEMORY VERSE:
And you shall know the truth, and the truth shall make you free.—
John 8:32 (NKJV)

SCRIPTURE: Job 19:25; John 4:42; 8:31–32; Romans 8:28; 2 Corinthians 5:1; 2 Timothy 1:12; 1 John 3:2, 14

LESSON IN A SENTENCE: It is possible to know truth from God.

THE BIG PICTURE (OR WHAT YOU'RE TRYING TO GET ACROSS):

Even in a postmodern world, there are some things we can know. Scripture uses a variety of words for "knowing" related to knowledge. Knowledge comes from many sources: intellectual, emotional, experiential and relational to name a few. To "know" someone or something is more than a passing acquaintance. It is more than just being able to memorize or repeat a formula. It is an intimate understanding that transcends your head, heart, and gut! Scripture is full of statements that express these truths to be known.

IN THIS LESSON STUDENTS SHOULD:

- Be introduced to the significance of "knowing" truths from God.
- Identify specific truths as found in Scripture.
- Be able to see benefits and consequences related to truths.

STUFF YOU NEED:

- Candy
- Mazes (if choosing option 2)
- 3 x 5 cards with scripture references written on them
- Dry erase board or butcher paper
- Markers

FOCUS

OPTION 1:

Truth or Lie?

This is a great game with little preparation and can easily be adjusted for time!

As your leaders arrive, ask each to think of a few truths from their own life and to make up a few lies. (If you have a small number of leaders, either have each leader think of several or enlist students to join!) Gather your group and have 3 leaders up front as "contestants." Before the "contestants" go up front, they agree as a group which one will state the truth while the other two will present lies. The three go to the front and in turn offer their statement. Have your students ask questions of each "contestant," trying to determine which person is actually telling the truth and which two are telling a lie. Continue playing with new "contestants" for at least three rounds or as long as they are still interested! (It's amazing what a simple game this is but how much your students will get into it—the sillier the better! For those needing a creative jumpstart, truths are relatively simple; believable lies can be more difficult. Consider things like "When I was in third grade, I shaved my eyebrows off." Or "When I took my dog for a walk I was not paying attention and fell in the canal.")

OPTION 2:

As your students arrive, have mazes and pens or pencils set out for them. You can pick up a book of mazes at the grocery or drug store. Be certain that each person gets to do at least one.

Say: We've already looked at one significant way to approach truth whether you realized it or not! Each maze had one solution and only one solution. Finding these solutions were aided by the mazes being two-dimensional. You had a view of the entire thing with nothing hidden as you were trying to find the solution.

DISCOVERY

They may have been able to find the solution to the mazes easily or they may have known who was lying and who was telling the truth, but how do we know other things? How do we know what is true?

God tells us there are things we can know. In fact, He left several specific truths in Scripture that we may "know" Him and His ways. The following scriptures happen to all have the word "know" in them. Realistically, this is a great lesson to tailor for the specific needs of your group. The concepts of knowing what God wants for us transcends the use of the word "know." It may be important for your group to know they need to love their enemies (Matthew 5:44) or not to worry (Matthew 6:28). Whatever it happens to be that your group needs, let this be a time when they can hear it in truth!

Write the following scriptures on 3 x 5 cards (one per card):

Psalm 46:10 (Know that I Am God)

Job 19:25 (My Redeemer lives, and prophetically will stand on earth)

John 4:42 (That Jesus is the Christ, the Savior of the world)

John 8:31–32 (You can know the truth)

Romans 8:28 (All things work to good for those who love God)

2 Corinthians 5:1 (God is preparing a place for believers in heaven)

2 Timothy 1:12 (That God is able to help us with our commitments)

1 John 3:14 (That we [believers] have passed from death to life)

Divide into groups of 4–6. Give at least one card to each group. Ask them to look the scripture up and write on the back of the card what they can "know." Have each group report back what we can "know" according to these scriptures. Write these on a list either on a dry erase board or butcher paper in a place that is easy for all to see.

ANCIENT PRACTICE: If you have never done a labyrinth with your group this would be a great time to offer this. A labyrinth may look like a maze at first but it is indeed quite different. There are no tricks, nor wrong turns that end in failure. A labyrinth is rather an intricate path. If you are fortunate enough to have a labyrinth nearby, schedule a time to take your group for this experiential time of walking in truth. You can check through the labyrinth locator portion of www.grace.org. If a labyrinth is not available, you may set one up in a room separate from where you are meeting. You may also purchase *A Prayer Path: A Christ Centered Labyrinth Experience* through Group Publishing (check out their web site for ordering.) You will want to choose a location away from distractions as much as possible. There are several good books and web resources to help you in finding a suitable plan for your own labyrinth.

Teacher's Note: In Hebrew the transliteration for "know" is "yaw-dah." This should sound familiar from its usage as slang—yada, yada, yada!

LIFE APPLICATION: Read back over the list of what you can "know" according to the scriptures looked up.

Ask: Do you think what we have listed here is true?

What does it mean for something to be true?

Perspective plays a huge role in how we understand things. The word truth itself can be subjective. It is true that my favorite ice cream is vanilla. Does this make it true for everyone? Students today are presented with more and more options of what may be possible and few filters to deal with the vast amounts of information.

Think back to the story of the blind men approaching an elephant. One encounters a leg and believes the elephant to be a pillar, a second feels the trunk and believes it to be a snake, a third grasps the tail and believes it is a rope, a fourth is brushed by an ear and believes it is a fan. Which man is correct? Only when they come together, while holding to their own experience, can they listen and learn in community to discover the real elephant!

God has placed us in community with the blessing of His revelation in Scripture. Ask: What about being a follower of Christ have you learned to be true from a community of believers?

MAKING IT PERSONAL: There are many mysteries in connection with God. There are many things we are told to be true that seem difficult to grasp.

Take a few moments and read again the list of what Scripture says we can know.

Break into prayer partners. Do you struggle with the truth of any of these? If not, with what Christian truth do you struggle? Share your struggle with your partner. Spend a few moments discussing these and close, inviting God to enter in and reveal what is true.

MEMORY VERSE ACTIVITY

Buy several used keys at a thrift store. Type and print the memory verse on strips of paper. Cut the strips, hole punch one end, and use yarn or ribbon to tie the verse to the key. Just before closing in prayer, ask the group who values freedom? The key to freedom is knowing how to acquire and keep it. Read the memory verse and hand out a key to each person.

CONNECTIONS: Jesus Himself says He is *the* truth. The language used here is that of a definite article. *The* truth is vastly different from *A* truth. While this may seem out of place in a politically correct postmodern world, we are no more pluralistic than life in Jesus' day. It is just as true, and just as counter-cultural, today as it was 2,000 years ago!

SONGS: "Leaving 99" by Audio Adrenaline on the album *Worldwide*

What Can You Know? —Midweek

MEMORY VERSE:
And you shall know the truth, and the truth shall make you free.—
John 8:32 (NKJV)

SCRIPTURE: Psalm 119:16; Galatians 2:5

LESSON IN A SENTENCE: It is possible to know truth from God.

FOCUS

Gather the lyrics to several of your students' favorite songs. Have a student or two help you with the choices to be certain they are current and in the genre your students actually like. Read the lyrics one line at a time (depending on your group, you may want to try one word at a time). As soon as they know what song it is and who sings it, have them call out the answer. Have plenty of small candies on hand to throw out for each person able to answer.

When you have run out of songs, ask how they knew the names of all of the songs.

DISCOVERY

Your students were handed keys at the end of the last meeting. Ask if any of them remember the memory verse at this point? (If not, look up John 8:32 and read this together.)

Assuming that we do not want to live under the Old Testament laws and legalism and that we do indeed desire to live in the freedom for which Christ came, died, and was resurrected, how do we know what is true in order to be set free?

As none of us walking around today were actually present with Jesus nor any of the apostles, we must rely on Scripture to gain insight into this question.

Look up Psalm 119:16 and Galatians 2:5.

Ask: How do these two verses fit together?

The gospel was spoken by Jesus, both in words and in His life. In knowing the gospel, we know truth. In knowing truth, we have been set free. We are not to forget what has been spoken by God.

Teacher's Note: Looking at Psalm 119:16, "word" is transliterated as "dabar." This is a widely used idiom that does not carry with it the more exclusive meanings of "word" such as law, testimony, precept, statute, commandment, or judgment. It comes from a verb meaning "to say" or "speak." It is broader in meaning and covers more. Whatever God says is indeed His word, and His word is true. This is in contrast to the statute mentioned. Statutes carry with them the concept of customs and often were engraved on metal or stone so they could be read and kept by all.

APPLICATION:

Ask: What does it mean for you to not forget God's Word?

From what do you need to be set free?

The gospel literally means good news!

Think through the connection between the memory verse and the two scriptures for this lesson. The gospel is the good news that sets us free. Knowing this, not forgetting this, and reminding ourselves of this allows us to live in freedom.

Most of us do not live daily as though we remember the Word of God. We continue to struggle and wrestle with things that hold us down. Ask again: What does it mean for you to not forget God's Word? The truth is that in not forgetting Jesus we are able to live in freedom!

QUOTABLE QUOTES:

Growing knowledge is not enough to save us, any more than bricks are enough to make a home. The Spirit of the crucified and risen Lord must dwell in the knowledge, or the knowledge itself becomes a prison.

—George Arthur Buttrick

Temples Do Come with Instructions

By Amy Jacober

MEMORY VERSE:
Do you not know that you are the temple of God and that the Spirit of God dwells in you? If anyone defiles the temple of God, God will destroy him. For the temple of God is holy, which temple you are.—1 Corinthians 3:16–17

SCRIPTURE: Hebrews 13:4; 2 Peter 2:9–11

LESSON IN A SENTENCE: The temple in which God dwells is to be kept by His instructions.

THE BIG PICTURE (OR WHAT YOU'RE TRYING TO GET ACROSS):
God gives directions for our lives not to punish or limit us but to set us free to be loved. If you have even been half paying attention, talk of spring dances, proms, and new love interests fill the conversations of your group. Along with all of this talk come the inevitable topics of prom dresses, curfews, what to drive, and yes, who to date. The too often unspoken topic (at least around the adults in their lives) is that of insecurities or anxieties over what to do once the dance is done. Most students are way beyond wondering if there should be a kiss at the door or not. God is quite clear that sex before marriage is not a part of His perfect plan. Even if the prom is not the hot topic in your group, this lesson can be framed around dating in general. Open communication and discussion is key as adolescents wrestle with what it means to remain pure.

IN THIS LESSON STUDENTS SHOULD:

- Know that the Holy Spirit lives within those who are believers.
- Learn that wherever God resides is considered holy.
- Identify sexual purity as one of many ways we are to keep our temples undefiled.

STUFF YOU NEED:

If you choose option 1 . . .
- ○ Marshmallows
- ○ CD player and music

If you choose option 2 . . .
- ○ Balloons
- ○ String, enough to tie the balloons to the ankles of your students.

FOCUS

OPTION 1:

Play a game of "Hot Potato" with a marshmallow as the item. This is like musical chairs only instead of people moving around the chairs, you pass an item. When the music stops, the person with the item is out! The final person to survive without getting knocked out gets the marshmallow as their prize!

Debrief, asking the group if anyone would like the marshmallow that has been passed around through everyone's hands, over and over again. Hold up the marshmallow and offer a drawn-out description of how squished and dirty it has become; it may be sticky from sweaty hands or simply dirty. Ask: Is there anyone who would prefer to have a nice, new, clean marshmallow to eat? Pass out the remainder of your bag while telling them that this is kind of like God taking us at times when we have become dirty and gross and making us clean and pure again. (Chances are you will have a student who just likes to be funny and will offer to eat the gross marshmallow. If/when this happens, use this as a teachable moment. You can point out that just like in our own lives, when we allow ourselves to become used and dirty, there will always be people willing to take us. God, however, desires that we allow Him to cleanse us and make us clean and whole once again.)

OPTION 2:

Give each person a balloon to blow up. Once they are blown up, give each person a piece of string to tie the balloon to their ankle. Be sure to tell them they must have at least a foot of string between their ankle and the balloon. (Some will try to be sneaky, anticipating the game, and tie it really close to their ankle. This is not a good idea, as in the excitement of the game someone can stomp on his or her ankle instead of the balloon!) The object of the game: try to pop the balloons of everyone else. Even when your balloon is popped, you may continue to try and get others. Call time on the game when only 1 or 2 people are left with a balloon intact.

Debrief asking: What was this experience like?

For those whose balloons were popped early, what was it like to be one of the only ones without a balloon?

Did it make it easier for you to go after others?

For the few who still have balloons, how did you manage to survive?

What was it like toward the end when the others had nothing to lose and were coming after you?

Every single person is born with something special from God. Today we are going to look at sexuality. This impacts every person! The world says it is something to give away as soon as possible. Just like each of you had others coming after your balloon to pop it, there will be people trying to get you to be sexually active early and outside of marriage. Also, just like this little game, some of those people will be your closest friends. Most of us have heard the rumors that the Bible says to not have sex before marriage, but we have no idea where it is found. Let's look at what Scripture really has to say around this subject.

DISCOVERY

The age and maturity of your group will determine the balance of time you spend looking at issues of sexual purity and issues of the body being the temple in a more general sense. This may be a good time to split into two groups, male and female. While the scripture is brief, the content is intense.

Ask: What does the world think about sexual purity? (Encourage them to not censor their responses, to get real with themselves and you.)

What do they think God says about sexual purity?

What does God say about sex before marriage?

Look up and read Hebrews 13:4.

Is it realistic to think that the marriage bed should be undefiled?

Read 2 Peter 2:9–11.

Ask: What is this saying?

Do you believe the Lord can really rescue you from temptation?

Read 1 Corinthians 3:16–17.

What does it mean to be the temple of God?

LIFE APPLICATION: Sex is everywhere in our world. It is in music, on TV, in movies, and the talk at school. Our students are inundated with messages from the standards of the world.

You have spent a little time looking at a few very specific scriptures. While we may know what the Bible says and be able to hold this in our minds, the messages from the world in our everyday lives are constant and strong.

Ask: Assuming we believe we are the temple of God and that it is His desire that we remain pure, why is it so hard?

Let this time open to questions and answers with your students. Be careful to not shame or shut them down for questions or uncertainties they may have.

MAKING IT PERSONAL: Each person will have a slightly different struggle. Some of your students will already be sexually active. Some of your students will never have kissed. Some will be obsessed with their own looks and trying to measure up to the standards of the world. Still others will be much more interested in looking at others. Offer a few moments of silent reflection, encouraging each person to not only consider that they themselves are the temple of God but that they also are called not to violate anyone else in any way.

MEMORY VERSE ACTIVITY

We have all thought of an amazing home at some point or another. Whether it is from watching MTV's Cribs or simply in driving through a posh neighborhood, dreams of something grand are present. Give each person a piece of blank paper. Tell them to create their dream home, the best place they can think of if money and location were no object. Give a few minutes for them to dream and create their masterpiece.

Ask: What do you think the dream home of God looks like?

Read 1 Corinthians 3:16–17. Granted, most of us did not create a temple as the ideal home, but God does! In fact, His ideal home is in you as His holy temple. To dwell means not just to live in as a place to eat and sleep but a place where you stay, where you slow down and spend time.

Using a thick marker, have each person write the memory verse over the dream home they created.

CONNECTIONS: Scripture has much to say regarding issues of sexual purity. A few other passages to check: Matthew 5:32; Acts 15:29; 1 Corinthians 5:1; 6:18; 7:2; 10:8; Ephesians 5:3; Colossians 3:5; 1 Thessalonians 4:3.

SONGS: "Fields of Grace" by Big Daddy Weave, on the album *Fields of Grace*

Temples Do Come with Instructions —Midweek

MEMORY VERSE:
Do you not know that you are the temple of God and that the Spirit of God dwells in you? If anyone defiles the temple of God, God will destroy him. For the temple of God is holy, which temple you are.—1 Corinthians 3:16–17

SCRIPTURE: Exodus 25–30, in particular Exodus 25:9

LESSON IN A SENTENCE: The temple in which God dwells is to be kept by His instructions.

FOCUS

OPTION 1:
This is a no-rule game. Have your students form one large circle. Set a ball, or several balls, in the center and tell them to begin playing. When they ask what to play, continue to respond by simply saying they can begin to play.

After a few seconds/minutes someone will inevitably pick up the ball and declare a game they already know or create a new game and establish the rules of play. Let the game go for 15 minutes or so and then call time.

Debrief, asking how they knew what to play? Say: There will always be rules and guidelines in life. Even when you are not given any rules, someone will establish them. The question becomes who is establishing the boundaries for your life? If guidelines are not set, others *will* set them for you.

OPTION 2:
OK, so this one really isn't for everyone, but if it is for your group, be certain to have a camera! Divide into teams of 4–6 with at least one person per team able and willing to get, well, messy/dirty/gross. Give each group a few of the following items: shaving cream, easy cheese, cotton swabs, a few pencils, and any other random small items you may find around. Instruct each group to create a hairdo on one of its members in the theme of a temple. Have your adult leaders judge and offer a prize to the winning team. (Be certain to give time for the one who was decorated to get cleaned up before beginning the content part of your lesson.)

DISCOVERY

Before the lesson, read through Exodus 25—30. Over and over again, there are specific instructions for the way the temple is to be built. Have pieces of construction paper taped on the walls around the room. Instruct your students to find these papers, look up the verse written on the top of the paper, and write the specific instructions told in the scripture on the remainder of the paper.

Chapters 25–30 of Exodus are simply full of very specific instructions. This is not a treasure hunt; unless you are completely not paying attention, it is obvious that God gives very specific instructions. Choose any section of verses between Exodus 25 and Exodus 30.

Depending on your group, you may want to read these passages in total or you may want to choose one or two verses with very specific, easily identifiable instructions.

For example:

Exodus 25:1–9, get gold, silver, and bronze, blue, purple, and scarlet material, fine linen and goat hair, rams' skin dyed red, porpoise skins, acacia wood, oil for lighting, spices for the anointing oil and for the fragrant incense, onyx stones and setting stones, for the ephod and the breastpiece

Exodus 25:4, get blue, purple, and scarlet material, fine linen and goat hair.

APPLICATION: God was certainly very clear that He had a specific way the temple was to be built, certain materials with which it was to be built, and certain things that were to happen there.

Ask: What was God giving instructions to have built?

Did anyone ever dream that God was so specific in His instructions?

What was the weirdest thing you think God specifically asked to have included?

If you were there, would you have ever questioned what God was asking?

What do you think would have happened if the people brought green material instead of blue and purple or pine instead of acacia?

Would you like it if God were that specific with you?

Read your memory verse together.

Ask: Did you know you were a temple?

What does it mean for you to be the temple of the Holy Spirit?

Do you think there are specific instructions for you as the temple?

Close with a time of brainstorming the ways in which God has offered specific instructions for our lives. Encourage your students to make it specific to your group. You may want to begin with a quick run-down of places your group struggles and then think through the specifics of how God would desire that you live.

Q U O T A B L E   Q U O T E S :

When we do anything from a sense of duty, we can back it up by argument; when we do anything in obedience to the Lord, there is no argument possible; that is why a saint can be easily ridiculed.

—Oswald Chambers

CROSS-CULTURAL ISSUES IN YOUTH MINISTRY

By Nathan Novero
FILM EDITOR/YOUTH WORKER

"I can't write this," I told her. "Why not," she asked. My friend had just requested that I write on the subject of "Cross-cultural Issues in Youth Ministry." Her request didn't surprise me. You see, I was born *brown*, a *Pacific Islander* to be exact. At least that's what the bubble option told me when I took the ACT during my junior year in high school. Before then, I was simply considered an "other," meandering across a predominately white and black Arkansas terrain. I was fully aware of my difference, but it was hardly a source of trauma during my upbringing.

Ironically, I've always considered my ethnic minority status an advantage. What better characteristic to remember a kid's name? Of course, there was one year when I shared this privilege with a Vietnamese foreign exchange student, but even then classmates had a fifty/fifty shot. I never had a problem finding my friends during football games, or rather, they never had a problem finding me. And what girl wouldn't want to accent her prom picture with a golden shade of brown (at least in my imagination)? My cultural diversity made me unique—for lack of a better word, it made me feel *special*. But it never birthed experiences I would categorize as "an issue".

"I haven't had issues," I explained. "You have the wrong guy."

"That's why I want you to write this article," she emphatically replied. And like lightning, I had a flashback. Did I hear thunder? Did I see a bolt of electricity? No, I saw a window, a window mounted on a door looking into an auditorium filled with screaming urban Latino teenagers. It was April five year before, and I had just volunteered to be a youth worker at a church in East Los Angeles. Before immersing myself in the frenzy, I decided to take a sneak peek to see what I had committed myself to. Gazing through that door's window I found myself frozen with fear. Here I was, a rural Arkansan Filipino attempting to relate to urban, Latino youth. My stomach emptied. My palms became clammy. At that moment, I was not a youth worker. I was a frightened teenager again, wanting nothing more than to be noticed, to be accepted, and to simply matter. In this moment of insecurity, I found security and a lesson I will never forget.

Cross-cultural youth ministry is not about the culture surrounding teenagers, it's the culture of being a teenager. The more I focused on external circumstances, such as being raised in Arkansas or Los Angeles, being a Filipino or Latino, raised in a rural town or an urban environment, the chasm between myself and the teenagers continued to increase. Every effort I made to understand their culture revealed how much I didn't—and the insecurities surfaced.

But who doesn't know these insecurities? Who hasn't felt like a timid teenager when surrounded by strangers? Who hasn't felt the junior high desire to be accepted, to be noticed, or to simply matter? Who doesn't feel like an awkward fifteen-year-old when you have a crush, or a fragile thirteen-year-old when you've just been embarrassed, or a cocky eighteen-year-old when you know you are "it"? This internal focus not only decreases the chasm, but erases it completely, reminding us that we are all still teenagers in many ways! Although many of you have not filled in the bubble for *Pacific Islander* on the ACT, you have all taken it, wondering how bad you will do or whether the cute girl or guy sitting behind you notices that you exist.

"Will you do it?" my friend asked. "Will I do it?" I asked. How could I say "No"? We've all been there.

APRIL 17, 2005

Toward the Finish Line

By Amy Jacober

MEMORY VERSE:
There is neither Jew nor Greek, there is neither slave nor free, there is neither male nor female; for you are all one in Christ Jesus.—Galatians 3:28

SCRIPTURE: Acts 10:1–35

LESSON IN A SENTENCE: God sees *all* people as valuable and calls us to do the same.

THE BIG PICTURE (OR WHAT YOU'RE TRYING TO GET ACROSS):
    Civil rights officially occurred a long time ago, and yet struggles over race continue in our world daily. Some of our students honestly think this is an issue of the past. They may assume that their generation or at the very least their group of friends are not racist and it is therefore a non-issue. God is very clear that He views us all in the same way and even more, calls us to follow His example. Following His example certainly means that we as individuals need to treat others equally. This may also mean that we need to consider system issues beyond our own actions. For some communities this topic will be more sensitive than others. For some, there will be differing opinions coming from family teachings. While this is an important area and the truth of Scripture is clear, proceed with sensitivity.

IN THIS LESSON STUDENTS SHOULD:

- ○ Understand that racial inequalities still exist.
- ○ Learn of a dramatic change in Peter's opinion of race relations.
- ○ Identify places in the world and/or their own communities where false dividing lines have been established.
- ○ Learn practical ways in which they may take a stand toward unity in Christ.

STUFF YOU NEED:

○ Crayons—borrow from the children's department. Broken and tiny are just fine!
○ A long piece of butcher paper
○ Paper for each student
○ Pencil for each student
○ Either a dry erase board or butcher paper and marker

FOCUS

OPTION 1:

As they arrive, hand each person a crayon of the same color. If your group is larger than 10, choose two colors, if larger than 20, three colors, etc. Once they are all present. Have your group gather around a piece of butcher paper. If you have handed out more than one color, have them gather in groups according to the color of their crayon. Ask them to draw collectively a map of the world and at least one item from each continent. I.e. for Europe they might know London is there and draw a doubledecker bus. What they choose to draw is really unimportant. When they are done, look at the pictures. Ask what would have made it better? (Chances are if you have a larger group and you have handed out more than one color, they will try to trade for variety. As best you can, prevent them from doing so.) Even the best pictures will be pretty boring if everything in the world is orange or burnt sienna! Offer the chance for them to trade with you so that they may color in or add to their picture to make it better with more variety.

OPTION 2:

Hand out paper and pencils and ask each person to make their top 10 list of favorite songs. Collect the papers. Read aloud a few of the lists. After reading a few ask the group what they would choose from one or two of the lists as the best song. Now ask them to imagine if that was the only song they could listen to, forever. No variety, no other favorites, nothing different. Ask: even if you love this song, do you think you would still like it in a month? In a year? In ten years?

Why is variety important?

DISCOVERY

Read Acts 10:1–35 aloud from The Message.

In groups of 4–6, have them read back through Acts 10:1–35 answering the following questions. (Either hand out 3 x 5 cards with the questions or re-type the questions as a worksheet for each student/group.)

Where does Cornelius live?
Where was Simon Peter?
What did Peter's dream mean?
What did they ask Peter to do?
What did Peter mean in verse 28?
What do you think Peter's dream means now?

Work together and come up with one sentence that tells the point of this story. Write this in a prominent placed in the room (dry erase board or butcher paper).

LIFE APPLICATION: Say: You may branch out from race at this point. While Peter is clearly talking about racial issues, there are many ways in which we declare others as "unclean" or inferior by our words and actions.

Based on what they have read and answered so far, ask each group to create a sketch that tells the same point of the story (the sentence you created) in a different way. Give 10–20 minutes for them to create a short sketch and then have each group offer their rendition.

As they are presenting their sketches, make a list in a visible place (either on butcher paper or a dry erase board) of all the people they have identified as society having labeled unclean. Once each group has finished presenting, refer back to your list. (There are many directions a list like this could go; think through the issues in your community. Is it race like in Acts, is it class, disabilities, education, the rich and poor, athletes and not so athletic, bullies, drug users. Who would your students consider to be not worthy of their time, inappropriate to have as friends, uncool or, at the heart of it all, inferior?)

Ask: How do we, in society, learn who is "clean" and who is "unclean"?

Do you think racial inequalities still exist? (While the civil rights movement was over three decades ago, and many believe all racial inequalities are a thing of the past kept alive only by those who say they are. Salaries, healthcare, education, housing, and many other hard facts would say differently. We have made great strides and at one time it was indeed the church setting the pace in this area. Racial divides are more evident in some parts of the country than others, but they still exist in our country as a whole.)

How have the racial issues changed from the time of MLK?

What does Peter's vision have to say to us in this area?

What other false dividing lines do we have?

Do you think this principle from Peter's vision carries over into all areas of division?

MAKING IT PERSONAL: Look back at the list you made as a group from the sketches and then what you added for those who are considered "unclean" in your community.

As a group, create a list of at least 5 practical steps each of you can take right now, in your community, to begin to stand with God and not declare "unclean" that which God has declared "clean." (This may be as simple as not making fun of those who dress in skimpy clothes or refraining from laughing at racial slurs. Be creative but be practical!)

Memory Verse Note: This memory verse is commonly used in lessons looking at division and God declaring there is no division. This verse in particular is talking about salvation. There was a time when being one of God's chosen was either by birth or by the choice of the master of the house. This verse reminds us of the new covenant under Jesus Christ. Salvation is available to all—male and female, Jew and Greek, slave and free. It is not talking about blanket equality (there are plenty of other places in Scripture that offer that lesson!) As we teach our students, it is important to teach what Scripture is actually saying and not what it may seem at first glance. This is not to undermine any authority; rather it is to establish the authority intrinsic in Scripture through the power of Jesus Christ and the indwelling of the Holy Spirit. Students (I would argue all people) become disillusioned when they realize you have fudged on a teaching. It causes them to wonder where else the application may have been stretched. Point out that God not only shows no partiality in our lives but God shows no partiality in His eternal desire for all to know Him personally!

CONNECTIONS: While there are many scriptures considering the equality of all, in our world today money determines more than most of us care to acknowledge. Check out Proverbs 22:2 and James 2:5 for both an Old Testament and New Testament look at this particular group often labeled as inferior.

SONGS: "If We Are the Body" by Casting Crowns, on the album *Casting Crowns*

Toward the Finish Line —Midweek

MEMORY VERSE:
There is neither Jew nor Greek, there is neither slave nor free, there is neither male nor female; for you are all one in Christ Jesus.—Galatians 3:28

SCRIPTURE: Romans 10:11–12

LESSON IN A SENTENCE: God sees *all* people as valuable and calls us to do the same.

FOCUS

Ask: What is the best gift you have ever been given? Give each person a chance to share the story of their gift.

After each has shared their story, give each person 5 strips of paper and a marker. Have each person write their five favorite possessions, one on each strip and place them in front of them. Once they are done, each person must trade at least one strip of paper for another's. Tell them to choose wisely as they are giving away one of their favorite possessions! Do this at least 2 more times. Ask if anyone feels like they have traded up? Who has been left with less than what they had at the beginning? Did anyone keep trading the "traded" item so they are still left with four of their own items? Once again, ask them to place the five strips of paper in front of them in order of the most precious to the least. Ask each person if there is anyone to whom they would be willing to give their most precious item?

Pull out the list from Sunday's lesson, the list of those considered "unclean" in your community. This time, ask if they would be willing to give their most precious item to any of these people. Ask: Would you realistically be willing to give any of your items to these people?

DISCOVERY

What is the greatest gift God ever gave? (Jesus Christ)
To whom did God give this gift?

Read Romans 10:11–12 together.

Both this verse and the memory verse for this week mention there being neither Jew nor Greek. Ask your group if they really know why this was so significant?

(Jews and Greeks may have been living in the same towns at this time but they were definitely not on good terms. Each considered themselves to be superior to the other based on nothing more than race.)

Ask your students if anything in particular stands out to them about this passage. This is a great passage for practicing *lectio devina*. (see www.lectiodevina.org)

As elements stand out for your students, slow down and spend the time to talk about them.

APPLICATION: The best gift God ever offered is a reconciled relationship with Him. That can happen only through His Son, Jesus Christ. Jesus came for *all*, regardless of race, education, class, or status. God's best gift was given for those considered superior *and* inferior—for *all*.

Assuming we know this in our heads and believe it in our hearts, why do we as Christians still struggle so much in these areas? (Try to keep this time focused on the Christian response. It is easy to slip into a discussion of the world at this point. While the world does struggle, Christians do as well. The difference is that we should know better!)

Close with a time in prayer for those you identified earlier in the week as "unclean." Pray also that your own hearts be softened and you begin to see others as God does.

QUOTABLE   QUOTES:

I note the obvious differences between each sort and type,

But we are more alike, my friends, than we are unalike.

—Maya Angelou

APRIL 24, 2005

Honor Your Extended Family

By Amy Jacober

MEMORY VERSE:
Let no unwholesome word proceed from your mouth, but only such a word as is good for edification according to the need of the moment, that it may give grace to those who hear.—Ephesians 4:29 (NASB)

SCRIPTURE: Acts 9:31; Romans 14:19; 1 Corinthians 8:1; 14:3, 26; 2 Corinthians 10:18; 12:19; Ephesians 4:12, 29

LESSON IN A SENTENCE: God calls fellow Christians not to division but to encourage each other.

THE BIG PICTURE (OR WHAT YOU'RE TRYING TO GET ACROSS):
It is not a great secret that between difficult grades, teasing at school, negative images on TV, harsh words said at home, not to mention all of the internal insecurities that our teenagers are often more torn down than built up. God calls us to something different. The Scriptures are clear in saying that not only are we to edify, to build one another up, but they even offer specific ways in which we may do this. This whole lesson really can be summed up in the memory verse alone. We cannot control all of what occurs in the world. We can offer an alternative and invite students to carry a new way of being into their daily worlds. Your time together can be one where unwholesome words are left at the door and a safe space is created, building up our students who have been torn down in so many subtle ways.

IN THIS LESSON STUDENTS SHOULD:

- Be able to articulate the difference between tearing down and building up.
- Learn that edification is a necessary part of the church.
- Identify several examples from Scripture of how to build others up.
- List ways they can build others up in their daily walk.

> ## STUFF YOU NEED:
>
> ○ Construction paper
> ○ Tape
> ○ Washable markers
> ○ Map of the world
> ○ Cards for thank you notes
> ○ Pens/pencils for writing

FOCUS

OPTION 1:

Many of us have done this somewhere in the past, but it is amazing that you can never really get tired of hearing good things about yourself. Ask your students to find a partner. Give each partner two pieces of paper, a few pieces of tape, and markers. Have each person write their partner's name on the top of the paper. Have them tape the paper on the back of their partner and then write at least one positive comment/compliment on the paper. After a few minutes, trade partners. Depending on your group size, trade until each person has written on every other person's paper or until they have switched at least 10 times. Give a few moments for them to read their papers. (Really stress that they need to write something genuinely nice and not sarcastic. You may need to have a leader or two wandering as they are writing to be certain nothing inappropriate nor a cruel joke is written.)

OPTION 2:

Borrow or purchase a Jenga (enough to have one game for every group of students). In groups of no more than 8, take turns with each stating an insult or negative comment they have heard in the last week. Have each student pull one block for each insult stated. If a group moves through the game quickly, have them play a second time.

Point out that for every insult or negative comment made, the structure becomes less stable. Eventually, it simply falls apart. As Christians, we are no different. We have the choice to either tear down or build up.

DISCOVERY

Create 4 stations around the room. Break your group into 4 groups and have each rotate through all 4 stations. At each station, have a leader posted. Begin by reading the scriptures and then proceed to the activity for that station. Be certain to time each rotation so that all students are able to go to each station within the allotted time for youth group.

STATION 1:

Have a map of the world on the wall. Mark a few places where fighting and war is currently taking place. Spend a few moments praying for all of those being impacted by the lack of peace in the world.

Acts 9:31—Churches all through Judea, Galilee, and Samaria had peace and were edified.

Romans 14:19—Let us purse that which brings peace and edifies one another.

STATION 2:

Spend a few moments expressing what they like about this youth group and your time together. Really encourage them to refrain from being sarcastic and to voice even the smallest of things they like or appreciate.

1 Corinthians 8:1—Knowledge puffs up, love edifies.

1 Corinthians 14:3—Prophecy speaks edification and exhortation.

STATION 3:

A psalm is a song of praise. The Book of Psalms is a collection of Hebrew praises, theological in nature and written poetically. Choose a few psalms to read or, if you have someone able to lead in music, read the psalm and then sing together the song based from it (such as Psalm 27:4; Psalm 40; Psalm 42:1–2; Psalm 51:10-12; Psalm 56:1–4; Psalm 63; Psalm 66:10; Psalm 84:10; Psalm 199:105; Psalm 122:1; or Psalm 150:6).

1 Corinthians 14:26—A song, a psalm, a teaching for edification

STATION 4:

Spend a few moments writing notes of encouragement to those within your church. Be certain each group writes to a variety of people serving in your faith community. You may need to prompt them as to the specifics of the preparation and sacrifice given by so many within the body of Christ.

2 Corinthians 12:19—Do all things for the edification of others.

Ephesians 4:12—equipping the saints, equipping the ministry, and edification of the body

LIFE APPLICATION: You have just spent some amazing time together edifying one another and the church as a whole. While you have done some specific things, there are many other options.

Ask: What other ways have you felt edified in the past?

In what other ways can we affirm one another and this church?

Choose at least one of these new suggestions and follow through with it this week.

MAKING IT PERSONAL: You may think edification comes easily once you have put your mind to it.

Invite each student to keep a journal this week. On one side of the page write each time you have insulted or torn someone down. On the other side of the page, write each time you have been insulted, hurt, or torn down. Some of you will be tempted to leave out some comments, saying they were only meant as jokes. Often the most hurtful comments are clothed in jest. These backhanded insults count just as much!

Pray that God opens your ears to really hear comments around you that do not build up others and to be aware of the consequences that follow.

CONNECTIONS: Just because you *can* does not necessarily mean you *should*. There are many things we all could say that in the end will may help us to look good but will tear others down. Take a look at 1 Corinthians 10:23 for a perspective from Scripture on this very topic.

SONGS: "Never Alone" by Jody McBrayer and Jadyn Maria, on the album *This Is Who I Am*

QUOTABLE   QUOTES:

Ideologies lead to debates, conflicts, violence, and often war, but faith leads to obedience, humility, faithfulness, and finally peace. Ideologies breed death, faith brings forth life.

—Henri J. M. Nouwen

Honor Your Extended Family — Midweek

MEMORY VERSE:
Let no unwholesome word proceed from your mouth, but only such a word as is good for edification according to the need of the moment, that it may give grace to those who hear.—Ephesians 4:29 (NASB)

SCRIPTURE: Ephesians 4:25–32

LESSON IN A SENTENCE: God calls fellow Christians not to division but to encourage each other.

FOCUS

Before your students arrive, make a straight line on the floor at least 15 feet long with masking tape. Ask for volunteers to walk the line (if you have a small group, encourage each person to try). Once you have a volunteer, tell them to take a good look at the line, especially the direction. Just before they begin, tell them you have one more little instruction. Blindfold them and spin them three times. Be certain that you really do set them in the right direction at the beginning. While no one may touch the person, the other students may offer words of encouragement and direction. (If you'd like to make it a bit more difficult, ask one or two students to be a distraction, offering false encouragement or insults along the way.)

Say: The Christian walk can be difficult in a world that offers little support and direction. We were not meant to do this alone. Nor were we meant to guess what it looks like.

DISCOVERY

Read through Ephesians 4:25–32.

On a piece of butcher paper, make a list of each specific thing we as Christians are instructed to do.

For example: In verse 25
Put away lying
Speak truth with your neighbors
In verse 26
Be angry but do not sin
Don't let the sun go down on your anger
Do this for each verse.

APPLICATION: One of the biggest complaints I hear from students is that the Bible is too vague. They know God wants for us to be good, but they don't know what that means! You have just created a whole list of very specific instructions.

Each of these can seem overwhelming on its own, and together they seem impossible! One of the best ways to approach the impossible is one step at a time. Work back through the list you made on the butcher paper.

There are always excuses we can give for not being able to do what God is asking. For each item, offer at least one excuse for not being able to follow through with this.

(Ask your students if they kept a journal this week about the times they have been hurt or insulted or times they have hurt or insulted others as suggested in the previous lesson. If yes, ask if they were surprised at the results. Edification is counter-cultural in our world, but it is not impossible.)

Say: Excuses, being insulted and torn down, it is no wonder that it is difficult to keep the Christian walk. God wants something different for His children. Take this time to cross through the excuses you have written on the butcher paper and commit to working on building one another up in all you say and do.

MEMORY VERSE ACTIVITY

On cardstock, print up the memory verse with the heading. Read the memory verse as a group. Go through each phrase. What is an "unwholesome word"? (Any insult, swear word, gossip, etc.) What words are good for edification? (Praises, encouragements, compliments, etc.) Why does it say according to the need of the moment? (At times, even if it is a compliment, the timing can make it divisive or tear others down. Think of the very serious moment in your talk when that energetic ninth grader decides to tell you that your haircut looks good!)

Use this verse as a way to set guidelines for your group. Only things which build others up may be said, and only at times when it is not interrupting or distracting. When someone violates this verse, shout "Ephesians 4:29"!

MAY 1, 2005

Jesus Is Our Advocate (Ascension Sunday)

By Amy Jacober

MEMORY VERSE:
It is Christ who died, and furthermore is also risen, who is even at the right hand of God, who also makes intercession for us.—Romans 8:34b (NKJV)

SCRIPTURE: Acts 1:1–11

LESSON IN A SENTENCE: Jesus is our advocate in heaven.

THE BIG PICTURE (OR WHAT YOU'RE TRYING TO GET ACROSS):

After the resurrection Jesus ascended to heaven. While this is not something we tend to speak of daily, it has significance for our lives. Two common mantras of teenagers are "no one understands me" and "no one is on my side." If not that exact wording, then something pretty close! The exact opposite is true. There is Someone Who not only understands and is on their side (and ours for that matter) but Who loves them dearly! A recognition of Ascension Sunday also helps to remind us all of the connection each Christian has to Christians all over the world, thinking on and studying some of the same scriptures at the same time. This is a lesson that would be very easy to get side-tracked by the details of the actual ascension. Be certain that you don't miss this time to talk of Jesus' intercession for us all!

IN THIS LESSON STUDENTS SHOULD:

- Know the account of the ascension.
- Learn that Jesus intercedes on their behalf.

STUFF YOU NEED:

- Lined paper
- Slips of paper for Mother's Day activity
- Pens/pencils

FOCUS

OPTION 1:

Play a good old fashioned game of freeze tag! While this seems to be just a silly harkening back to childhood and playground games, the segue for this game comes as you call them in after playing. Ask: How did any of you become un-frozen in this game? (Simple response: help was given from someone else.)

Say: In this game no one could play and survive by themselves; it requires the help of others. Jesus holds a similar role in our lives.

OPTION 2:

So many questions, so little time!

In groups of no more than 10, play the question game. Have each group stand in a circle and designate a starter. The first person looks directly at someone and asks a question. The person asked does not answer—rather, he or she looks at someone else and asks another question. This repeats until someone is out! A person gets out if he or she (1) answers the question, (2) hesitates more than 3 seconds, (3) ask a question back to the person who asked you (unless there are just 2 of you left), (4) repeats a question, or (5) gives a statement instead of a question. Keep playing until there is only one person left.

Say: We all have questions. Sometimes it feels like we are asking them just for the sake of asking them. Sometimes it feels like there is no one to listen or to help us find answers. In this lesson we're going to look at the role Jesus has in our lives when it comes to all of our questions.

DISCOVERY

Ask: What do you think of when you think of the Holy Spirit? Why do we have/do we need the Holy Spirit?

Read Acts 1:1–8.

Split into two groups.

Ask group 1: What did Luke say in this passage?

Ask group 2: What did Jesus say in this passage?

All together, read Acts 1:9–11.

Re-read this passage, inviting students to assume the perspective of one of the characters in this passage: of Luke, the author, of Theophilus, of Jesus, of the men of Galilee.

Teacher's Note: This passage is addressed to Theophilus. While it is a personal name, it means "friend of God." The exact identity of this "person" is never revealed, and there are two common strands of thought. The first is that this letter is written to all Christians. The second is that it is written to a person of high standing politically or socially and therefore a pseudonym is being used to protect him from persecution. A third thought is that it is as a desire or wish written to a non-believer, a desire or wish that he or she would indeed believe in Jesus and be a friend of God.

In the greater church calendar today is known as Ascension Sunday. By tradition, it is the 40th day after Easter. This is also traditionally tied to Pentecost Sunday, linking the day Jesus ascended and the day the Holy Spirit descended.

LIFE APPLICATION Ask students to share what they experienced as one of the characters in this passage. (This may be done verbally or by offering a short time for your students to journal their thoughts.) What new things did they learn?

Ask: What will followers of Jesus do according to verse 8?

We may not all have had the opportunity to shake Jesus' hand nor to have a cup of water beside a well with Him. We do, however, have the Holy Spirit. This is no trite substitution. This is the third member of the Godhead, no less deity than God the Father or Son.

We all need help in life. We all have questions. Jesus is in heaven advocating for us while the Holy Spirit is present with us, right here, right now.

MAKING IT PERSONAL: Verse 8 lets us know that we will be witnesses in Jerusalem, Judea, Samaria, and to the ends of the earth. It is not a question of if we will be a witness, rather a question of what kind of witness.

Think through your life right now. What have you done in the last week, the last few days, today? What would those who have been around you say about your beliefs and life?

Think of one thing you would like to change. Ask Jesus to advocate for you and the Holy Spirit to strengthen you to commit to a change. Remind your students that asking to be rich or to ace a test with no study is inconsistent with what we know about prayer. Jesus is our advocate, but by His will not ours. The Holy Spirit was sent that we might be comforted and strengthened in this world.

EXTRA! EXTRA!: Find some time at the end of this lesson and remind your students that next Sunday is Mother's Day. Encourage them to do something nice for their mom in the upcoming week leading to next Sunday. Let them know that, as a youth group, you have a very simple but fun way to show appreciation. Ask each student to write a sentence or two about their mom/grandma/step-mom/aunt—something they appreciate, something they love, something that makes them laugh! You may want to create slips of paper with a space for their name and the beginning of a sentence: "My favorite thing about my mom is. . . ." Be certain to have them include their name. Collect each of these and type them up in the week to follow. Send a letter of appreciation to all of the women in the lives of your students and include your typed up collection of anecdotes.

CONNECTIONS: The ascension is further referenced in Ephesians 4:8–13.

SONGS: "Show Your Love" by Jars of Clay, on the album *Who We Are Instead*

QUOTABLE   QUOTES:

The best and most beautiful things in the world cannot be seen or even touched. They must be felt with the heart.

—Helen Keller

Jesus Is Our Advocate —Midweek

MEMORY VERSE:
It is Christ who died, and furthermore is also risen, who is even at the right hand of God, who also makes intercession for us.—Romans 8:34b (NKJV)

SCRIPTURE: Nehemiah 2:9–20

LESSON IN A SENTENCE: Jesus is our advocate in heaven.

FOCUS

Begin with a Sherpa walk! Have each person find a partner. Give each couple a blindfold. Designate a place across your property or in another part of the building as a destination. Have one partner blindfolded while the other partner is leading him or her to the destination. The trick is that no words may be spoken and the partners may not touch. They can use clapping, noises, or any other creative form of communication. Once they have made it to the designation, switch roles for the return trip.

Once all of the partners have returned, Ask:

Who had a hard time?

Who had a partner who led them into trouble (a wall, a ditch, etc.)?

Did anyone think their partner was leading them astray only to be pleasantly surprised?

What would have made this easier?

DISCOVERY

Do you know any government officials? If you do, invite him or her in for a 5–10 minute talk with your students. Prepare them ahead of time that you are going to be talking about getting a major building project approved and executed. Ask how easy or hard this kind of action is.

Split into groups of 4–6. Have each group read Nehemiah 2:9–20. Ask each to re-write the passage as a news article of no more than 1/2 a page. Feel free to use journalistic license to fill in the details and make the stories as creative as possible. Be certain they include the major details and use who, what, where, when, why, and how to cover the bases.

Have each group read their version out loud. Just like with news today, the same story gets covered by every channel. Listen to each story, paying attention to where they are similar and where they differ. Are there any discrepancies? Is there a better understanding once you have heard them all?

Teacher's Note: Nehemiah was a governor in his day. He was interested in both physical and political reconstruction and moral reform. For Nehemiah, there was no conflict of interest in ruling out of what he believed. Ever the politician, he was no renegade. He prayed and used his political savvy to accomplish that which God was calling him to do.

Before reading, tell your students that this is a story about a governor trying to help. The walls of Jerusalem had been destroyed by Nebuchadnezzar in 586 B.C. They were almost rebuilt after 464 B.C. under the reign of Artaxerxes. Nehemiah is burdened for Jerusalem, both physically and morally. As the cupbearer to King Artaxerxes, he uses his position and risks punishment by sharing that he truly is sad. Artaxerxes asks what is the matter and before you know it, Nehemiah has shared his burden and is granted permission to rebuild the walls.

APPLICATION: Ask: Have you ever been asked to do something and you had no clue how you were going to do it?

Each of you took a walk earlier blindfolded. Do you think you could have done this if you didn't have any help?

Nehemiah knew he was to lead in having the walls of Jerusalem rebuilt. He secured permission from the king (a wise political move) and proceeded to find those to help in his project. There were certainly those who questioned what he was doing, if not downright ridiculed him!

God placed something great in the heart of Nehemiah. This certainly did not end with him! When God places something in your heart, the same God in heaven will speak to you and advocate. As best you can, get in a circle with your students. Tell them to take a few moments in silence to consider what it is that God is calling them to do that they would be able to share with this group. After a few moments, go around the circle and have each person share one thing. As you are doing this, ask each person to pay particular attention to what the person to his or her right is saying. Once each person has shared Say: just as Jesus intercedes for us in heaven, we can follow His example and intercede for one another right now. Ask your students to pray for the person to his or her right. After a minute or two, close thanking Jesus that He intercedes for us all of the time, even when we forget.

Teacher's Note: Intercession is one of those words that gets thrown around in church circles a lot! At its most basic, it is the act of intervening or mediating between two parties. In a Christian context, it is the act of one person praying to God on behalf of someone else. Romans 8:34b tells us that Jesus makes intercession for us. If you have a group able to have deep or more abstract discussion, consider discussing the concept of Jesus interceding, of Jesus praying for each of you. Have they (have you) ever considered the truth of this? How would this change the way you live to truly embrace the truth of this scripture?

Dear Youth Pastor:

My husband and I have been blessed with three wonderful children! Our youngest is a beautiful ninth grader this year. People often say that there is just something "different" about her and can't quite put their finger on what it is. While she is in ninth grade, her IQ is lower, and she reads and reasons at a third grade reading level.

We had concerns as the time came for her to be in a youth group. I would guess most parents with a special needs child feel the same. Sadly, many parents assume there is no place for their child (and consequently them) within a church. It is important to know that just as every person is unique and an individual, every mentally retarded child is not a cookie cutter of one another. What I hope for you to hear can be expressed in a couple personal experiences and ten pointers.

In our church, one of the leaders approached us and said our daughter was now the age to be able to be in her discipleship group. While we appreciated the offer, we knew she didn't know what she was getting into. We also knew that Emily would change the group entirely! We thanked this leader, expecting a very polite (and probably relieved) exchange as we refused the offer. Her response both surprised and blessed us. She said that, as the leader of this group of high school young women, "If my girls can't accept her, I'm doing something wrong."

Bringing a special needs child into a group can either polarize or authenticate the "answers" given by the group. Giving the right church answers can be done by anyone—living them is another thing. In the past year of her involvement, Emily has been blessed by this group, but more than that, her leader tells us, she has been a blessing to the group!

My husband I decided long ago that Emily is not the focus of our family; she is part of it. Emily is not the center of our lives—Christ is. In many families the special needs child can consume all the attention and the others get ignored. What we have observed is that the same can be true for a youth group. The special needs child can create resentment if all the attention is focused on her. Having your youth group revolve around the special needs teenager becomes a youth group revolving around a special need and not around Jesus.

While many things are easier said than done, I've put together a "top things to know" (in no particular order) as you minister and share God's love with teenagers and their families!

(1) If you require students to treat/handle a special needs child in a particular way, resentment can be created. The best way is for the leader to model interactions in order for this to be authentic. People with special needs can see through inauthentic gestures.

(2) Good communication with parents is vital! Ask lots of questions. They can be as simple as "Is there anything I need to know?" or "How is your child doing?" Share your phone number and invite parents to call with questions and concerns. Make sure parents know you are open to suggestions of how to accommodate, serve, and love their special needs child.

(3) Learning takes longer than a lesson; it is a lifelong process. Please don't dumb the message down, but don't overwhelm with too much information either. Special needs kids deal with the same issues of love, fear, acceptance, and identity as every teenager, so be open to one-on-one conversations about the topic being studied.

(4) The more you can partner with parents (keep them informed of what you are teaching and how they can reinforce the concepts at home), the greater the likelihood true growth will take place in kids' lives. Encourage parents as much as possible to take responsibility for the spiritual growth of their child. (This can be tricky depending on the faith of the parents.)

(5) Group trips and outings might require additional directions from parents. You may have to monitor or give specific help regarding bathing, personal hygiene, medications (and any potential reactions), personal boundaries, safety (Will they stay with a group? Will they go with a stranger?). It is often a good idea to incorporate the buddy system to help the special needs child. Be clear on money issues. This is not the time to try and teach responsibility lessons. A few dollars a day rather than the whole lump sum at once will save both of you a lot of headaches!

(6) Ask the family if there has been any kind of an emotional or physical trauma in the past that could affect behavior in the present. Ask what you can do to handle or prevent those situations.

(7) Games are a huge part of any youth ministry and every teenager's life. A special needs teenager really can know his or her own boundaries—challenge by choice. It may help for you to know what their physical limitations are. Learn how to not allow them to use their limitations to get out of playing. (This once again focuses on the need more than the person.) They shouldn't sit out if they don't need to. A special note: as much as we all like to think that the most responsible helper in our group could be a buddy, during night games, most often kids won't stick with those in need as the adrenaline kicks in. Find ways to have everyone participate or be included but not put anyone at risk.

(8) Check on accessibility for activities at camps, on field trips, wherever! If the special needs are physical, someone on the ministry leadership team should learn to drive a wheelchair-accessible van and be trained in managing the equipment.

(9) Be prepared to serve all the kids. During free time, don't just have football but have board games, cards, or other alternative activities for those with physical disabilities. If you're not certain what they can do or what they like to do, ask them!

(10) Finally, don't forget to include special needs kids in the group dinners or one-on-one soda times after school that you do with all of the other students. All kids thrive from personal attention. Actively recruit people who have a heart for special needs kids, as this can help relieve the leader to focus on the entire group. They can help validate that all kids are important to the ministry while adding stability and richness to the experience

I hope these family stories and my tips help you get a handle on working with special needs youth! Thanks for all you already are doing, and may God open your eyes, hearts, and ministries to those who are too often overlooked.

MAY 8, 2005

The Wise Counsel of Women (Mother's Day)

By Amy Jacober

MEMORY VERSE:
Charm is deceitful and beauty is vain, but a woman who fears the LORD, she shall be praised. —Proverbs 31:30 (NASB)

SCRIPTURE: 1 Samuel 1—2:1–11, 19

LESSON IN A SENTENCE: God teaches each new generation through the words and lives of mature, faithful believers.

THE BIG PICTURE (OR WHAT YOU'RE TRYING TO GET ACROSS):
Mothers have always had a difficult job. Children simply do not come with instruction manuals! In spite of this, mothers have been charged with loving, teaching, providing for, and protecting their children, among many other duties. Some have done this well, and others have struggled. Some of your students will have wonderful relationships with their mothers; others will not, and still others may not have a relationship with their biological mother at all. While we are looking at the story of Hannah, it is as much about Hannah as a woman of prayer as it is about Hannah the mother of Samuel. Samuel is not who caused her to pray. Motherhood was indeed a blessing, but her faith in God was settled long before the arrival of her son. While Hannah's desire was for a child, we can relate in that we all have desires deep within our hearts. Whether male or female, young or old, Hannah offers to us the example of her life in faithful prayer.

IN THIS LESSON STUDENTS SHOULD:

- Learn from the example of Hannah's life.
- Know that God provides support through others around us, but only He can satisfy.
- Prayer is not a magic trick to getting what we want.

STUFF YOU NEED:

- Pictures of famous influential women from newspapers or magazines
- Tape
- Numbers (to be placed next to the picture of each woman for identification)
- Paper
- Pencils
- Small prize (e.g., $5 gift card to the local coffee shop)

FOCUS

OPTION 1:

This will take a little prep work during the week. Tape pictures of at least 10 famous influential women around the room with a number beside each. (Try to avoid using only singers. Make some of them easy and some women making significant contributions at the time but perhaps with little recognition.) Once your students arrive, hand each a piece of paper and a pencil. The first to be able to correctly list by number the names of each woman and get their paper back to you wins a small prize. Once you have a winner, be certain to go around the room to each picture, identify the woman, and tell what significant contribution she is making.

Debrief by saying that all of these women have made contributions to our world in one way or another. We're going to take a look at a woman in the Bible who made a huge impact in her day and from whom we can still learn centuries later.

OPTION 2:

Invite one or two women from your congregation to share their stories about motherhood. In particular, request that they share their top three joys and top three struggles in motherhood. Many if not most of our teenagers never stop to think that they did not come with instructions! They are convinced that parents know exactly what they are doing and often it entails trying to destroy the lives of their children! Reality is, many women spend hours on their knees with their faces before God in prayer, just like Hannah. Consider inviting women who are not typically involved in youth ministry. This is a great way to connect with the congregation and allow your students to know another adult apart from the youth ministry team. At the end, offer a question/answer time for students to ask any questions they may have. (Tip—for women not accustomed to speaking, you may want to conduct an interview or offer pre-planned questions.)

DISCOVERY

This section may be a bit tough, as there is quite a bit of scripture. Resist the temptation to skip or shorten this part. It is Hannah's consistent life of prayer that teaches the lesson. This requires a look at the entire story up to the birth of Samuel. Break into at least five groups of no more than 6. (If you have a larger group, create more groups and assign the same scripture to more than one group or break the scriptures into smaller portions.) Have each group read their portion of the story and present what happens to the whole group. Encourage them to be as creative as possible! Present through sketches, movie posters, storyboards, or whatever manner the group chooses. In each presentation, be certain the following questions are answered.

1 Samuel 1:1–10: How did Hannah's husband (Elkanah) feel about her? Why did Hannah weep in anguish?

1 Samuel 1:11–18: What did Eli (the priest) think Hannah had done? What was Hannah really doing?

1 Samuel 1:19–22: What prayer of Hannah's was granted? What did Hannah plan to do with Samuel?

1 Samuel 1:23–28: What does Hannah pray in this section?

At the conclusion of the presentations, have a female leader read Hannah's prayer from *The Message*.

Hannah prayed:
I'm bursting with God-news!
I'm walking on air.
I'm laughing at my rivals.
I'm dancing at my salvation.

Nothing and no one is holy like GOD,
no rock mountain like our God.
Don't dare talk pretentiously—
not a word of boasting, ever!
For GOD knows what's going on.
He takes the measure of everything that happens.
The weapons of the strong are smashed to pieces,
while the weak are infused with fresh strength.
The well-fed are out begging in the streets for crusts,

while the hungry are getting second helpings.
The barren woman has a houseful of children,
while the mother of many is bereft.

God brings death and God brings life,
brings down to the grave and raises up.
God brings poverty and God brings wealth;
he lowers, he also lifts up.
He puts poor people on their feet again;
he rekindles burned-out lives with fresh hope,
Restoring dignity and respect to their lives—
a place in the sun!
For the very structure of earth are God's;
he has laid out his operations on a firm foundation.
He protectively cares for his faithful friends, step by step,
but leaves the wicked to stumble in the dark.
No one makes it in this life by sheer muscle!
God's enemies will be blasted out of the sky,
crashed in a heap and burned.
God will set things right all over the earth,
he'll give strength to his king,
he'll set his anointed on top of the world!

—1 Samuel 2:1–10

Teacher's Note: Hannah is best known for being a woman of prayer. That she certainly was. Her very name means "favor" or "grace." She was a woman who found the favor of God.

LIFE APPLICATION: What was one consistent theme in the life of Hannah?

What kind of mother do you think Hannah was?

Ask: Do you know of anyone older than you (either by a lot or just a little) from whom you would like to be learning? What is it about what that person has to offer that makes him or her so compelling?

Hannah was an amazing woman of prayer, passing her faith to her son. She had something to pass on! Read 1 Samuel 2:19. Samuel did not stop being her son when he was taken to the temple. In fact, Hannah continued to care for her son both in prayer and as a mother, bringing a robe to him each year.

MAKING IT PERSONAL: What things have you learned from your own mother, grandmothers, or aunts?

Just like Hannah and Samuel, we as children do not outgrow the teaching of our elders. Your own mom, grandma, aunt, or older family friend will always have wisdom to pass along. Encourage your students to invite their mom to a one-on-one date with them. This can be as simple as a Coke after school at the mall.

Close with a prayer for the mothers and all women who teach, love, and serve the students in your ministry.

ANCIENT PRACTICES: Spend a few extra moments in a guided prayer for the mothers, grandmothers, aunts, and surrogate mothers in the lives of your students. You may want to place tea lights around the room or on a back table. Invite each students to get up and take a few moments alone lighting the candle, offering their prayer up to God for their mom.

EXTRA! EXTRA!: I remember my first Mother's Day like it was yesterday. I was 25 and I had nearly 40 teenagers! The church I was serving had a tradition of offering flowers in the service, certainly to every mother, but also to every grandmother, aunt, and adult female in general. The flowers were presented with music playing, and each woman in the congregation was presented with a flower from a student in the youth group. When it came to the end the youth group gathered and called me to them. One young woman spoke for them, stating while they knew I had no children of my own, they offered their love to me as my adopted family whom I had mothered in a truly biblical sense— as that of teacher, boundary setter, accountability, caretaker, and offering my love. It was an amazingly powerful gift to me at such an early stage of my calling, reminding me that I needn't abandon being a woman in order to follow where Christ leads. While you may not be able to re-create this exact scene, use this time to honor both the biological mothers in your church family and those women who tirelessly pour into the lives of your students as well.

SONGS: "You Are a Child of Mine" by Mark Schultz, on the album *Stories and Songs*

QUOTABLE   QUOTES :

Every single act of love bears the imprint of God.
                                                    —Author Unknown

The Wise Counsel of Women — Midweek

MEMORY VERSE:
Charm is deceitful and beauty is vain, but a woman who fears the LORD, she shall be praised. —Proverbs 31:30 (NASB)

SCRIPTURE: Psalm 78:1–8

LESSON IN A SENTENCE: God teaches each new generation through the words and lives of mature, faithful believers.

FOCUS

Break into teams of 5–10 people. Have each team create a list of all the things you can "pass" (you can pass a basketball, you can pass a car on the freeway, etc.) Give teams 3 minutes to create the longest list they can. When time is called, have each read one item on their list in turn. If that item is on the list of anyone else, both the team reading and the team matching must scratch it off their list. Keep going until every team has only its unique items left on their list. The team with the greatest number of items on their list wins. Give the winning team candy as a prize.

Debrief by saying that things get passed every day. Sometimes we do the passing, sometimes we receive the pass. While most of the things on our lists were physical things that get passed, the Bible talks of faith as something that gets passed along from more mature believers to the young.

DISCOVERY

Ask: Have you ever lost something? When? What is the story?

Have you ever hidden something or had something hidden from you? What's that story?

We spend a lot of our lives looking for things—things we have lost, things we've misplaced, things hidden, and things taken. Many of us spend our lifetime looking for something more important than just stuff. What would it be like if we always had someone right beside us to help us look and find? That's just what God had in mind.

Read Psalm 78:1–8.

Split into at least 2 groups.

Give one group the following two questions:

Re-read Psalm 78:1–5.

What are parents supposed to pass to their children?

If parents are supposed to keep the ways of God from being hidden, why are so many of us still trying to figure it out?

Give the second group the following questions:

Re-read Psalm 78:6–8.

Assuming we are a part of the generation, what is our responsibility to those who come behind us?

Why does God want each generation to pass on His ways?

What keeps us today from passing on His ways to everyone around us?

Depending on your time, either have the groups report their scriptures, questions, and what they discussed or, after 10-15 minutes, have the groups switch questions.

APPLICATION: If money, age, education, and opportunity were no object, what are all of the things you would like to pass to the generation just behind you?

Take the same scenario and make a list of all of the things you would like to tell adults about what you have already learned.

Think back to what Psalm 78 said. Are you passing on things that will draw others closer to God and walking in His ways? Cross everything off both lists that have no connection to God whatsoever.

Have each person choose one thing from the remainder of the lists and think of how this honors God specifically and a way they can live out the principle in order to pass on to others through their words and lives.

MAY 15, 2005

We Are Never Alone (Pentecost Sunday)

By Amy Jacober

MEMORY VERSE:
I will put My Spirit within you and cause you to walk in My statues, and you will keep My judgments and do them. —Ezekiel 36:27

SCRIPTURE: Acts 2:1–13; Ephesians 5:15–21

LESSON IN A SENTENCE: The Holy Spirit came to live within each of us.

THE BIG PICTURE (OR WHAT YOU'RE TRYING TO GET ACROSS):

The Holy Spirit is often the most neglected person of the Trinity. While eternally present just as the Father and the Son, the Holy Spirit was sent at Pentecost, after the ascension, to walk with believers. There are days when we all feel like we cannot make it. Realistically, in our own flesh, we could not. The Holy Spirit is comforter, guide, counselor, and the One Who convicts. As the song goes, "Not by might, not by power, but by My Spirit says the Lord." It is by the Spirit of God that we are able to walk through our daily lives. It is by the Spirit that we remain humble in our giftedness, that we can remain hopeful in our trials, and we can remain strong when our own flesh is weak. God never meant that we live in this world apart from Him. In His continual effort at reconciliation, the Holy Spirit restores the relationship and community God intended all along.

IN THIS LESSON STUDENTS SHOULD:

- Know that God puts His Spirit within each believer.
- Be able to identify a few specific roles of the Holy Spirit.
- Find comfort and accountability in the constant presence of the Holy Spirit.

STUFF YOU NEED:

If you choose Option 1:
- A sheet or plastic tarp
- A new plastic rain gutter
- Ice cream and toppings—enough to fill the rain gutter
- Spoons (enough for each person present)

FOCUS

OPTION 1:

A little messy but certainly an opportunity to find something good in what may seem like chaos! Begin with a large sheet or tarp. Set a new plastic rain gutter in the middle. (If you have a large group, you may need two of everything!) Give each person present a job: ice cream scooper, topping master, sprinkler of nuts, banana slicer, cherry placer, and last but not least, whipped cream topper! (FYI—while none of these are particularly safe for the rambunctious student, whipped cream is a favorite weapon of those with high energy! Choose your students wisely!) Once the jobs are given, set about making a huge rain gutter sundae! As the masterpiece is completed, give a spoon to each person and dig in! (If you are looking for a further way to debrief, give each student a long teaspoon and tell them they can eat all they like *but* they may not feed themselves. They must find a partner and work together to feed one another.)

OPTION 2:

Break your students into groups of 4–6. Tell them they are each a part of a public relations team competing for a job. The first order of business is to create a team name. Give 5 minutes for the creativity to begin! As they are working on their team name, give them an envelope with the following instructions.

Your assignment is as follows: As a newly formed public relations team you have been hired by the Christian church. It is not uncommon for people to be able to talk about Jesus and God the Father. The Holy Spirit however is less discussed. Your job is to present, in no more than 60 seconds, Who the Holy Spirit is.

DISCOVERY

Tell your students that you are talking about a feast today! Explain that Pentecost was a feast celebrated by the Jews. It was to offer the first fruits to honor God. In biblical days, often those who lived in the remote areas made a special trip to Jerusalem to join the celebration!

Ask: Have any of you ever been at a party when an unexpected guest arrives?

Have any of you ever crashed a party?

What is that like? How does that impact the mood of the party?

What do you think would happen if God crashed the party?

Read Acts 2:1–13.

Ask: What happened?

You may want or need to read this again. Try to picture yourself at this feast in Jerusalem. As the passage is read again, what do you feel? What do you hear? What are the smells in the air? What do you think is happening?

Verse 13 says that some were mocking, saying the people were full of sweet wine. If you were there, how would it make you feel to be made fun of for the most amazing experience with God? How would it feel to be so misunderstood when you had done nothing wrong? Would you ever want to encourage anyone else to go through this same kind of experience?

Most scholars agree that Paul wrote the letter to the church at Ephesus. Among many other directions, he encourages them to be filled with the Holy Spirit.

Read Ephesians 5:15–21.

Ask: What do verse 15 and verse 17 have to say about those who are foolish or unwise? What does verse 18 say we are to be?

Say: We can learn a thing or two from this letter. Being filled with the Spirit means you may be mistaken for being foolish or unwise. You may be opening yourself up to being made fun of or misunderstood.

Teacher's Note: While most of us are vaguely familiar with Pentecost being the time after the ascension when the Holy Spirit arrived, it began as a tradition much earlier than that! It was a feast! The feast of firstfruits to be exact. Just like God to show up for the party! Even more than that, Pentecost is widely considered as the beginning of the church as we know it today, becoming famous as the birthday of the church! The term comes from a Greek word *pentekos-tos*, meaning "fiftieth." It was a feast that occurred fifty days after Passover. Exodus 34:22, Deuteronomy 16:10, and Leviticus 23:17–20 can help shed a little light on the feast of Pentecost.

LIFE APPLICATION: What do people get made fun of for today?

Take a few moments and make a list of all the things you have heard in the last week, that you have experienced, or that you know is going on. Write these up on a whiteboard. Once you have a list, go back through and ask if there are any of the things listed that are up there simply because someone doesn't understand the person or situation. For example: making fun of someone for the way they dress. What you might not know is that the person has a parent with cancer at home and what they are wearing simply does not matter at this time.

MAKING IT PERSONAL: Ask: Would you ever choose to live in a way where you knew you would get made fun of?

Re-read Acts 2:13 and Ephesians 5:18.

What do these verses seem to suggest?

What do these verses mean for you?

Say: While it is certainly not God's goal to have each of us be teased and mocked every day, reality is we live in a world where following Jesus and being filled with the Holy Spirit is misunderstood, even by many of those who call themselves Christians.

Close thanking God that you don't have to be understood by anyone but Him!

CONNECTIONS: For a few other considerations of the Spirit, see John 14:17; Romans 8:9; 1 Corinthians 3:16; 1 John 2:27.

SONGS: "Sing a Song" by Third Day, on the album *Offerings 2 Album*

"Right Here" by Jeremy Camp, on the album *Stay*

Q U O T A B L E   Q U O T E S :

We must be ready to allow ourselves to be interrupted by God. . . . We must not . . . assume that our schedule is our own to manage, but allow it to be arranged by God.

—Dietrich Bonhoeffer

We Are Never Alone —Midweek

MEMORY VERSE:
I will put My Spirit within you and cause you to walk in My statues, and you will keep My judgments and do them. —Ezekiel 36:27

SCRIPTURE: Ephesians 1:12–14

LESSON IN A SENTENCE: The Holy Spirit came to live within each of us.

FOCUS

This is an exercise in allowing another to hold you up! It is about balance, coordination, and a bit of strength while mostly about learning to trust!

Have your students partner up as best as possible with those close in size. Facing one another, have them touch hands and take one step sideways. (This should be so easy at first that it seems pointless!) Have each set of partners take a step back, put their hands up again and step sideways while touching hands. Continue this process with each turn taking yet another step back. After just a few turns, they will need to lean quite a bit in order to move while touching. (As they lean further and further apart, you may want to have a spotter on all fours crawling between them in case of a fall.) See which set of partners can lean the furthest and still move sideways. Offer a box of pizza rolls to each of the winners! (Get it? Leaning tower of "pizza"!)

DISCOVERY

Ask: Do you ever feel alone in this world? Like the deck is stacked against you and no matter what...God seems to only be at church or worse, on the retreats that happen twice a year?

Have your students consider these three questions while they are reading the passages; (1) Who is the "Him" mentioned? (2) What does it mean to be sealed with the Holy Spirit? (3) What are we guaranteed? Have available several translations of Scripture. Tell them to keep reading until they can confidently answer all three questions. You may want to write Ephesians 1:13–14 on separate pieces of paper from several translations (NKJV, NASB, NIV, NRSV, CEV, *The Message*, Phillips, etc. If you don't have several translations handy, check out www.biblegateway.com)

Spend a few moments answering the three questions based on what they found.

ANCIENT PRACTICE: Any discussion is often a confusing matter. While this passage is short, it is rich. You may want to consider a *lectio devina* as an alternate way of learning from this passage with your group.

APPLICATION: We all have times of struggle and doubt. The Scriptures teach us that while those are bound to come, we are not alone. God has sent His Holy Spirit. Not only has He sent His Spirit, but He sent His Spirit to dwell in us! For followers of Jesus, we do not walk through difficulty alone. It is sometimes hard to see this. While we are blessed to be alive and in a prosperous country, at times that can make it feel all the more like we are the only ones struggling. It can feel like the rest of the world is just fine here and now.

Ask: Why do you think the Holy Spirit was sent?

What does a promise, a guarantee of all that awaits in heaven mean to you right now?

How might it change the way you live daily if you were to have and be aware that the Holy Spirit was with you at all times?

On a slip of paper (like a bookmark size and shape) write one thing you feel like you simply cannot do by yourself right now. This can be anything from understanding math well enough to pass a test to not being able to resist going out drinking on a Friday night. If you need to write a few code words so only you know the meaning, feel free. On the other side, write Ezekiel 36:27. God has directions for our lives. He has also provided the support each of us needs, even when it is not what we wanted.

Say: You are never alone if you are a follower of Jesus. The Holy Spirit is not only here with believers now to walk through good and bad times, but as a guarantee that there is something more to come!

MEMORY VERSE ACTIVITY

A rather silly object lesson but quite effective!

Bring cream or jelly-filled donuts or snack cakes. Before eating them, ask if anyone knows how the filling gets inside?

Any thoughts on how the Holy Spirit gets inside of you? Check out Ezekiel 36:27. While hundreds if not thousands of bakeries have managed to figure out the secret to getting the filling inside, there is only One who can send His Spirit to live in us! God Himself is the One to put His Spirit in us.

Getting Ready to Dare Great Things

By John Losey

MEMORY VERSE:

"If you have raced with men on foot
and they have worn you out,
how can you compete with horses?
If you stumble in safe country,
how will you manage in the thickets by the Jordan?"

—Jeremiah 12:5 (NIV)

SCRIPTURE: John 14:12; Hebrews 12:1–3; Judges 6:12–15

LESSON IN A SENTENCE: Regardless of what job or career you end up living, God has called us all to live extraordinary lives. We can start living that life here and now.

THE BIG PICTURE:

God has called you to do great things in any situation in which you find yourself. If you are a believer, then you have eternal life. God asks us to prepare ourselves to live extraordinary lives for all eternity. That starts now. Don't compare your life and goals to those around you. God has higher expectations and knows you can do far more than you think you can. It will not be easy, but you can start preparing to dare great things right away.

IN THIS LESSON STUDENTS SHOULD:

- ○ Understand that, regardless of what career they choose, God has called them to do great things with their lives.
- ○ Realize that this life will not be easy, and they should expect difficulty in living extraordinary lives.
- ○ Begin to prepare themselves for this life right now.

STUFF YOU NEED:

○ Spot Markers for Option 1
○ 1 pack of 100 3 x 5 cards/group of 8 for Option 2
○ 1 box of paper clips/ group of 8 for Option 2
○ 1 large book or Bible /group for Option 2

FOCUS

OPTION 1:

Traffic Jam—(groups of 8–16)

Set out enough "spot designators" (some sort of marker: paper, carpet squares, backpacks) so that there is one more spot than group members. Arrange the spots in a straight line (see diagram).

Split the group in half so that the two halves are facing each other with the open space between them.

The object is to have the group on one side move to the other and vice versa only using the legal moves.

Legal moves—(1) A person may move into an empty space in front of him/her. (2) A person may move around one person facing him/her into an empty space.

Illegal moves—(1) Any move backwards. (2) Any move around someone facing the same direction you are. (3) Any move not into an empty space.

Once they have completed the puzzle once, have them do it again. Be sure to have them stand in different places in the line to start. If time permits, have them repeat the challenge but without talking.

Leader's Note: Notice when mistakes are made. Even after the group makes a mistake they can continue to make several legal moves until they are truly stuck. The earlier they realize their mistake, the sooner they can get back on track. Notice if they adopt additional rules or guidelines that help them stay on track. This is a great activity to explore the idea of how decisions they make now might impact their lives later on. Hint for solving the puzzle—before you make a move, consider all the possible moves and the consequences they have for future moves.

When they have completed the puzzle (or given up), have the groups discuss several of the following questions:

Was this activity challenging? Why or why not?

How did you go about solving this puzzle?

How did you know if you made a mistake?

When did you know you made a wrong decision? Did you know right away?

Besides the official rules, did you discover any additional rules or guidelines that were helpful to solving the puzzle?

OPTION 2:

Clips and Cards—(groups of 8)

Give each group a pack of 3 x 5 cards, a box of paperclips, and a large, heavy book (Bible?)

Challenge them to see how tall they can make a tower/structure out of the clips and cards that will still hold the book. Give them a 10-minute time limit.

After 10 minutes test the structures.

Take away all the clips and cards that are not part of the structure and challenge them to build a taller structure with the same amount of materials. Give them 10 minutes to complete this task.

If time permits, repeat step 4.

Have the groups discuss several of the following questions:

What did you think when you were first given this challenge?

How did you go about constructing the structure the first time?

What did you think when you were asked to build a taller structure with the same amount of resources you used to build a smaller one?

What do you think about what you accomplished?

DISCOVERY

Read Judges 6:11–15

The angel of the LORD came and sat down under the oak in Ophrah that belonged to Joash the Abiezrite, where his son Gideon was threshing wheat in a winepress to keep it from the Midianites. When the angel of the LORD appeared to Gideon, he said, "The LORD is with you, mighty warrior."

"But sir," Gideon replied, "if the LORD is with us, why has all this happened to us? Where are all his wonders that our fathers told us about when they said, 'Did not the LORD bring us up out of Egypt?' But now the LORD has abandoned us and put us into the hand of Midian."

The LORD turned to him and said, "Go in the strength you have and save Israel out of Midian's hand. Am I not sending you?"

"But Lord," Gideon asked, "how can I save Israel? My clan is the weakest in Manasseh, and I am the least in my family."

What is Gideon doing when the Angel sits under the tree?

Why is he in a winepress?

Teacher's Note: Threshing wheat was usually done in the open where the wind could carry the chaff away and the grain would fall to the ground. A winepress was usually a hole in the ground. Gideon is fearful of the Midianites stealing his grain, so he was hiding in the hole in the ground.

How does the Angel greet Gideon?

Does Gideon think the name "mighty warrior" fit? (see verse 15)

Do you think the name fits Gideon at this time?

Why do you think the Angel calls him by this name?

Teacher's Note: If you know the story of Gideon, you know that he becomes the "mighty warrior" the Angel predicted he would be. God thought much more of Gideon than he thought of himself.

Read Jeremiah 12:5:

"If you have raced with men on foot
and they have worn you out,
how can you compete with horses?
If you stumble in safe country,
how will you manage in the thickets by the Jordan?"

Teacher's Note: Just before the Lord speaks these words, Jeremiah is complaining about how difficult and unfair life has been. This is God's response to his complaint.

This is God's response to Jeremiah's complaint. How do you think Jeremiah was expecting God to respond?

What's the difference between racing other people and competing with horses?

What's the difference between walking in safe country and walking in the thickets?

What do these verses tell us about what God thinks Jeremiah can do?

What do you think God is trying to tell Jeremiah

LIFE APPLICATION: God seems to think a lot of both Gideon and Jeremiah. God has a high opinion of what we can do with the life He has given us all the resources we have.

Read John 14:12 (NIV).

I tell you the truth, anyone who has faith in me will do what I have been doing. He will do even greater things than these, because I am going to the Father.

What were some of the things Jesus was doing?

What do you think about this promise of Jesus?

How do you think this promise impacts your life?

MAKING IT PERSONAL: Read Hebrews 12:1–3:

Therefore, since we are surrounded by such a great cloud of witnesses, let us throw off everything that hinders and the sin that so easily entangles, and let us run with perseverance the race marked out for us. Let us fix our eyes on Jesus, the author and perfecter of our faith, who for the joy set before him endured the cross, scorning its shame, and sat down at the right hand of the throne of God. Consider him who endured such opposition from sinful men, so that you will not grow weary and lose heart.

Teacher's Note: The "great cloud of witnesses" is referring to the great heroes of the faith listed in the previous chapter. The following verses are advice on how to prepare ourselves to live heroic lives as well. Have the students use these verses as an evaluation/training plan for living extraordinary lives.

What are the things that hinder or hold you back from doing great things? Choose one of these things to "throw off" or get rid of this week (things that are part of you; bad habits).

What things "entangle you" or get in your way as you try to do great things? Choose one of these snares to avoid this week (things that are around you; bad or unhealthy environment or friends).

What are some major challenges you will be facing in the near future? How can you prepare yourself to face the difficulties and work through them? (Perseverance is knowing that things are tough and going through it with a positive attitude.)

How are you going to fix your eyes on Jesus and learn from His example? Jesus endured much because He could focus on the joy on the other side of the pain and difficulty. What qualities of Jesus can you focus on when life gets tough that will help you see the joy set before "so that you will not grow weary and lose heart."

Getting Ready to Dare Great Things —Midweek

MEMORY VERSE:

"If you have raced with men on foot
and they have worn you out,
how can you compete with horses?
If you stumble in safe country,
how will you manage in the thickets by the Jordan?"

—Jeremiah 12:5 (NIV)

SCRIPTURE: Ephesians 4:1–6

LESSON IN A SENTENCE: Regardless of what job or career you end up entering, God has called us all to live extraordinary lives. We can start living that life here and now.

FOCUS
Career counselor:

Have you ever noticed in high school there are only a handful of careers ever mentioned? Doctor, lawyer, teacher, music star, athlete—these pretty much cover the main categories.

Have each person present think of at least 10 different jobs in the world. Write each of these on a separate 3 x 5 card. Encourage your students to really be creative—recipe taste tester for a magazine, movie reviewer, paint color namer, traffic controller, tracker of volcanic activity, tractor driver, and mechanic, etc.—the more obscure the better!

Once you have gathered all of these, have your students get in pairs. Let each pair draw ten cards. (Throw out any duplicates and know that you will have extras at the end.) Tell each pair they must come up with one thing, one task, one contribution within the church that would uniquely match the gifts of the person with each career. For example, if the person is the recipe taste tester, he or she must know how to cook. This person can offer free cooking classes to the community for outreach or choose to pass on some skills in cooking to a small group as relationships are built and a time of prayer could follow each cooking class. A person who tracks volcanic activity can offer a seminar on the wonders of God's creation and the power we are only beginning to understand. A tractor driver and mechanic may volunteer to take a group on a mission trip to work with migrant farm workers and offer help on their equipment. Encourage them to be as creative as possible!

Once they are through working, have each pair choose their top three favorite careers matched with the contribution each may give to the church. Present each of these to the group.

Ask: When it comes to church work, what careers or training usually come to mind?

DISCOVERY

Read Ephesians 4:1–6.

Re-read verse 1.

Ask: How do verse 2–6 help to explain what it meant by "calling" in verse 1?

Say: The point of this passage is not to encourage you to find the one and only occupation that is worthy or good. It reminds us that what we do is not who we are.

The word vocation actually comes from the Latin *vocatio* which means "to call." Vocation and calling are the same. There is not an exclusive list of jobs in Scripture. There is a calling not to a job but to a purpose. No matter what job you do, your purpose in life remains the same. You can have five different careers, with the same vocation, the same calling.

APPLICATION: Ask: Keeping this in mind, that vocation and calling are the same, what other parts of your life will impact your calling? A few examples are your church life, family, marriage or singleness, and society.

Say: Vocation is related to what you do for a living but it is much more than that. Right now you are in school and have all of the responsibilities that go with that. One day soon, you will be choosing a career. You do not have to wait until you have a full-time paying job to think about your vocation or your calling in life.

Spend a few moments discussing different purposes or callings you may have heard about or witnessed in your life (to fight injustice, to offer mercy, to bring beauty to an ugly world, etc.)

Ask: How would an occupation differ from a calling? How would it be similar?

Once you have helped your students to think through a few of these, invite them to ask God to begin showing them their purpose in life, their calling or vocation. Pray that God would not only begin to reveal this but that God would help them to find ways to begin living their purpose right now.

QUOTABLE   QUOTES :

It is when I turn to Christ, when I give up myself to His personality, that I first begin to have a personality of my own.

—C. S. Lewis

MAY 29, 2005

So What's Fair

By John Losey

MEMORY VERSE:

Now all has been heard; here is the conclusion of the matter: Fear God and keep his commandments, for this is the whole duty of man. For God will bring every deed into judgment, including every hidden thing, whether it is good or evil.—Ecclesiastes 12:13–14 (NIV)

SCRIPTURE: Matthew 19:30; 20:1–16; Ecclesiastes 9:11; Romans 3:23; 6:23

LESSON IN A SENTENCE: Life is not fair but God is in control; we might not like the results if life were really fair.

THE BIG PICTURE (OR WHAT YOU'RE TRYING TO GET ACROSS):

"Who ever said life was fair?" We've all heard this phrase but seldom consider what good news this is. When we complain about the unfairness of a situation usually it's because we feel that we didn't get something we deserved and really wanted. Consider the other side. Do we complain when we don't get the punishment or consequences that we have earned or deserved. This lesson will help students look past the frustration and anger that often accompanies an unfair situation. They will be encouraged to look at the Big Picture; God is in control and, instead of being "fair" and giving us the punishment our sin has earned us, He offers grace, the unfair gift of eternal life.

IN THIS LESSON STUDENTS SHOULD:

- ○ Realize that life is not always fair.
- ○ Understand that what's fair may not always be what is pleasant or positive.
- ○ Discover that they can choose their attitude when they find themselves in unfair situations.
- ○ Rest in the reassurance that God is in control and will make all things right.

STUFF YOU NEED:

- ○ Prizes for Option 1
- ○ Bibles
- ○ Game supplies depending on the option and/or activity chosen.

FOCUS

OPTION 1:

Choose a game that will result in one clear winner (see suggestions below). Promise a wonderful prize to whoever wins the competition (make a big deal out of this. It will help the discussion later). Present the winner with the promised prize, but also give the same prize to all the other competitors. Discuss several of the following topics/questions with the group:

What did you think about the game/competition?

How did the winner feel when they received the prize? What about the rest of the group when they received the prize?

What did you think when the rest of the competitors were given the same prize as the winner?

Is this fair? Why or why not?

What does "fair" mean?

Who decides what's fair?

GAME IDEAS

- ○ Bible Quiz
- ○ Twinkie eating contest (first to eat 10 or most in a minute)
- ○ Giant Twister contest. Last one standing wins. Use several twister sets or make your own from canvas paint drop cloths and spray paint
- ○ "Simon Says"—Instead of elimination, assign points every time someone messes up. The person with the least amount of points at the end wins.

OPTION 2:

Set up a simple race or obstacle course. Ask for several volunteers to participate. Just before you start the race give at least one of the faster students a simple but safe handicap (Have them carry a chair, tie their shoelaces together, make them hop) At the end of the race discuss several of the following questions with the group:

What did you think about the game/competition?

Did the "right person" win the race?

Was this race "fair?" Why or why not?

In organized athletics (any level from high school football to the Olympics) does the right person or team always win? Can you think of any examples where the results of a competition weren't fair?

What does "fair" mean?

Is life always fair? Why or why not?

DISCOVERY

Before you begin reading the scripture passages, have the group come up with a definition of "fair." It should be something about getting what you earned or deserve.

Read Ecclesiastes 9:11 (NIV).

I have seen something else under the sun:
The race is not to the swift
or the battle to the strong,
nor does food come to the wise
or wealth to the brilliant
or favor to the learned;
but time and chance happen to them all.

How does this verse relate to the race we just completed (if you did option 2)?

Is this accurate to your experience in life?

Do you think the writer understands what it's like to experience situations that are not fair?

Let's look at the advice the writer gives to living life in a world that doesn't always make sense and is often unfair.

Read Ecclesiastes 12:13–14 (NIV).

Now all has been heard;
here is the conclusion of the matter:
Fear God and keep his commandments,
for this is the whole duty of man.
For God will bring every deed into judgment,
including every hidden thing,
whether it is good or evil.

What qualities of God do these verses point out?

What does it mean to "fear God"?

What does it mean to "keep his commandments"?

How do these verses help us deal with unfair situations?

Read Matthew 19:30.

But many who are first will be last, and many who are last will be first.

Discuss how that verse relates to fairness.

Read Matthew 20:1–12 (NIV).

"The kingdom of heaven is like a landowner who went out early in the morning to hire men to work in his vineyard. He agreed to pay them a denarius for the day and sent them into his vineyard.

"About the third hour he went out and saw others standing in the marketplace doing nothing. He told them, 'You also go and work in my vineyard, and I will pay you whatever is right.' So they went.

"He went out again about the sixth hour and the ninth hour and did the same thing. About the eleventh hour he went out and found still others standing around. He asked them, 'Why have you been standing here all day long doing nothing?'

"'Because no one has hired us,' they answered.

"He said to them, 'You also go and work in my vineyard.'

"When evening came, the owner of the vineyard said to his foreman, 'Call the workers and pay them their wages, beginning with the last ones hired and going on to the first.'

"The workers who were hired about the eleventh hour came and each received a denarius. So when those came who were hired first, they expected to receive more. But each one of them also received a denarius. When they received it, they began to grumble against the landowner. 'These men who were hired last worked only one hour,' they said, 'and you have made them equal to us who have borne the burden of the work and the heat of the day.'

Have a few students try to retell this story in their own words.

How would you feel if you were one of the workers who started early in the morning?

How would you feel if you were one of the workers who started at the 11th hour?

Is this fair? Why or why not?

Read Matthew 20:13–16.

"But he answered one of them, 'Friend, I am not being unfair to you. Didn't you agree to work for a denarius? Take your pay and go. I want to give the man who was hired last the same as I gave you. Don't I have the right to do what I want with my own money? Or are you envious because I am generous?'

"So the last will be first, and the first will be last."

How does this story relate to the competition we did earlier (if you did option 1)?

From the landowner's perspective is this story fair? Why or why not?

LIFE APPLICATION:

Read Romans 3:23 and 6:23.

What do we really deserve? What have we earned?

What if God was "fair" and gave us what we deserved?

Have the students reflect on the following. (Give them several minutes of silence)

Before you demand to be treated fairly think about what that might really mean.

When you are being treated unfairly how can you use that to focus on God's gift of grace?

MAKING IT PERSONAL: Have a few of the students share their reflections. Ask the students to do one or more of the following between now and the next meeting:

Keep a "fairness" journal. Write down when they feel they have been treated unfairly, why they felt that way and how they responded.

Challenge the students to choose their attitude. When they begin to feel frustrated about an unfair situation, ask them to remember the "unfairness" of grace and be thankful instead. Have them share how it worked or didn't at the next meeting. (See 1 Thessalonians 5:18; Philippians 4:4.)

So What's Fair? —Midweek

MEMORY VERSE:
Now all has been heard; here is the conclusion of the matter: Fear God and keep his commandments, for this is the whole duty of man. For God will bring every deed into judgment, including every hidden thing, whether it is good or evil.—Ecclesiastes 12:13–14 (NIV)

SCRIPTURE: Matthew 5:44–45

LESSON IN A SENTENCE: Life is not fair but God is in control; we might not like the results if life were really fair.

FOCUS

Rent the movie *Bruce Almighty*. If you have not seen this before, you will want to preview the film so that you are able to know in context what is happening. (There may be some question in using this film. It does not show a godly man with struggles by any means. It shows a man who is lost and living as a lost man. While he does make progress in the film, there are still some choices left unresolved. Deep struggles and questions are couched in humor.)

There are many scenes throughout the film that depict a sense of a human perspective on what is fair and what is not. One example would be as follows:

Toward the beginning of the film is a scene where Bruce (the main character of this film) pitches a fit back at his apartment in front of his girlfriend. In this scene he says that God is like the mean kid with a magnifying glass and he is the ant. The entire tantrum revolves around a verbal explosion of venting that God is not fair—that he has not done anything wrong, in fact that he thinks he is a fairly average nice guy and yet God is picking on him! (Is this sounding like any of your students?)

Ask: How "real" is this scene? Maybe not this extreme, but can any of you think of a similar situation where you or someone you know tried to be good, someone who mostly did the right things and figured God owed him or her?

Ask: Pretend God has asked you to sit down for a chat. He wants to know what you would do to be certain everything happens just as it should in the entire world. How do you respond? (Remember this must include being all loving, that all people have been created in His image, etc.)

DISCOVERY

Ask: Who deserves bad things to come into their lives?

How do we define bad things? (Take a few minutes and write some of these up on a whiteboard.)

Read Matthew 5:44–45.

Ask: On whom does God cause the sun to rise? The rain to fall? What does this mean?

Say: Many Christians today have a false impression that being follower of Jesus means that life gets better and all our troubles are gone. We barter with God: If I follow you, fix this problem in my life. "If I choose not to cheat on a test because I know that is not what you would want, then God, you need to give me an A." Or "God, if I am nice to others and work hard, you should provide the friends and money I need to be happy." A big one tends to be "If I wait until I am married to have sex, then you should give the perfect boyfriend or girlfriend to me right now." We may not say things like this out loud, but we certainly think them or at least live our lives like this.

Ask: Does the Bible ever say life is supposed to be fair? Does the Bible ever say followers of Jesus will have an easier life or get everything we want?

LIFE APPLICATION: Think of one place in your life where you have tried really hard to live the right way, to be above reproach.

Ask: Why are you trying to live the "right" way in this area? What do you expect to gain?

Say: We talked last time we were together and determined that indeed life is not fair. In fact, it is a good thing that life is not fair. We do so many wrong things every day, that were life "fair" we would constantly be having negative consequences in our lives. Just like Bruce in the movie, we are not always careful for what we ask and we rarely think through the consequences of how it may not be the best for us nor what negative impact it may have on others.

Choose one area in your life to offer over to God in submission for at least one week. What this means is intentionally choosing to do the right thing because it is the right thing, not to get anything in return. It may be not talking back to your parents, not skipping school, not spending hours surfing the web instead of doing homework—whatever. Tell one person here so that he or she may pray for you and hold you accountable.

Close in prayer thanking God that He indeed is not impartial. That in His mercy He is not perfectly fair as He does not punish us as we should be for every wrong thing we do. In His love, He walks with us in a world where the rain indeed falls on the just and the unjust.

Learning to Talk to God

By Amy Jacober

MEMORY VERSE:
Do not be rash with your mouth, and let not your heart utter anything hastily before God. For God is in heaven, and you on earth; therefore let your words be few. —Ecclesiastes 5:2 (NKJV)

SCRIPTURE: Matthew 6:9–13; Luke 11:2–4

LESSON IN A SENTENCE: God wants for us to have meaningful conversations with Him.

THE BIG PICTURE (OR WHAT YOU'RE TRYING TO GET ACROSS):

We begin learning right at the very beginning of our lives. Babies born around the world learn the language of their families and communities. Many of us grew up with a parent or grandparent teaching us some rendition of "Now I lay me down to sleep. . . ." For most of us, we know prayer is important but our childhood bedtime prayers were the last time we really were "taught" anything about how to have a conversation with God. Jesus longs to talk with us. He longs not for small talk or just chitchat, but daily moments in intimate conversations. Jesus was also aware that sometimes we aren't certain of the way to even begin those kinds of conversations and therefore end up avoiding a time to talk at all. For your students it can be even worse! They hear adults pray with eloquence and the words just seem to roll off their tongues. (Not to mention a few of us adults get equally intimidated by such seemingly perfect prayer!) Jesus doesn't require that we sound perfect and polished. He simply wants to talk with us. Jesus gave the Lord's Prayer as a model for us to begin the conversation.

IN THIS LESSON STUDENTS SHOULD:

- Understand that God wants to talk with us.
- Know that the Lord's Prayer is a model offered to us to begin a conversation with God.
- Learn where to find the Lord's Prayer—both versions—in Scripture.
- Think through the meaning of each part of the Lord's Prayer.

STUFF YOU NEED:

○ Copies of the sketch (ideally rehearsed ahead of time)

FOCUS

OPTION 1:

Have students open with a presentation of the following sketch.

The Lord's Prayer
By Sarah Ware

The scene begins with a girl kneeling at the side of her bed. She has been praying the Lord's Prayer every night before she goes to bed since she was a little girl. This night, her traditional ritual is interrupted when God answers her back.

Running Time: 4 min.- 5 min.

Players (2): Voice of God
                     Girl

Girl:	"Our Father who art in heaven . . ." (interrupted by God's voice)
God:	Yes.
Girl:	"Our Father who art in heaven . . ."
God:	Yes.
Girl:	(faster) "Our Father who art in heaven . . ."
God:	I heard you the first time two times. I'm omniscient, not deaf.
Girl:	Don't interrupt me. I'm praying.
God:	But you called me.
Girl:	Called you? I didn't call you. I'm PRAYING. "Our Father who art in heaven . . ."
God:	There! You did it again!
Girl:	Did what?
God:	Called me. You said, "Our Father who art in heaven." Well, here I am!
Girl:	(She looks around panicking—looking under pillows and blankets.) Where is here exactly?
God:	Everywhere. (Girl covers herself with a blanket to try and hide.) Along with omniscient, I'm also omnipresent, and the

blankets aren't doing anything for your style, so let's proceed, shall we?

Girl: Proceed? I didn't mean anything by it. I was just saying my
prayers for the day. I always say the Lord's Prayer before I
go to bed at night. It helps me sleep better. Or, at least it did.

God: Right. Why don't you keep going then?

Girl: I would if somebody wouldn't interrupt me! (She covers her
head in fear.) "Our Father who art in heaven . . ." (She pauses
waiting for God to interrupt. She continues with the prayer
once she feels that it's safe.) "Hallowed be thy name . . ."

God: (interrupting once again) Do you know what that means?

Girl: Of course I do! It means your name is, . . . it means your
name is . . . "hallow-ed." (She pauses, waiting for an
answer.) Fine! I don't know what it means.

God: Yeah, I knew that already. Omniscient, remember?
Hallowed means holy and wonderful.

Girl: Look, this is taking a lot longer than it usually does, and I
have a big day tomorrow. I need to get some sleep, so if we
could move this along, that would be great.

God: Okay, contrary to what you believe, I am the center of the
universe. Not you. You're on my time. Please continue.

Girl: "Thy Kingdom come, Thy will be done on earth as it is in
heaven."

God: And how have you helped to bring this about?

Girl: Well, I go to church.

God: Going to a donut shop doesn't make you a donut.

Girl: Why are you picking on me? I'm just as good as everybody
else in that church!

God: I'm sorry. I must have been mistaken. I thought you were
praying for MY will to be done. If that's going to happen, it
will need to start with the ones who are praying for it—like
you.

Girl: Why does it always have to be your way? What about my
kingdom?

God: (God laughs) My dear, if your kingdom were to come,
everyone would wear lots of pink and gossip all the time.

Girl: I do have some hang-ups.

God: It's a start at least.

Girl: "Give us this day our daily bread, and forgive us our sins as
we forgive those who sin against us."

God:	(Cough) Becky.
Girl:	Forget it. I'm not forgiving her.
God:	But your prayer! What about your prayer?
Girl:	Okay! "Forgive us our sins as we forgive everyone but Becky." (She sticks her tongue out.)
God:	Settle your heart, and forgive Becky. Then the sin and hate will be Becky's problem, not yours. You'll feel better.
Girl:	Oh, you're right. You always are.
God:	Of course.
Girl:	Besides, I want to be right with you more than I want to egg Becky's car.
God:	There! How do you feel now?
Girl:	Better. But I'm really tired. I think it's time for bed.
God:	Wait! You're not finished yet.
Girl:	"And lead us not into temptation, but deliver us from evil."
God:	Easily done. Just don't put yourself in a place where you can be tempted.
Girl:	I don't get it.
God:	Don't knowingly find yourself standing in front of Becky's car in the middle of the night with twelve dozen eggs and a roll of toilet paper. Nothing good can come from that. Oh! And forget about using me as an escape hatch.
Girl:	Okay, I get the first part, but what is this about an "escape hatch"?
God:	You know exactly what I mean. You get yourself in a bad situation, then it's (mockingly) "Lord help me and I promise I'll never do it again!" Ring any bells?
Girls:	I've never done that!
God:	Ahem.
Girl:	Today. Oh, I'm ashamed, Lord! Really! Until now I always thought that if I just prayed the Lord's Prayer every day then I could do whatever I want. I never thought about its meaning.
God:	Go ahead and finish your prayer.
Girl:	"For Thine is the kingdom, and the power, and the glory forever." Amen.
God:	Amen.

DISCOVERY

Ask: How many of you find it difficult to talk to God sometimes? How many of you pray just like the girl in this sketch, never dreaming God might actually be listening, let alone respond?

We live in a fast-paced world that does not encourage us to slow down! We also live in a world that encourages us to "accomplish" and move on! Learn this, memorize that, conquer the latest video game only to push us to finish it and find the next best thing. Sometimes, the next best thing is what we already have and we just have to slow down long enough to realize it!

Have everyone open their Bibles to Matthew 6:9–13 and Luke 11:2–4. Choose two readers in your group to read each passage nice and loud as the others follow along.

Teacher's Note: Your students might be reading for the first time (and you may too!) that there are two versions of this prayer. This is a great time to talk about the different translations used as well (debts, sins, transgressions). In case your group is wondering where the missing words "For Thine is the power and the glory forever" have gone. The version containing this ending is actually from a non-canonical Christian writing called the Didache. It was written in Syria in the early second century.

LIFE APPLICATION: Ask: Did you know there were two accounts of the Lord's Prayer in the Bible? (Some of them may have heard the Lord's Prayer before and not even known it was in the Bible!)

Why do you think it might be good to have a model to follow for a prayer?

Say: Many of us do stumble over what to say when praying. The disciples were no different. Jesus in His infinite wisdom taught them (and us) a way to think about really being able to pray.

Teacher's Note: Many of us turn to this prayer as a model. It is important to not be too caught up in the order of the words and thoughts. If adhered to legalistically we can easily slide into the very thing Jesus was trying to prevent in this model. Consider the prayer in the wider context of Matthew 6:5–13 and 6:1–18. Jesus was contrasting empty words with gut-level honesty. He is calling us to get real and lose any language that reeks of shallowness, exhibitionism, or hypocrisy.

MAKING IT PERSONAL: Print up the Matthew version of the Lord's Prayer, leaving space between each phrase. Invite your students to write in their own version or response to each section. Have them find a comfortable place in your room. You may want to put on a more mellow praise and worship CD to encourage them to take this time seriously. Remind them that the whole point of the prayer was to teach people to not say empty words but to get real in their prayers.

For example:

Our Father in heaven, Hallowed be Your name,
Your kingdom come. Your will be done on earth as it is in heaven.

Continue for the entire prayer.

Close your time saying the Lord's Prayer together.

CONNECTIONS: Luke offers even more insight on prayer. In Luke 11:2–13 is a teaching on prayer looking at why to pray and what to pray.

SONGS: "Pray" by Darlene Zschech, on the album *Kiss of Heaven*
"Let My Words Be Few" by Matt Redman, on the album *Pour Over Me: Worship Together Live 2001*

QUOTABLE   QUOTES :

When I neglect to pray, mine is the loss. Forgive me, Lord. Amen.

—Peter Marshall

Learning to Talk to God —Midweek

MEMORY VERSE:
Do not be rash with your mouth, and let not your heart utter anything hastily before God. For God is in heaven, and you on earth; therefore let your words be few. —Ecclesiastes 5:2 (NKJV)

SCRIPTURE: Ecclesiastes 5:2; Matthew 6:7

LESSON IN A SENTENCE: God wants for us to have meaningful conversations with Him.

FOCUS

Gibberish! No, that's not what you are thinking; it's the game you are going to play. Similar to charades, only it requires at least two people to "act" a scene. The trick is, instead of having a regular dialogue; the entire thing must be done in gibberish. The rest of the group should be able to guess the scene being played from the acting and be able to translate every line spoken in gibberish. It may seem impossible, but with a little creativity, you can pull it off.

DISCOVERY

Ask: How many of you have ever had a sibling or a friend when you were younger play the copycat game? You know, where whatever you say, the same thing is coming out of their mouth just a few seconds later. (If you can handle it without wanting to scream, play for just a few minutes.) Call an end to the game just before someone gets hurt!

Ask: How annoying is that?

How annoying was it to play Gibberish?

Have you ever thought about God having ways He prefers (and quite frankly, ways He prefers not) for us to talk to Him?

Read Ecclesiastes 5:2–3; Matthew 6:7

Re-write these verses in your own words.

APPLICATION: We can all pretty much agree that rambling, copycat, gibberish talk is at best annoying, if not a total waste of time for everyone involved!

Say: Both Ecclesiastes and Matthew instruct us to let our words be few. Ask: Why then do you think some prayers go on forever?

Repeating things over and over in a prayer does not help God really hear it! He hears the first time. Often our prayers are less conversations and more a verbal outpouring, and as soon as we are through talking, the prayer is done. Have your students think of one thing for which they would like to pray right now. (Just one! The temptation is to be so busy with what we have to say in prayer that we never listen.) Once they have that one thing, tell them you are going to give five minutes of silence. Most of us do not pray about one thing for five minutes. You may be through "talking" after the first minute or so. The prayer, however, is not over. Give space for God to speak, to respond to the one thing about which they are praying.

Teacher's Note: Of course intercession is an important part of the Christian walk. Interestingly, in the last few years to ask for something, to petition, has been labeled as selfish. When looking at the model Jesus offers (the Lord's Prayer) the entire prayer is a petition. It maintains the order of God first, human needs second. Even in this, it asks for God's name to be honored, for His kingdom to come, and for God's will to be done on earth as it is in heaven.

JUNE 12, 2005

Dealing with Adversity

By Alicia Claxton

MEMORY VERSE:
Consider it pure joy, my brothers, whenever you face trials of many kinds, because you know that the testing of your faith develops perseverance. —James 1:2–3 (NIV)

MEMORY VERSE ACTIVITY: Write the memory verse on a large sheet of butcher paper or posterboard and hang it up at the front of the room. Tell students they have 3 minutes to look over and memorize the verse. Once time is up, have students stand in a circle facing one another. Use a beanbag or ball as the "hot potato" and tell students that when the ball is passed to them they must say the next word of the verse immediately or they will be out. Start the activity by saying the first word of the verse, then throwing the ball to someone else in the circle. That person must immediately say the next word or step out of the circle. After each mistake, the verse is started over. Continue to pass the ball until the memory verse is successfully said from beginning to end with no mistakes. Have a prize for those still in the circle when the verse is completed.

SCRIPTURE: Romans 5:1–5

LESSON IN A SENTENCE: In this life we will face adversity, but God is able to sustain us and make us stronger through the challenges.

THE BIG PICTURE:
Failed tests, broken relationships, poor health, shattered dreams—life is full of adversity. We will all face trouble in our time here on earth and we need to be reminded that God is at work even in the midst of our trials. He doesn't desire that we be afflicted, but He will use all circumstances in our lives to deepen our faith in Him.

IN THIS LESSON STUDENTS SHOULD:

- Accept that adversity will come and begin to see how it can help them grow.
- Recognize God's hand at work in the midst of adversity.
- Be willing to learn and apply God's Word more with each new challenge.

```
STUFF YOU NEED:

    ○ Butcher paper or posterboard (see Memory Verse
      Activity)
    ○ Blindfold (see Focus – Option 1)
    ○ Rope or string (see Focus – Option 2)
```

FOCUS

Depending on group size, choose option 1 or option 2. Be sure to watch your time and not get too carried away with this part of the lesson.

OPTION 1: SMALL TO MEDIUM-SIZED GROUP

The Lighthouse. For this activity, you will need to go outside or in an open room. Ask one student to be the "lighthouse," one to be the "ship," and the others to be "obstacles." The object is to get the ship, which is blindfolded, from the starting point to the lighthouse by having the lighthouse call out commands that will lead them to safety. Meanwhile, the obstacles such as rocks, storms, enemy ships try to keep that from happening. For example, the *rocks* are stationary and make no noise, but if touched the ship goes down and is out of the game; the *storms* can move around and make noise, but they cannot touch the ship; *enemy ships* can move and try to get the ship to run into them, but they cannot deliberately touch it. Make sure you or one of your students acts as a shield for the blindfolded ship so they don't get injured. Allow group to do this activity several times, switching positions each time.

OPTION 2: LARGE GROUP

Crossing the River. This activity requires your group to think and work as a team. You will need to mark boundaries using string, rope, masking tape, or something that clearly shows the banks of the river (the river should be about 5–6 feet across). Tell your group to gather on one side of the river. If you have a large group of students, you can divide them into teams and have them compete against each other. The object of the game is to get everyone across the river within the time limit (3–4 minutes) but each time you play there is a different twist such as:

Get your whole team across the river but *only the first person can touch the water.* (Solutions include having the first person carry each member over; having the first person lay down and members walk across on their back—be careful with this one.)

Get your whole team across the river but *only the feet of the tallest person can touch the water* (Solutions include having members one by one stand on the feet of the tallest person and walk across together; having each member crawl or walk across on their hands without letting their feet touch the ground.)

Get your whole team across the river in alphabetical order by last name. *Only one person can be touching the water at a time, and no one can cross the river more than twice.* (This one just sounds complicated, but based on the wording each member can walk across the river one at a time in order by last name.)

Transition to the lesson: Both of these games illustrate the reality of trials or obstacles that threaten to keep us from a victorious life in Christ. Lead into the Bible study by saying something like, "In life, we are going to face trials that may confuse and challenge us. Adversity can discourage us and keep us from seeing the truth that God is at work in the midst of our struggles. The Lord promises to sustain us and He desires to teach and strengthen us through each trial."

DISCOVERY

Ask students to define adversity in their own words. The official Webster's definition is: misfortune, trouble, affliction. According to that definition, they should all agree that adversity is a reality for everyone—no one is exempt, we will all face troubles at some point in our lives. So if we know it's coming, how should we respond as believers? Our goal as believers should not be to avoid adversity but to allow God to grow us up through each trial.

Have a student read Romans 5:1–5, then ask the following questions:

Who is the author of this letter to the Romans?

According to verse 1, with whom do we have peace through our Lord Jesus Christ? What does it mean to have peace with God?

What does Paul tell us to rejoice in according to verses 2 and 3? Why would he tell us to rejoice in two extremes: *"hope* of the glory of God" and *"sufferings"*?

What does suffering ultimately produce in our lives when we let God work through it (verses 3–4)?

Did Paul experience adversity or "sufferings" in his life? What examples can you think of? Based on what we know about Paul, did those sufferings produce perseverance, character, and hope in his life?

Paul begins this chapter by celebrating our reconciliation with God through the Lord Jesus Christ. For us as believers, all of life points back to our relationship with God—our hope for eternity, our earthly sufferings, and everything in between. In our greatest moments we eagerly strive to glorify God and testify to His goodness, but we must learn that even our sufferings can be opportunities to glorify Him. By the power of the Holy Spirit at work within us, our lives are strengthened in suffering, "because we know that suffering produces perseverance; perseverance, character; and character, hope!"

LIFE APPLICATION: Ask students to define perseverance. What is the value of perseverance in this life? If further explanation is needed, use the example of athletes in training—they endure pain and discipline their bodies in order to build perseverance. Perseverance gives them the ability to stay in the game despite physical challenges. Spiritually, perseverance gives us the ability to stay in the race despite adversity.

Ask students to define character. What is the value of character in this life? If further explanation is needed, continue with the example of an athlete—the goal of training and exercising perseverance is to build physical strength. Strength gives them the ability to not only endure but to overcome physical challenges. Spiritually, character is our strength of heart and mind and is formed by the work of the Holy Spirit within us. He gives us the strength to not only endure but to overcome adversity.

Ask students to define hope. Why is hope necessary in our earthly lives? If further explanation is needed, continue with the example of an athlete—the motivation and inspiration for an athlete in training is the hope that they will win or at least finish the race. Hope is essential for our spiritual health and success as well. We place our hope in Christ for this life and for the life to come.

PERSONAL APPLICATION: Roll out two large sheets of butcher paper on the floor and place markers around them. Label one "The Wall of Pain" and the other "The Wall of Praise." Challenge students to think about the trials they are facing right now (relationship problems, school challenges, family issues, unknown future) as well as challenges they have faced in the past. Invite them to come and write down the trials they are facing now on "The Wall of Pain," then write examples of some adversity that God has helped them overcome on "The Wall of Praise." Encourage them to spend a few minutes in prayer thanking God for His work in their lives and asking Him for wisdom as they continue to deal with adversity.

If there is time left over, challenge students to look over "The Wall of Pain" and "The Wall of Praise" and spend some time praying for each other and praising God for what He has done in the lives of those around them.

After a few minutes, close this session in prayer.

CONNECTIONS: If you have extra time at the end of this session or have students who want to study more about dealing with adversity, encourage them to study the life of the apostle Paul and see the challenges he faced. The Book of Acts is a good source for information on the events of Paul's life.

Dealing with Adversity —Midweek

MEMORY VERSE:
Consider it pure joy, my brothers, whenever you face trials of many kinds, because you know that the testing of your faith develops perseverance.—James 1:2–3 (NIV)

SCRIPTURE: Matthew 7:24–27

LESSON IN A SENTENCE: In this life we will face adversity, but God is able to sustain us and make us stronger through the challenges.

FOCUS

Before class, gather up some "building materials" such as building blocks, toothpicks and marshmallows, bubble gum and graham crackers, deck of cards. Place a small set of building blocks or Lego's in one bag, a stack of toothpicks and some marshmallows in another bag, a pack of bubble gum and some graham crackers in another bag, and a deck of playing cards in another bag. Close up the bags so students cannot see what's inside. Divide students into 4 teams and give each team a bag of building supplies. Instruct them to build the sturdiest structure possible with the materials they have. Give them 4–5 minutes to strategize and complete their structure. Then let each group present their work. Ask for a representative from each team to come up front. Tell them they get one shot at blowing down the other teams' structures. See if any structure is still standing after the "windstorm."

Transition to the lesson by saying something like, "In life, storms will come and threaten to blow us apart. But we have a promise in Christ that we can overcome even the toughest trials. In this session we will look at how to build our lives so that we can stand in the face of adversity."

DISCOVERY

Ask for a volunteer to tell their best version of "The Three Little Pigs." What are some basic principals we learn from that story?

Long before there were three little pigs, Christ introduced us to the principle of stability. You can't build your house upon the sand and expect it to endure a mighty storm. However, the house built upon the rock cannot be destroyed.

Ask a student to read Matthew 7:24–27.

What is Jesus referring to when He talks about the "sand"? *(things of this world)*

What is the "rock" upon which we are to build our lives? *(God's Word)*

What do the wind and rain represent in these verses? *(adversity; trials)*

What does Jesus say we must "do" to be like the wise man that built his house upon the rock? *(We must hear and put into practice the words and principles of God.)*

LIFE APPLICATION: Ask students to list some things that people build their lives on that are like "sand."

Ask students to share some promises from God's Word that they have leaned on in times of trouble.

PERSONAL APPLICATION: Encourage students to look back over Matthew 7:24–25 and spend a few minutes thinking about the stability of their own lives and how sturdy they will be when adversity comes. Invite them to spend some time praying and asking God to make them stronger and better prepared for each new challenge. After a few minutes, close this session in prayer.

As a reminder of this lesson, consider giving students a small rock to put in their pocket or purse.

MY DAUGHTER

By Rick Steele
PROFESSOR/ PARENT

Dear Youth Pastor:

My 19-year old daughter, Sarah, is a college freshman this year. She loves it, because for the first time in her life, her peers treat her like a friend and equal, not like an oddity or an outcast. Sarah is confined to a wheelchair, or rather, Sarah is liberated by her wheelchair from confinement to bed. Her body is almost completely immobilized by a rare muscular-skeletal disorder. She takes numerous medications each day. Some are hormones, which she needs because her pituitary gland had to be removed during brain surgery when she was 8. Others help to prevent urinary tract infections, to which she is prone, and from which she once nearly died. She also suffers from sleep apnea and pulmonary deficiencies, so she now sleeps with a contraption that helps her breath more efficiently. Keeping Sarah alive and functioning has been a full-time job ever since she was born, and it's a joy to her mother and me to see her doing so well in college—living (with assistance) in a dorm, studying hard, making friends, planning a career, and being as "normal" as possible.

I am writing to you because you are working with one or more young people with "special needs," and want some pointers on how to help them and their families. Let me begin by thanking you for being willing to do youth ministry at all, which is always challenging, and especially for committing yourself to including kids in your program with physical or emotional disabilities or chronic medical conditions. You are already my hero! But there are some things you need to know in order to translate your heroism into successful ministry. I will put them in terms of some of my family's favorite sayings—things we have learned from living long under difficult conditions.

(1) People are clueless. They don't know the details about the child's medical condition. Why should they? And they can't imagine the work that goes into care-giving. How could they? Your first task is to get educated. Ask the family for printed literature or a reliable website that explains their child's medical condition, and learn as much about it as you can. But don't stop with general knowledge. Each case is different, so ask the family questions about *their* experience. Be tact-

ful, but don't be shy. They will probably be eager to talk to someone who is sincerely interested, especially if you are going to have some responsibility for their child's welfare. And then invite them on some fun family outing of their choice—a movie, a concert, a museum, an amusement park. Tell them you want to get a glimpse of their world from the inside. Learn their routines and get a feel for the hassles they face all the time: transportation, parking, mealtimes, toileting, and so forth.

(2) A disability *inhabits* an individual, but it *belongs* to the whole family. When a child has special needs, everybody in the home is affected. It determines what they can and cannot do, where they can and cannot go, their schedules, and their energy levels. It shortens their tempers, drains their finances, and often makes them feel like strangers, even among their extended family, their closest personal friends, their workplace colleagues, and their fellow churchgoers. So to minister effectively to the child, you must learn how his or her special needs shape the family dynamics—both for good (and there is much good!) and for ill. And you must plan on ministering to the other members of the family, who may be feeling rage, resentment, fear, grief, disappointment, exhaustion, over-protectiveness, and so forth.

(3) After a crisis, life gradually returns to normal—but it's usually a *new* normal. People like to feel "normal." Almost by definition, a family with a special needs child already feels *abnormal* with respect to the world around them, but even they settle into routines that give life a comforting sense of order. When crises occur, however, even their abnormal normality is disrupted for a time, and its consequences may require them to develop a new, and even more abnormal, state of normality. Your job is to walk with them through the bewilderment and eeriness of each crisis and each new adaptation, to let them know by your presence that they are not alone, and to help them find their way into whatever "new normal" life holds in store. Be there, and get the kids in the youth group to be there, too, preferably with casseroles.

(4) The angel is in the details. You know the old cliché: Grand plans are great, but the devil is in the details. This is especially true for families of special needs kids. People may tell them they are "welcome," but they don't do the 1001 little things that constitute hospitality: situating the wheelchair so the kid can see and hear, planning meals that account for dietary restrictions, determining the availability of an accessible restroom, choosing appropriate games and activities, and, in short, anticipating obstacles and impediments, and finding ways over,

around, or through them. As the minister, that's your job, and you will be an angel to the child and her family if you do it.

(5) We don't want your pity. We do want your compassion. Pity is often debilitating to those who receive it, because it accentuates their difference from everybody else. In contrast, compassion is empowering, because it emphasizes the human connections linking the sufferers and those they love. And compassion is exercised not only in kindness and sensitivity and faithfulness to those who suffer, but in bold advocacy of their needs and rights to the clueless. Part of your ministry to special needs kids will be in ways that they may never see: in nagging the church board to lay out the money for making the building accessible (especially the restrooms and the communion table!) and to plan worship services, educational curricula, and special programs that make it possible for those who live "abnormal" lives to belong. Don't expect to be popular with the church, and don't expect much thanks from the family. Your reward will be from Someone Else.

God bless you in your ministry,

Sincerely,

Richard B. Steele
Redmond, Washington

JUNE 19, 2005

The Wise Counsel of Men (Father's Day)

By Amy Jacober

MEMORY VERSE:
And if it seems evil to you to serve the LORD, choose for yourselves this day whom you will serve, whether the gods which your fathers served that were on the other side of the River, or the gods of the Amorites, in whose land you dwell. But as for me and my house, we will serve the LORD. —Joshua 24:15 (NKJV)

SCRIPTURE: Joshua 24:1–15 (Joshua 24:16–28)

LESSON IN A SENTENCE: God intends that His followers pass down the faith to their children, and their children's children.

THE BIG PICTURE (OR WHAT YOU'RE TRYING TO GET ACROSS):
We talked about mothers just a few short weeks ago. Fathers have an equally difficult role! God is clear that faith and teaching are not intended to happen apart from the family. All through Scripture are the stories of the blessings where faith in God has been the standard in the family and, sadly, of consequences where faith in God has been cast aside for the ways of the world. While it is highly likely you will have students who are in families where one or more parent is not a believer, in God's ideal, it is the entire household that serves the Lord! Some of your students may have absent fathers or fathers who don't treat them well. Keep your group in mind as we celebrate a God-ordained role in our lives within the reality of a broken and fragmented world. Fathers come in all shapes and sizes, strengths and weaknesses. While some certainly make better choices than others, God calls all men (and women) to choose for themselves who they will serve. For better or worse, how they choose impacts those around them.

IN THIS LESSON STUDENTS SHOULD:

- Know that we have a rich heritage of faith in our forefathers.
- Learn the context in which Joshua declares the loyalty of his household.
- Understand that your personal faith has an impact on the people around you.

STUFF YOU NEED:

If choosing option 1:
  ○ Invited guests
If choosing option 2:
  ○ Butcher paper
  ○ Markers
  ○ Lined paper
  ○ Pens/pencils
  ○ Envelopes
  ○ Postcards

FOCUS

OPTION 1:

Invite one or two men from your congregation to share their stories about fatherhood. In particular, request that they share their top three joys and top three struggles in fatherhood. Our teenagers don't come with instructions for their fathers any more than they did for their mothers! Even more so, our society and culture offers certain stereotypes that often do not match God's ideal. Many men pray for their children daily. Consider inviting men who are not involved in your youth ministry. You may also want to invite fathers at different stages of this role in their life, one with an infant or toddler, one with school age, one with an adult child. This is a great way to connect with the congregation and allow your students to know another adult apart from the youth ministry team. At the end, offer a question/answer time for students to ask any questions they may have. (Tip—for men not accustomed to speaking, you may want to conduct an interview or offer pre-planned questions.)

OPTION 2:

Break into groups of 4–6. Give each group a piece of butcher paper and a few markers. Ask your students to think about the rules in their house—the big ones and the small, the ones that make sense and the ones that don't! Encourage them to include everything like no phone calls after 10 P.M., squeeze the toothpaste from the bottom, and don't put empty cartons back in the fridge. Once the list is complete, read back over these. Are there any that are unique to a household? Ask each group to eliminate the ones they never want to have as rules in their house. Are there any rules they would like to implement that are not currently in their house?

How do the rules in a house get established?

DISCOVERY

God's people have been through a lot to get to the point of being in the Promised Land! Joshua has led the Israelites to victory against many enemies. Victory is always sweet. Unfortunately those good feelings never seem to last long enough. In fact, many of us forget them as soon as the next challenge is underway. Joshua is well aware his days are coming to a close. As a wise man he reminds all the people of the promises and fulfillment of promises from God over the years. As a leader, he reaffirms whom he and his house will serve.

Read through Joshua 24:1–15.

This is a longer passage full of lists and names. While it may seem pointless, it offers example after example of the commitment of God.

Give small groups of students one or two verses and ask them to write out the promise and fulfillment of that promise found in the verse.

Joshua 24:1–2; 3–4; 5–6; 7–8; 9–10; 11; 12–13.

Some at this time were turning to the gods of those they had defeated, the gods of the world around them. Joshua not only reminds the people of the one true God, but of all He has promised and fulfilled.

Read Joshua 24:14–15.

Ask each small group to re-write this in their own words.

Say: Now that the history has been established and Joshua has declared the present, let's look to the future.

Read Joshua 24:16–25.

Ask: What happens in these verses?

(The people begin declaring that they will serve God. Joshua will not let them get away with empty declarations! He firmly states that you can serve one and only one, and this needs to be God. Joshua renews the covenant between the Israelites and God as one of his last acts.)

Teacher's Note: This renewal of the covenant is Joshua's way of trying to protect his people as a transition is coming. Just a few verses later (Joshua 24:29) Joshua dies. The leadership is transitioning from Joshua to a whole new system of judges. As a wise man, he was more concerned with passing on faith in the Lord than in maintaining himself as a leader.

LIFE APPLICATION: Promises made and kept, promises broken—life seems to be filled with both.

What promises do you know of that have been made and kept? (You can think of this question on a number of levels—as a society, a youth group, a family, etc.) What promises do you know of that have been made and broken?

Say: Joshua reminded the people of the promises God had made and kept.

Ask: Can you think of any promises God has made and kept for you?

God is a keeper of promises. Many of us, however, struggle in this area. Even for Christians, remaining faithful can be a struggle. What do we end up serving in this world in place of God? Make a list on a whiteboard where everyone can see.

MAKING IT PERSONAL: Joshua declares that a choice must be made! The gods of others must be put away, and he chooses for himself and his house that they will serve the Lord.

Hand out lined paper, envelopes, and pencils to each person. Ask each person to think through what or whom it is they are currently serving. Just like the wise counsel that came from Joshua, we too are asked to consider the faith in Christ that is passed down, to decide this day whom we will serve.

Say: Write a letter to God first confessing what or whom you have been serving and secondly either making or renewing a commitment to which He is calling you. When finished, place the letter in the envelope, seal it, and put your name on the outside.

While you've got them in writing mode, collect the letters in the sealed envelope (don't forget to have them write their name on it!) and trade them for a blank postcard. Save these letters to give back to them at a later date. (If you are like most youth ministers, the best of intentions are taken over by forgetfulness! You may want to set these letters in a place you can find and write on your calendar to hand them back in a month.) Have each person spend a few moments writing a short note to their dad, grandfather, or uncle thanking them for taking care of them and teaching them some of the lessons of life. Be certain they address these. Collect them before they leave and mail them to their fathers this week.

CONNECTIONS: Following God has been a choice long before Jesus came. God has not been silent in this area, but He will not force you to be in a relationship with Him. Consider Exodus 32:26, Deuteronomy 30:19, and 1 Kings 18:21.

SONGS: "Moment Made for Worshipping" by Steven Curtis Chapman, on the album *All About Love*

The Wise Counsel of Men —Midweek

MEMORY VERSE:
And if it seems evil to you to serve the LORD, choose for yourselves this day whom you will serve, whether the gods which your fathers served that were on the other side of the River, or the gods of the Amorites, in whose land you dwell. But as for me and my house, we will serve the LORD. —Joshua 24:15 (NKJV)

SCRIPTURE: Psalm 71:17–18

LESSON IN A SENTENCE: God intends that His followers pass down the faith to their children, and their children's children.

FOCUS

Give each person a 3 x 5 card. If they could think of one life lesson to pass to others, what would it be? (Answers can range from "Don't eat corn-on-the-cob just before riding a rollercoaster" to "Tell the people you love that you love them as often as you can while you can.") Ask them to write this down with their name. Fold the card and place them all in a bag. Once you have all of the cards, read each life lesson out loud and have the group try to match the lesson to the person!

DISCOVERY

God calls us to pass on what we have learned to each new generation.

Read Psalm 71:17–18.

Ask: According to this scripture, what are we to do?

Prepare your group that you have invited a special guest to share with them. If you have a particularly rowdy group, you may want to review a few guidelines of being polite for older guests. Invite a senior (as in senior citizen) or two to your group. Ideally, invite a male and female. Ask them to share what life was like for them as teenagers, what God has taught them over the years, and what they have seen change the most both in the world and in church. Ask what they think was better when they were younger and what they think is better now. Don't rush through this time.

APPLICATION: Think back over the cards of the life lessons. Are these really the things you would like to pass on to others? Ask: To what kind of things do you think David was referring when he said he would declare the strength and power of God to this generation.

While this verse is talking about being old with gray hair, you have some great things to pass down right now.

Ask: What could you do right now to pass down what God has already taught you?

Make a list on the whiteboard. Choose one that you can do as a group and place this on your calendar for the next few months.

Ask each person to consider one thing they could do themselves apart from the group. (This may be to tutor younger kids, to help with VBS, to work in the nursery, to teach guitar to anyone who may want to learn, etc.) We all have things to pass on. God is calling us to do so!

QUOTABLE   QUOTES:

Life was a lot simpler when what we honored was father and mother rather than all major credit cards.

—Robert Orben

JUNE 26, 2005

Stewardship

By Amy Jacober

MEMORY VERSE:
But who am I, and who are my people, that we should be able to give as generously as this? Everything comes from you, and we have given you only what comes from your hand. —1 Chronicles 29:14 (NIV)

SCRIPTURE: 2 Corinthians 9:6–15; 1 Peter 4:10-11; Ephesians 5:15–16; Psalm 24:1

LESSON IN A SENTENCE: Everything belongs to God and we honor Him by using wisely the gifts and resources He has entrusted to us.

THE BIG PICTURE:

Everything good comes from God—our talents, our resources, even our time here on earth. We are not owners, but stewards of these blessings and we will be held accountable for how well we manage what has been entrusted to our care. We honor God by investing ourselves as well as our resources into His eternal work.

IN THIS LESSON STUDENTS SHOULD:

○ Be able to define the difference between ownership and stewardship.
○ Recognize the gifts and resources God has entrusted to each of them.
○ Be willing to offer their time, talents, and resources in service to God.

STUFF YOU NEED:

○ 3 good prizes, 3 average prizes, 3 silly prizes, 6 paper sacks (see Focus - Option 1)
○ Play money (see Focus - Option 2)
○ Index cards

FOCUS

Depending on group size, choose option 1 or option 2. Be sure to watch your time and not get too carried away with this part of the lesson.

OPTION 1: SMALL GROUP

Before class, gather up 3 good prizes (CDs, gift certificates, books, etc), 3 silly prizes (pack of gum, pencil, stickers, etc) and 3 average prizes (bottle of Coke, candy bar, etc). Put each prize in a brown paper sack so that they all look alike. Leave out the 3 average prizes, which will be used to get things started. At the beginning of class, ask for 3 volunteers to come up and be a part of the introduction. Show everyone the 3 big prizes, then put them back into their bags and shuffle all the bags around. Hand the first volunteer his/her average prize, such as a bottle of Coke or candy bar. Ask if they are happy with the prize they have in their hands or if they would like to trade it in for a chance at a better prize. If they decide to trade it in, have them close their eyes while you shuffle the bags one more time. Ask them to hand over the average prize and pick out the prize they will take home. Once they choose a bag, have them show the group what they've won. Continue this way until each of the volunteers has played.

Transition to the lesson by saying something like, "In this game, the participants were given a gift and they could choose whether they wanted to hold on to it or invest it for a chance at something greater. In our lesson we are going to talk about the gifts God has given each of us (time, talents, and resources) and see how He would have us invest them."

OPTION 2: LARGE GROUP

Make up your own version of the NBC reality show, "The Apprentice." Divide students into teams of 6–8 per group. Give each team $1,000 of play money to be used for their business venture. Give everyone the same assignment: elect a team manager or CEO, come up with a name for their organization, decide on what kind of business they will be, and how they will use their $1,000. Give them about 10-15 minutes to work together, then have each team manager present their organization and tell how they spent their money. Give out prizes for creativity.

Transition to the lesson by saying something like, "In this activity, you were given a sum of money and challenged to invest and manage it wisely. In our lesson we are going to talk about the gifts God has given each of us (time, talents, and resources) and see how He would have us invest and manage them."

DISCOVERY

Ask students to define the difference between ownership and stewardship. If they can, ask them to give an example of each.

"In this life, we are stewards (not owners) of what we have. It all belongs to God." Ask a student to read Psalm 24:1. "He has entrusted us with blessings and opportunities for the purpose of glorifying Him. There are three important things that we have each been given and will be held accountable for how we manage: our time, our gifts/talents, and our resources."

Have a student read Ephesians 5:15–16. Ask the following questions:

How does verse 15 encourage us to live? What are we to "make the most of" in verse 16?

What does it mean to make the most of every opportunity? Why is it so important that we not waste time?

Do you think we will be held accountable for the way we spend our time? Why or why not?

Have a student read 1 Peter 4:10-11. Ask the following questions:

What "gift" is Peter referring to in verse 10? How should our gifts be used?

What is the result when we use our gifts as God intended?

Who supplies the strength, power, and opportunity to use our spiritual gifts?

Do you think God also gave us talents and natural abilities to be used for His glory?

Do you think we will be held accountable for the way we use our gifts and talents? Why or why not?

Have a student read 2 Corinthians 9:6–15. Ask the following questions:

What does it mean to sow and reap? What is Paul referring to when he speaks of sowing and reaping generously?

What kind of giver does God love, according to verse 7?

According to verse 10, what does God promise to provide for those who honor Him with their resources? What does God desire that we do with our resources, according to verse 11?

How do we honor God with our financial resources? What is the difference between giving a tithe and giving an offering?

Do you think we will be held accountable for the way we invest our resources? Why or why not?

"God provides us with time, gifts/talents, and resources, and He gives us opportunities to use them for His glory. We make decisions every day about how we will invest what has been entrusted to us. "

LIFE APPLICATION: Have students list some ways they can use their talents for God's glory. Ask them to think about and discuss the following question: Can our talents be used outside the church and still bring God glory (such as athletics, creative arts, singing "secular" music, etc)…*Teacher's Note: This can be a good discussion because many young people question their God-given talents and how they can and can't use those abilities. Be ready to help them process this important issue from a biblical perspective.*

PERSONAL APPLICATION: Give each student an index card and pen. Challenge them to think about how they use their time. Are they investing quality time into their relationship with God? Next challenge them to make a list of the gifts and talents that God has blessed them with. Ask them to think about how they use those gifts and talents. Are they investing them wisely? Finally, challenge them to think about their financial resources. What resources do they have, and are they investing resources into eternal things?

CONNECTIONS: If you have extra time at the end of this session or have students who want to study more about this topic, instruct them to read The Parable of the Talents in Matthew 25:14–30.

SONGS: "Life Means So Much" by Chris Rice

Stewardship —Midweek

MEMORY VERSE:
But who am I, and who are my people, that we should be able to give as generously as this? Everything comes from you, and we have given you only what comes from your hand. —1 Chronicles 29:14 (NIV)

SCRIPTURE: 2 Kings 4:42–44; Matthew 14:15–21

LESSON IN A SENTENCE: Everything belongs to God and we honor Him by using wisely the gifts and resources He has entrusted to us.

FOCUS

Use this activity to help prepare your students for the Bible study. Keep an eye on the time as you lead this activity.

Play the "Stock Market Game." Before class, make an oversized spinning wheel (simple materials such as cardboard can be used) and divide the wheel into 6–8 slots. In each slot put a different scenario such as "The economy boomed and your stock increased by $0.10 per share" or "Bad day at the office: the CEO resigned and your stock fell by $0.05 per share." Make as many good or bad scenarios as you like on this board. Also, gather up a couple of dollars worth of pennies.

Divide group into teams of 5–10 students. Each team should gather up as many pennies as they can find between them. Then they must decide what major company they would like to invest their money in. Write the name of each company on a large sheet of butcher paper and the amount of stock each team has bought (each penny they have buys them 1 share of stock). Have teams take turns spinning the wheel and adding or subtracting stock according to the outcome of each spin. After a few turns, have each team calculate their gains or losses. Give teams who gained money the pennies they earned and have teams that lost money turn in the pennies they owe.

Transition to the lesson by saying something like, "In this game, the success of your stock depended more on the luck of the wheel than on the value of your original investment. Even with limited resources, some of you were able to multiply what you started with. In our lesson we're going to look at how God can take our life investments (our time, our talents, and our resources) and multiply them to accomplish amazing things for His glory!"

DISCOVERY

Ask students to define a miracle. Then ask if they have ever seen a miracle happen or known someone who has experienced a miracle. Have them share stories. Tell them that this lesson will revolve around two miracles where God multiplied that which was offered in faith.

Have a student read 2 Kings 4:42–44. Ask the following questions:

Who was the man of God in this story? What did he ask the servant to do in verse 42?

Why was the servant reluctant to do what he'd been asked?

What made Elisha so sure that the food would be enough for everyone?

What was the result of Elisha's faith?

Have a student read Matthew 14:15–21. Ask the following questions:

What were the disciples concerned about in verse 15? How did they suggest this problem be solved?

What was Jesus' response to their suggestion?

How much food did they have? How many people did they need to feed (according to verse 21)?

How did Jesus handle this situation? Was He able to provide for the needs of everyone there? Was there any food left?

"We may sometimes feel that what we have to offer is insignificant in light of the needs around us. But we must remember that what we have is more than enough in the hands of our Savior. By His power, whatever we offer is multiplied to accomplish mighty things. As a good steward and a faithful servant, our desire should be to offer all we have for His glory and trust Him with the result of those investments."

LIFE APPLICATION: Ask students to list some things they would consider to be "wise investments" of their time, talents, and resources.

PERSONAL APPLICATION: Give students a sheet of paper with the following questions on it. Challenge them to spend some time in honest reflection as they answer each question.

Do you feel like what you have to offer is too insignificant for God to use?

Do you believe that God is the One who made you and gave you the gifts, talents and resources that you have?

Do you believe that God is able and willing to take what you offer and multiply it for His glory?

Can you think of some ways God has used you in the past (your talent, your words of encouragement, your willingness to serve).

Encourage them to spend a few minutes in prayer, thanking God for entrusting them with the means and opportunity to honor Him with their lives. Challenge them to ask the Lord for wisdom to know how to best use the time, talents, and resources they've been given.

After a few minutes, close this time in prayer.

More than a Show

By Amy Jacober

MEMORY VERSE:
So rend your heart, and not your garments; return to the LORD your God, for He is gracious and merciful, slow to anger, and of great kindness; and He relents from doing harm. —Joel 2:13

SCRIPTURE: 2 Chronicles 7:11–14

LESSON IN A SENTENCE: God values sincerity over an exhibition.

THE BIG PICTURE (OR WHAT YOU'RE TRYING TO GET ACROSS):

We all know students (and a few adults!) who look the part of the perfect Christian. They have a scripture to prooftext anything you may say, they are always aware of the sins of others, and point out how they are in sharp contrast. They are often also the ones who volunteer for your ministry all of the time, and they want everyone around to know they are the one helping you! These same superChristians are also the ones to protest the loudest when things seem out of sorts. They offer a grand show to let everyone know how offended, how hurt, and how deeply they are impacted by the wrongs of the world. To put it in today's terms: drama, drama, drama! In stark contrast, God calls us to humility in all we do, including when we are broken, angry, or hurting over an injustice in the world. We are not to do things to draw attention to ourselves. Rather we are to rend our hearts and humbly seek God's face in all we do.

IN THIS LESSON STUDENTS SHOULD:

- ○ Be able to tell the difference between an exhibition and sincerity.
- ○ Know that God is calling them to turn from their wicked ways for real.
- ○ Talk about what makes it such a struggle to repent sincerely and name some ways to overcome this.

STUFF YOU NEED:

If choosing option 1, anything you choose to help hype the
performance
If choosing option 2, 2 chairs and 1 blanket
○ 8 pieces of butcher paper
○ Markers

FOCUS

OPTION 1:

Enlist one of your leaders to come and perform: sing, dance, juggle,
whatever! Make a REALLY big deal out of it. Tell your students how
great this person is; it's a talent up to this time which has been hidden
from them. Depending on how elaborate you want to be, make flyers
the week before or have this person in costume to add to the effect.
Once you have really built this up, your students are seated and ready,
introduce your leader with fanfare! Be certain that, whatever they
choose to perform, they are bad! As adults, try not to laugh, and watch
your students try to figure out what is happening!

Debrief: Once the trick is up, ask your students what just happened.
Often, the hype is more that the reality. The show and build up is greater
than the actual performance. Ask: What other times in life can they think
of where the exhibition, the show, is greater than the reality?

OPTION 2:

Bad pick-up lines continue to be a source of amusement! For this
activity you will need 2 chairs and a blanket large enough to cover the
two chairs. You will play the role of the host for this activity. Ask for
two female volunteers and at least 2 male volunteers (be certain to
choose males who are not too shy or who are easily embarrassed).
When they arrive up front, send the guys away with another leader for
a few moments. Once the guys are gone, explain to the group that the
guys are going to offer their best pick-up lines to the ladies. If one or
the other girl accepts his pick-up line, he will be able to sit on the
"bench." The leader with the guys is explaining that they will be offering their best pick-up lines in order hopefully to be invited to sit on the
bench. Pick-up lines are things like "Are you tired? (pause) Cause
you've been running through my mind all day!" Even if you don't
know any, your students will! Set the two chairs next to each other
with space in between. Put the blanket over the chairs and have each
girl sit on the chairs and pull the blanket tight so that it looks like a

bench. (Remember, the chairs are pulled far enough apart, leaving space for the bench effect.) Send the first guy back in. Have him offer his pick-up line to see if he has earned a place on the bench between the ladies. When one of them says yes, and he goes to sit, the girls stand! The guy will try to sit on the "bench" where there is no seat. Get ready for feet to fly in the air and laughter to follow! Timing is everything, so be certain you tell the girls not to stand too soon! Repeat this process for as many male volunteers as you have.

Debrief: We all hear cheesy comments trying to get us to do things every day. We all know of times when someone was showing off just for the sake of showing off. Ask: Other than this being a set-up, would these pick-up lines have worked in real life? Why or why not? Life tells us we have to have a hook, clever packaging, or presentation over what is actually being offered. God has a counter-cultural way of looking at this issue.

DISCOVERY

Break your students into groups of 4. Have each group read through 2 Chronicles 7:11–14. Have each group create two lists: what God does, and what Solomon and the people are to do. Ask: What if any of these things are we to do today?

Verse 14 is by far the best-known verse in this section. Have your group go phrase by phrase, trying to sort out what this means. Depending on your group, either do this activity as a whole, or assign each group one phrase and allow them to wrestle with this. On butcher paper, write each phrase at the top and allow space below for bullet point responses to be written. Pass out these papers and markers. As you work through each phrase in order, tape these papers to the wall.

"If My people . . ." Ask: Who are God's people? Does this mean the Israelites? Those who follow Him? All people created by God?

". . . who are called by My name . . ." What does it mean to be called by "My name"? Who does the calling?

". . . will humble themselves . . ." What does it mean to be humble? How do people humble themselves?

". . . and pray and seek My face . . ." What is the difference between praying and seeking God's face? Is it possible to pray not seeking God's face?

". . . and turn from their wicked ways . . ." What are the wicked ways of the world from which you think we need to turn? How probable do you think this is?

"... then I will hear from heaven ..." Do you really think God hears our prayers? Why or why not?

"...and forgive their sin ..." What does God mean that He will forgive their sin? Are consequences eliminated for forgiven sins?

"... and heal their land." Is it possible for God to heal the land? What would it take to have this happen?

ANCIENT PRACTICE: Confession is good for the soul, or so the saying goes. There are two familiar references to confession, Proverbs 28:13 and James 5:16. Confession is both a way to relinquish the burden of carrying one's actions/sins and a way of preventing future actions/sins. It is coming clean not only before God but those God has placed in your life. It is not an easy discipline and requires a level of maturity and trust that is uncommon in our culture. This said, it is indeed scriptural and a part of our ancient Christian heritage. If you feel your group is mature enough, offer a brief look at confession and discuss the benefits of such a corporate activity. Confession (as with all good things) may also be abused. It is not to be used as a "get out of jail free" card nor is it to be a therapy or gossip session. It is taking responsibility for one's actions and repenting, asking others to come alongside for accountability and prayer. It may be equally as helpful, once you have discussed the positive elements of confession, to look at the ways it may be abused.

Teacher's Note: This passage deals with the time under the reign of King Solomon before the kingdom is divided. Solomon was known as a wise and wealthy king. He was revered for his prowess politically, economically, architecturally, and spiritually. He was not a king who left God behind. Interestingly enough, it was under this reign that verse 14 was written—a caution for the people, affirming a covenant, not chastising nor punishing. When things were going well, God sends a reminder of that which allows it to continue to go well.

LIFE APPLICATION: You have now walked through, phrase-by-phrase what God is calling for His people to do. These were His people, not during a time of rebellion, but during a time of a reminder of the covenant made.

Ask: Who do you think does things that hurt themselves, their family, or friends on occasion? The answer should be everyone!

Why do we live like we don't need to confess and turn from those wicked ways? Many of us look to the really bad people and know they need to get right before God, but this passage is not directed to the rebellious ones who have fallen away or chosen to live in sin. It is directed to "His people called by His name."

One of the groups touched on this but let's revisit one section ". . . and turn from their wicked ways. . . ." We live in a culture consumed with image and how people look on the outside. Ask: What would it look like if this world turned from its wicked ways for real? Is it possible to simply look the part? Where in our world, in our culture, do you see things that seem good on the outside, but once you know the inside, you know they are not sincere?

MAKING IT PERSONAL: Ask the group to be silent for just a moment. It is easy to think of all the ways the world puts on a show. Each of us, at one time or another, is just as guilty of pretending to be more sincere than we really are.

Say: You don't have to answer any these out loud unless you feel led to, but listen to each question and think about how you would respond.

Do you like it when others are being fake around you?

How do you think God likes it when you are being fake?

Can you think of a time when you know you messed up and you were more concerned with the show you were putting on with your apology or decision to stop doing something than what was really happening in your heart?

Have you ever seemed sincere on the outside when inside you knew you felt or believed totally different?

How can you learn to not put on a show but to be more sincere?

Close in prayer, asking God to remind us that we don't have to be perfect to come to Him, but that He does want us to, and He expects us to be sincere. He knows what is in our heart anyway!

CONNECTIONS: Jesus has strong words to offer on this subject. In Matthew 23:27 He states exactly what He thinks of those who look good on the outside but have insides that do not match!

SONGS: "Lose This Life" by Tait Band, on the album *Lose This Life*

More than a Show —Midweek

MEMORY VERSE:
So rend your heart, and not your garments; return to the Lord your God, for He is gracious and merciful, slow to anger, and of great kindness; and He relents from doing harm. —Joel 2:13

SCRIPTURE: Joel 2:1–13

LESSON IN A SENTENCE: God values sincerity over an exhibition.

FOCUS

Before your students arrive, write out the following 13 items on cards. Have a separate piece of construction or butcher paper for each item. Have students volunteer and give one item to each for him or her to draw; the rest of the group guesses what is being drawn. When each item has been drawn and guessed, write the item in clear letters below the picture and tape them on the wall in order. Be certain to give the items in the order listed. (You can also play this as a competition by dividing into two teams. Each team takes a turn at drawing the item you have given keeping tack of the time. The group to have guessed their items in the least amount of time wins!)

(For the purpose of this lesson, you will not want to play the game on a dry erase board.)

1—A trumpet blowing
2—A dark, rainstorm
3—A wildfire
4—Stampeding horses
5—A chariot race
6—People about to faint
7—People climbing a wall
8—Weapons
9—Thieves
10—An earthquake
11—An army commander giving orders
12—Fasting, weeping or mourning
13—Ripping clothes

Ask: Is there anyone who would like to experience all of the things we have just drawn?

DISCOVERY

This passage is one where each and every verse conjures up strong images! Use this to your advantage. After having completed the game, read Joel 2:1–13 aloud. (The prose of this passage reads like a reader's theatre with no alteration. You may want to choose two strong reader's to read through this, alternating verses as they proceed through the passage.)

Look back to the drawings on the wall. Did anyone make the connection that each one is an image from each verse?

The drawings are rather primitive and crude as they were being drawn in haste and for a game. Read back through the passage slowly, verse by verse. Ask your students to close their eyes as you read each verse and then ask what they picture in their mind's eye?

For example: "Blow the trumpet in Zion, and sound an alarm in My holy mountain! Let all the inhabitants of the land tremble; for the day of the Lord is coming, for it is at hand" (Joel 2:1).

Ask: What do you imagine this to look like?

This passage is one of destruction and struggle over and over again, ending in a clear direction. Regardless of the circumstances we are to rend our hearts, not our garments.

APPLICATION: What on earth does it mean to rend our hearts and not our garments? What on earth does it mean to rend anything?

Rending is a tearing or pulling apart. It is used as a sign of mourning (Genesis 37:34; Leviticus 21:10; 1 Samuel 4:12; and 2 Samuel 3:31) and repentance (Genesis 37:29; Joshua 7:6; 2 Chronicles 34:27; Joel 2:13).

Ask: What does it mean to rend your heart and not your garments?

What does it look like when others are "rending" their garments?

In Joel 2:13, rending is a sign of repentance. It is used here to talk about God wanting not an outward action or show of repentance but for the heart to be what is torn apart as an inward action in response to repentance.

Ask: What does it mean for you to rend your heart and not your garment?

Close asking God to show you where in your life you need to move from having empty outward signs of repentance to having a truly inward change.

Q U O T A B L E   Q U O T E S :

One who does not know where one stands, stands nowhere. . . . You can't learn from others unless you learn first from who and what you are. Only teenagers, and shallow ones at that, may be excused for turning against all that has shaped them. Openness does not mean emptiness.

—Andrew Greeley

We must adjust to changing times and still hold to unchanging principles.

—Jimmy Carter

WHY POP CULTURE MATTERS

By Dick Staub
CULTURE WATCHER/EXPERT

If you love kids and you love Christ, you better get close to popular culture. I learned this lesson in 1966 when I sat at Fillmore West, sandwiched between two guys on an overstuffed couch, both of them smoking marijuana, all of us listening to Jefferson Airplane. I was there because I had just read the Gospels for the first time, and observed Jesus spending considerable time in "the world" I had been taught to be separate from. In my confusion, way before the trendy bracelet told me to, I asked myself "what would Jesus do?"

I was driven to this question by what I observed around me. To some the 60s were about sex, drugs, and rock and roll, but I also saw an age of spiritual yearning expressed in an influential popular culture. "We are stardust, billion-year-old carbon, caught in the devil's bargain, and we've got to get ourselves back to the garden" is how Joni Mitchell put it.

For the most part the church was either cocooning itself from this long-haired hippie culture or trying to do combat with it. It was an age that sowed seeds for what is now in full bloom.

Today we who love Christ and kids find ourselves caught in the vortex of a perfect storm, where three forces are converging: a misguided spiritual search, an influential popular culture, and a marginalized church.

Misguided Spiritual Journey

Some 82 percent of Americans say they are on a spiritual journey. Of these, 52 percent say they have talked about it in the previous 24 hours. Yet it is a search with self rather than God or truth as the object. While being a "seeker" is trendy, one astute observer has called this generation "snackers." Such a trivial pursuit deceives people into thinking they are serious about God. Most aren't.

Influential Popular Culture

Since the 60s, popular culture has become more influential, traveling faster on the road of new technologies. It is powerful, pervasive, and persuasive. It has become the common language of the next generation and it mediates the spiritual conversation in our land. Phyliss Tickle of

Publisher's Weekly reports, "More theology is conveyed in, and probably retained from one hour of popular television, than from all the sermons that are delivered on any given weekend in America's synagogues, churches, and mosques." Media guru Michael Wolfe adds, "I really believe entertainment in a lot of ways has become a way for people to come together. It has, in fact, become—I'm convinced of this—a replacement for religion. And I think that in the same way people used to quote Scripture they're now quoting 'Seinfeld.'"

Such an influential popular culture presents a threat because it often conveys beliefs and values antithetical to a Christian worldview. It presents an opportunity because it is the common language of our culture, which once learned, allows Christians access to a spiritual conversation already taking place, but are we ready?

Marginalized Church

As the influence of popular culture has risen, the church's influence has declined. Christian reactions to popular culture have been schizophrenic and the result is what Brian Godawa calls a generation of "cultural anorexics" or "cultural gluttons." The cultural anorexic is cut off from culture and cannot seize the opportunities it represents. The cultural glutton is consumed by culture and is vulnerable to its threats. While evangelicals set out to transform the culture and have grown in attendance, there is ample evidence that it is we who have been transformed by culture in that our beliefs and behavior mirror the culture. Like the early church in Corinth, the culture is influencing the church more than the church is influencing culture.

Bad News

This is having a devastating impact on the next generation. A 1998 National Opinion Research Study found that of 18–22 year olds only 16 percent had any ongoing contact with the faith in which they were raised. Thirty years ago in *The God Who Is There*, Francis Schaeffer warned, "I find that everywhere I go, children of Christians are being lost to historic Christianity. They are being lost because their parents are unable to understand their children and therefore cannot help them in their time of need. We have left the next generation naked in the face of twentieth century thought by which they are surrounded."

Today the twin towers of an influential popular culture and an anemic, inauthentic American Christianity hasten the next generation's departure from the faith. So what are we to do?

Needed: Culturally Savvy Christians

Influencing the culture and our kids requires a return to our roots in Jesus who fully engaged culture. The Culturally Savvy Christian is the ultimate answer to the "what would Jesus do" question. What is a Culturally Savvy Christian?

(1) A Culturally Savvy Christian is serious about faith, desires to do God's will, exhibits a transformed mind and behavior, and follows Jesus into the world as a loving, transforming presence in the company of friends.

(2) The Culturally Savvy Christian is savvy about culture and understands the Christian's multifaceted calling to be: artists and appreciators of art who enjoy resonance with culture, aliens who experience dissonance with the fallen-ness of culture, and ambassadors who express good news at the intersection of faith and culture.

(3) The Culturally Savvy Christian is skilled to negotiate the relationship between faith and culture—discovering the messages of both faith and culture, discerning the similarities and differences, and deciding on an appropriate course of action that maintains fidelity to faith and the fullness of human experience and expression in culture.

Research shows this is a generation that justifies leaving their faith because they: claim to have not experienced God in the church, find their "tribal" connections stronger outside the church than in it, see little relevance for their life in what is talked about in church, and observe little in their parents' life that makes them want to be a Christian.

The next generation is crying out for examples of Christians who pursue Jesus in the company of friends, who are qualitatively different from culture, but who are also called and equipped to engage culture in ways that connect the truth to the questions being raised in culture. They are crying out for models of Culturally Savvy Christians who are serious about faith, savvy about culture, and skilled to operate authentically in both. For more information visit dickstaub.com.

JULY 10, 2005

The Water in Which You Swim Does Matter!

By Amy Jacober

MEMORY VERSE:

But Ruth said: "Entreat me not to leave you, or to turn back from following after you; for wherever you go, I will go; and wherever you lodge, I will lodge; your people shall be my people, and your God, my God."—Ruth 1:16

SCRIPTURE: 1 Corinthians 9:19–23

LESSON IN A SENTENCE: Our world colors the way we understand God.

THE BIG PICTURE (OR WHAT YOU'RE TRYING TO GET ACROSS):

Ruth knew it, Paul knew it, culture does matter. It matters in how we understand the unchanging truths of God in an ever-changing world; it matters in how we share those truths with others. Paul was well aware of the culture of his day, politics, education, poetry, and philosophy. While music, video games, movies, magazines, and fashion may not seem quite the same, for today's contemporary world, they are the expressions of culture. All of us, but teenagers in particular, are inundated with images and cultural trends every day. At times the messages are subtle, at other times they slap you in the face! When sharing our faith, either our current lessons (both successes and struggles), or what it means to be a follower of Christ for the first time, we must be speaking the same language. Culture is what determines how well we understand the words we are speaking to one another. There is also a danger in this—it is possible to be so consumed with understanding the language of culture that we forget that we are to be in it and not of it. It is for the sake of the gospel that we become all things to all people!

IN THIS LESSON STUDENTS SHOULD:

- Learn that it is important to understand their world but not be consumed by it.
- Understand that the gospel is the reason to be in the world.
- Know that relating to others on their terms does not mean one's own faith is lost.

STUFF YOU NEED:

○ 3 x 5 cards
○ Pens/pencils
○ Scissors
○ Paper (ideally butcher paper or some other longer sheets of paper for paper dolls)
If you choose option 1:
○ Construction paper
○ Glue
○ Pictures of famous people, bands, logos, etc.
○ Lined paper
○ Pencils
If you choose option 2:
○ Strips of paper
○ Pencils/pens
○ Popcorn
○ Movie candy

FOCUS

OPTION 1:

This one will take some time cutting pictures from magazines and newspapers. On at least 4 different colored sheets of construction paper, glue 10 pictures of famous people, bands, and name brand logo/icons. (If you have a larger group, you will want to create more sheets.) These will not be hard to find in just a few magazines! If you are nervous about who is "in," just pick up one of the many teen magazines or ask for help from a few of your student leaders. Once you have them glued on, number each picture and then make a key—for example: green sheet, #1 Nike, #2 J-Lo, etc. Make a key for each different colored paper.

Break your students into groups of 4–6. Give each group a lined sheet of paper and pencil. Hand out the colored sheets of paper with pictures upside down. Have them flip them over at the same time and name as many of the people/bands/logos, etc. as they can. Be certain they label their list with the color of sheet they have! After 60 seconds, trade sheets. Do this at least 4 times. Once they are done, go through the sheets giving the answers. The group with the most correct answers wins!

OPTION 2:

Movie line trivia! As your students arrive, hand each person at least one strip of paper. Ask them to write down their favorite movie line, the name of the movie from which it comes, and their own name. Set chairs up in two sections, like a theatre. This would be a great time for a little popcorn! Be certain the two sections are even and gather the strips of paper with the movie lines into one bag. Have one person from each section come up and draw a line from the bag. Read it aloud for their team. If no one knows the answer, the guess goes to the other team. (Be certain each person pays attention to who wrote the line; they may not offer a guess or the opposite team gets the point!) Keep track of points and offer your favorite movie candy for the team with the most points by the end.

DISCOVERY

Culture is the way in which the world communicates with itself. Knowing songs, movies, fashion, video games, and just about any other element of popular culture is not going to be a stretch for most of your students.

Say: Paul talks of being in this world. In fact, he talks of being in this world for a particular reason.

In groups of 3, read 1 Corinthians 9:19–23. Instruct each group to (1) write no more than one sentence summarizing what Paul says in verses 19–22 and (2) answer why Paul did what he did (huge hint in verse 23!).

You may want to offer this passage from *The Message* as an alternative.

> Even though I am free of the demands and expectations of everyone, I have voluntarily become a servant to any and all in order to reach a wide range of people: religious, nonreligious, meticulous moralists, loose-living immoralists, the defeated, the demoralized—whoever. I didn't take on their way of life. I kept my bearings in Christ—but I entered their world and tried to experience things from their point of view. I've become just about every sort of servant there is in my attempts to lead those I meet into a God-saved life. I did all this because of the Message. I didn't just want to talk about it; I wanted to be in on it!
>
> —1 Corinthians 9:19–23 (*The Message*)

Teacher's Note: Culture is everywhere! In some circles "culture" refers to the ballet and opera, the high elements of fine arts. Your community comes with its own cultural rules and norms. Many of these are not easily recognized, as they have become such a part of the world in which you live. It's like being asked to describe what it is to breathe air.

You don't know any different, so it becomes difficult to say. Culture can be seen as the patterns in life for behavior and beliefs. Teenagers have a culture within a culture. Their clothing styles, slang vocabulary, and what TV shows they watch are carved out of the larger society's idea of what is popular. While we as adults absolutely do not need to act, look, and sound like teenagers, just like Paul, we do need to be able to understand their perspective and know what they mean when they use certain words.

LIFE APPLICATION: Say: Paul talks of being a Jew to the Jew, becoming weak to the weak, and a servant to all. He is acutely aware of the culture in which he lived, but also the culture of those around him!

Ask: What would this look like today?

Should every Christian adopt this kind of attitude and behavior or could it be dangerous?

Have each group of three come up with a situation in which they might meet or spend time with someone totally different from them. Have them write this on a 3 x 5 card. (It may be having an exchange student as a lab partner, being a complete extrovert and meeting and talking with an introvert at lunch, holding to your convictions but talking with those who party, etc.) Trade cards with another group. Ask: What would it look like for you to follow the example of Paul and become "all things to all people" for this situation? What would make it hard? What part(s) could be easy? What could become a place where you might stumble?

Flashback! OK, not too far back, but at least to your opening activity. For many of us, we are already deeply a part of this culture. A huge difference is that we've learned how to compartmentalize what we do and who we are.

Ask: Why was it so easy to know the pictures or movie lines? How could you use these very common, everyday kinds of things as a beginning place to be able to talk about Jesus?

Teacher's Note: You may want to spend a little time talking about and thinking through some popular culture ideas at this point. There are many great resources on the internet to help you think through issues (and quite frankly, there is so much it is impossible for most of us to keep up with everything!). One among many is www.dickstaub.com. There are others listed in the web resources section in the back of this book.

MAKING IT PERSONAL: This can be pretty scary! We do not live in a world that encourages us to conform, to look like, sound like, or act like anyone else, or do we? Magazines are full of ways to be unique—

to find your own style! Part of the difficulty comes when everyone is shopping at the same five stores, watching the same movies and TV shows, and listening to the same radio stations. For all of this unique individualism we promote, it has really become a clever way to have us relate.

This can be used to our advantage. Invite your students to listen to culture this week. Ask them to keep a journal each time they hear a line in a song, a scene from a TV show, something in a magazine or on a billboard, wherever that God, Jesus, or some manner of spiritual question is being asked. (Spiritual questions being things like what happens after we die? How do we make it in a world that seems so hard? Where do I find my value?) Say: The culture in which we live is asking questions. Paul calls us to be all things to all people. It is difficult if we spend our time judging or ignoring others instead of trying to understand their perspective.

Say: It is easier to become consumed in our own worlds and not even notice what is going on around us. As you keep a journal this week, try to understand what the people may be thinking who sang the song or wrote the script. Begin to pray for them, even though you don't know them. Begin to look for ways right in your own school or neighborhood where you can learn others' perspective for the sake of the gospel!

MEMORY VERSE ACTIVITY: This may seem a bit childish at first, but make a paper doll chain. Fold a piece of paper and cut out the shape of a person to make the paper dolls. If you have a roll of butcher paper, make the longest chain through which your scissors will cut. As you hold up the paper dolls, talk about what it means to be all things to all people. Cut the dolls apart and give one to each person present. Ask each student to think of one person as they write the memory verse on the paper person.

CONNECTIONS: It may feel like a stretch for some of your students to consider becoming "all things to all people." It may even feel a bit hypocritical. Remember, Paul does not say to take on the way of life of another, simply to try and understand it. Can you think of anyone else who does this same thing?

Different messages are offered to different people depending on what they can handle and their maturity. No one would try to teach calculus to the average six-year-old! It is not a bad thing to teach about God in a way that is understandable. As each person grows and matures, the conversations and lessons can change. It is not about trying to be deceitful; it is about trying to not speak over the heads of others. Check out John 16:12; 1 Corinthians 3:2; Hebrews 5:12; and 1 John 2:13.

SONGS: "Mistaken" by Warren Barfield, on the album *Warren Barfield*

QUOTABLE   QUOTES:

I think that, regardless of our culture, age, or even personal handicaps, we can still strive for something exceptional. Why not expand our sights instead of restricting our lives and accepting the lowest common denominator of a dormant existence? Faith . . . in God . . . will permit us to take a chance on a new path, perhaps different from the one we now follow. It may be surprising where it leads.

—Jimmy Carter

The Water in Which You Swim Does Matter! —Midweek

MEMORY VERSE:
But Ruth said: "Entreat me not to leave you, or to turn back from following after you; for wherever you go, I will go; and wherever you lodge, I will lodge; your people shall be my people, and your God, my God.—Ruth 1:16

SCRIPTURE: Mark 4:30–34

LESSON IN A SENTENCE: Our world colors the way we understand God.

FOCUS

Make a list of famous pairs. These can be people or things—peanut butter and jelly, Dorothy and Toto, or current couples in the news. Write these down on separate strips of paper. Be certain you have enough so that every person will be able to have one half of the pairs. Once your students are there, tape one of the strips of paper on his or her back. As soon as everyone has one, they have to ask yes or no questions to try to figure out what is on their back and then wander until they find their match!

Ask: How did you know those things went together? (Most of your students will just stare blankly at you. They go together because, well, they just go together!)

Say: Many of us know things or believe things and we're not even certain why. We have grown up in a culture where our world, our communities, our family, and popular culture have taught us all along what it means to be who we are. This doesn't stop even when it comes to God. How we understand God, what we think goes with being a Christian, is colored by growing up in this country. This isn't good or bad, it just is. It is important, however, that we realize this.

DISCOVERY

Read Mark 4:30–34.

Ask: What is a parable?

Do we ever talk in parables today?

Of course we talk in parables. Most of us just don't call them that!

Ask: What do you know about mustard seeds and plants?

Unless you are living on an herb farm, most of us can hear this one and what we know of plants helps it to translate, but it's still not a clear picture for us. If this one doesn't communicate much to you, what subjects could?

On a whiteboard, make a list of all of the interests and stuff of daily life that could be used for a parable. These can be anything from riding the bus, going to the beach, washing dishes, rollerblading, playing soccer, etc.

Teacher's Note: Parables are used throughout Scripture. Jesus certainly was a fan of this kind of storytelling, this kind of narrative teaching. Part of what makes a parable so popular and so helpful is in the very definition of what a parable is. It is a story, a comparison that is only trying to get across one point. It does not offer many comparisons or several interpretations. By the end of the story, you know exactly the point the person was trying to make.

APPLICATION: There are some things about God and being a follower of Jesus that are certainly the basics. Ask your students to brainstorm simple basic truths that those who follow Jesus need to know and understand. Write these on the other side of the whiteboard.

Ask: What does Mark 4:33 mean?

We are to share in ways that make sense, in ways that connect with the worlds in which people really live. This may mean coming up with stories that tell basic truths but in whole new ways.

Once you have these lists side by side, have two groups of partners get together (peanut butter and jelly joins chips and salsa!) to make a group of 4. Their job is to take one of the topics or settings and match it with a basic truth and write their own parable. Once these are written, have each group share their story. (If your group is not much into writing, have them create a sketch and perform it for one another, or have them draw a cartoon of the parable they have created.)

Ask: Did anyone keep a log this week of times they heard about God or Jesus in their daily lives, on TV or songs, in magazines? The world is full of ways subtle messages and/or questions are being presented. In some ways, even if the message is not always clear or true, the world is teaching us about God, or at least its perception of God.

Invite your students to really listen. (Chances are, most of them will have either blown off or forgotten you asked them to keep a log. Don't take this personally!) You may want to offer a few of your observations from the past few days of things you have heard or seen. As we hear and see the questions being asked, we are able to tell stories in ways that will be heard. Remind them, according to Mark 4:33, they are modeling Christ in this way.

It Is Good!

By Amy Jacober

MEMORY VERSE:
And He (Jesus) said to them, "The Sabbath was made for man, and not man for the Sabbath."—Mark 2:27 (NKJV)

The Sabbath was made for humankind and not humankind for the Sabbath. —Mark 2:27 (NRSV)

SCRIPTURE: Nehemiah 13:15–22

LESSON IN A SENTENCE: Sabbath is not only good for us; it is a commandment!

THE BIG PICTURE (OR WHAT YOU'RE TRYING TO GET ACROSS):

There has been a shift in the last few years about an awareness of most of us being overwhelmed, overworked, and just plain too busy! We may be aware but there is still much work to do in the area of actually changing this pattern in life. God calls us to rest—actually *commands* us to rest. This can come as a welcome relief to stressed-out, overwhelmed students, or seem like a nice idea needed for a later time when it is really needed, or something impossible to put into their PDA. Teenagers are truly gifted at being able to spend huge amounts of time doing absolutely nothing. Some of your students do not get the chance to relax on a regular basis. They run from school to practice, to their volunteer tutoring, to dance practice or guitar lessons, and then to their part time job so they can afford all the clothes, CDs, video games, or whatever it is they are into. Even family takes a back seat to all of these activities. Churches can either be a help or a hindrance in this area. Part of our role in this is to not only teach about Sabbath but to live it as leaders and set it as a priority in our programming choices.

IN THIS LESSON STUDENTS SHOULD:

- ○ Understand what a Sabbath is.
- ○ Learn that keeping Sabbath is more than taking a nap all day.
- ○ Be able to see benefits and consequences related to the Sabbath.

STUFF YOU NEED:

If you choose option 2:
  ◌ Collection of either Darwin awards stories or stupid
    criminal stories

FOCUS

OPTION 1:

As your students arrive, have your normal routine set in place—music playing, snacks if you normally do snacks. Give any announcements and housekeeping details right up front. Once everything is taken care of, ask each student to find a comfortable spot in the room where they are not touching anyone. (They can stay in chairs, sit in the floor, against a wall in a bean bag or wherever they can find space.) Change the music to something slower and instrumental. Invite your students to relax, to slow down, to set aside the worries of the day. Let your students know that they get to sit, in silence, for ten minutes. Ask then to stand when they think 10 minutes have passed. (As this is going on, keep track on your watch of when 10 minutes are up, but also as people begin to stand, make a note of how many minutes have actually passed.) (If you have a particularly active or a younger group, you may want to shorten this activity to 5 minutes.)

Ask: What was this like for you? Did it feel like a long time or a short time?

Say: Most of us talk about being stressed out, too busy, overwhelmed with school and activities. It's amazing that even when we stop for just 10 minutes, it becomes uncomfortable and we want to fill the time.

OPTION 2:

Keeping the Sabbath is a command, not a suggestion. We have commands all around us. While it is an easy step for Christians to move into legalism (which Jesus warns sternly against), there are many guidelines we seem to take as loose suggestions. Not following what God desires has consequences.

The internet is full of reports of people who just don't seem to get the guidelines set up in this world. They try to make their way around the rules and, well, they get caught. There are several ways you can do this one. Look up the most current Darwin awards or any other listing of stupid criminals that you can find on the internet. Collect at least 10 stories. Either as a whole or in smaller groups, read the stories of the stupid criminals. (This is a great activity to use with power point or media shout if you have it!) Have your students rank the stupid criminal stories from 1–10. Ask if they know of any others to add to your prestigious list!

After you have finished, Say: While these stories are funny and the criminals, well, not the sharpest tools in the shed, we make mistakes just as stupid every week if not every day. Very few Christians actually observe the Sabbath. It's a guideline that was set by God for our benefit and we break it all of the time. We may not get caught like these criminals, but there are consequences.

DISCOVERY

Say: Sabbath is a command. We are supposed to rest or there are consequences.

Ask: Why would God tell us (and even set the example) of taking time to rest? Do you really think this was needed back before the days of cell phones, Ims, and after-school activities or jobs?

Look at Nehemiah 13:15–22 to see what was happening thousands of years ago.

Break into groups of 3–4 and ask each group to read though the passage and list every thing they can find that the people were doing or that Nehemiah criticizes them for doing to break the Sabbath.

Say: Nehemiah is inflexible in insisting that the Sabbath should be kept! What does he say he will do in order to ensure all the people are going to keep the Sabbath?

Read verse 22 again. Ask: Why do you think Nehemiah is asking God to remember him according to His mercy?

Teacher's Note: The word Sabbath alone carries with it deep and rich meaning. The word Sabbath comes from the Hebrew *Shabbat*, meaning to cease or to stop. Have you ever heard the phrase "Shabbat Shalom" or "Shalom Shabbat"? Hebrew *Shalom* carries with it the meaning of peace, but even deeper than that. It means peace, a wishing for well-being, restoration, reconciliation with God, and salvation. What a greeting, and a communicated desire for a day set apart for rest and as a sign of the covenant relationship between God and His people.

LIFE APPLICATION: Nehemiah had a whole list of things he knew shouldn't be done on the Sabbath. Ask your students to make a list of modern-day equivalents to the prohibitions offered by Nehemiah.

Re-read verse 22 one last time.

Say: Nehemiah is asking God for two things. The first is to remember him. The second is to spare him! He is praying to God for mercy as he tries to guarantee that all the people will be observing the Sabbath.

Ask: Why do you think Nehemiah was so strong on being certain the Sabbath was observed?

Say: Nehemiah talks of a few of the consequences for not keeping the Sabbath.

Make a list of the consequences of not observing a Sabbath today.

Ask: Why is it so hard in our world today to observe the Sabbath?

MAKING IT PERSONAL: Ask: Why is it so hard for you to find a way to observe the Sabbath?

Refer back to your focus activity, either a few moments of silence or looking back at stupid criminals. Silence is rare in our noisy world. While it is awkward and uncomfortable at first, God calls us to slow down. If you looked at the stupid criminals, these criminals got caught. They really did some stupid things and could not get away with it. God is clear that there are consequences to not taking a Sabbath. This is not a hard command, where He is telling you to push a boulder up a hill! Just like the stupid criminals, we want to do things our own way, not realizing that the commands are set up to help us and there are consequences to violating them, whether we realize it or not.

Invite your students to consider following the ancient practice of Sabbath for real. They may think they can't because they are too busy. Encourage them to try just for this week. And then, recommit each week to try to carve out some space for rest in the Lord.

ANCIENT PRACTICE: While seemingly impossible in our over-scheduled world, invite your leaders and students to take a Sabbath, a real one. Sabbath takes planning: it means that homework needs to be done early, that chores have to be done ahead of time. Sabbath takes protection. It means being certain that you don't allow every responsibility and/or offer to encroach upon that time, just because you know you have some "free" moments. Sabbath is to be a time when you rest from your normal routine (even if your routine is not routine at all, but simply constant motion running from one activity to the next). It is when you stop trying to get stuff done for you and enjoy God and the world He has created for you. It does not mean sitting silently on your bed for the whole day. We live on the other side of the cross. Observing Sabbath, while still a commandment, is not about finding every tiny rule for exactly what can and cannot be done. Sabbath was made for humankind. What brings you rest? What draws you closer to God? Playing guitar with a few friends? Painting? Surfing? Skateboarding? A nap? A walk after dinner with your family?

CONNECTIONS: The Sabbath is a concept we get originally from the Old Testament. It was to remind us of creation and was therefore holy (Exodus 20:8–11), and later of the redemption from slavery (Deuteronomy 5:12–15). It became a time of rest from one's usual pursuits and a day of remembering God or spending time in worship. Jesus observed the Sabbath through worship. Of course He—like Jews today—observed it on Saturday (actually sundown on Friday through sundown on Saturday). For early Christians, a shift occurred. Sabbath was originally a reminder of the covenant of God with His people. Jesus changed that as He was and is the covenant. Sabbath then became a symbol of future rest (Hebrews 4:1–11). The observance was moved to the "first day of the week" to commemorate Jesus' resurrection.

SONGS: "Clear" by Watashi Wa, on the album *The Love of Life*
"When I Enter Your Rest" by Joann Rosario

QUOTABLE QUOTES :

One ought, every day at least, to hear a little song, read a good poem, see a fine picture.

—Goethe

It Is Good! —Midweek

MEMORY VERSE:
And He (Jesus) said to them, "The Sabbath was made for man, and not man for the Sabbath."—Mark 2:27 (NKJV)

The Sabbath was made for humankind and not humankind for the Sabbath. —Mark 2:27 (NRSV)

SCRIPTURE: Genesis 2:1–3; Exodus 20:8–11; Hebrews 4:1–11

LESSON IN A SENTENCE: Sabbath is not only good for us; it is a commandment!

FOCUS

OPTION 1:
   If you have an active group needing to burn a little energy, play freeze tag. At the end, talk about the "freezing," the time when they had to stop, to cease from the running and the chaos of the activity and simply rest for a few moments. (Remember from the previous lesson, Sabbath means to cease!)

OPTION 2:
   This is an old favorite that many of you may have grown up doing! Have some sort of container with a lid, preferably clear but that certainly isn't necessary. Depending on the container you choose, find a large object that takes up most of the space. (A tennis ball in a margarine-sized container works perfectly!) Set the large object in the container and fill the rest of the space around it with popcorn. Be certain you can place the lid back on the container completely.
   On a whiteboard have your students make a list of all the things that fill their days and week (school, sleeping, brushing teeth, talking on the phone, internet, horseback riding, fishing, skating, whatever!) Dump out the contents of your container. Read through the list and slowly place a little bit of popcorn in for each item mentioned. At the end, point out the tennis ball; this represents God. If you don't take some time to stop your normal routine, you will never be able to fit God in. Show this by placing the tennis ball on top of the popcorn. The lid will not fit with it this way! Dump the popcorn back out. Place the tennis ball in first. Read back through that same list, placing a little bit of popcorn in the container for each item listed. By setting the ball in first and fillingd the rest of the container around the ball, the lid will go right on with no problem!

Say: When we set priorities, when we make certain we are going to observe Sabbath and spend time with God, the rest of life is able to fall into place.

DISCOVERY

Split into three groups. Give one group Genesis 2:1–3, give the second group Exodus 20:8–11, and give the third group Hebrews 4:1–11.

Give each group time to read through the passages.

On a piece of posterboard, have the words who, what, where, why, when, and how written. Give a separate posterboard to each group. As they read through their passage, have them fill in the blanks for each question. For some of the passages, they may have to read above or below the verses to get the context and be able to really answer the questions.

When all three groups are finished, have each group present their posterboard. Be certain to tell them to listen carefully for how these three passages relate to each other!

Ask: Can anyone tell how these three relate?

APPLICATION: God set the example for Sabbath right from the beginning, and it was good! This was affirmed both in the commandments and the lives of His chosen people. Sabbath did not end with Jesus. In fact, He observed it in worship and celebration! As people of God, we are to rest!

Ask: Why is rest so important? What are you like when you become too busy for too long?

Consider a Sabbath, a ceasing from the normal routine of your life. Think back through your week. Is there something that can be let go, something that can be moved or a way you can better use your time in order to carve out space to rest?

Spend a few closing moments sharing with a partner what a Sabbath would look like for you. Pray for one another that you may be able to observe as God commands, realizing that it is indeed good!

Persecution—Rain Will Fall

By Amy Jacober

MEMORY VERSE:

And He has said to me, "My grace is sufficient for you, for power is perfected in weakness." Most gladly, therefore, I will rather boast about my weaknesses, that the power of Christ may dwell in me. Therefore I am well content with weaknesses, with insults, with distresses, with persecutions, with difficulties, for Christ's sake; for when I am weak, then I am strong."—2 Corinthians 12:9–10 (NASB)

SCRIPTURE: 2 Corinthians 11:23–28

LESSON IN A SENTENCE: Struggles and persecution are a part of the Christian life.

THE BIG PICTURE (OR WHAT YOU'RE TRYING TO GET ACROSS):

Somewhere along the way we have been taught that following Jesus meant that our lives would get easier. As we grew in our faith and obeyed God, we would be blessed. What most of us were not taught is that truly following Jesus can be difficult if not down right oppressive. We are blessed in the USA to be able to attend church and choose to openly profess Christ without political or economic sanctions. We may be teased or left out of some social networks, but this is relatively mild compared to many other places in the world. This lesson will have a dual focus. One is to remind ourselves that even we will feel some form of persecution, keeping in mind that we are not meant to fit into this world, this is not our home. The second focus is to create an awareness of just how difficult it can be to faithfully follow Jesus in other parts of the world.

IN THIS LESSON STUDENTS SHOULD:

- ○ Know of Paul and some of what he went through for the cause of Christ.
- ○ Hear that hardships are a part of any Christian life, even those who are faithful.
- ○ Learn of the persecuted church around the world and be encouraged to pray for fellow believers.

STUFF YOU NEED:

If you choose option 1:
  ⊙ Soft balls for dodge ball

If you choose option 2:
  ⊙ White board or butcher paper
  ⊙ Markers

FOCUS

OPTION 1:

If you have an active group, a game of dodge ball is perfect for this lesson! There are several variations on this game; feel free to take these basic rules and adapt them for your group. Break into two teams of equal numbers. Have the teams line up shoulder to shoulder and face one another. On an imaginary middle line between the teams, place several soft balls (use nerf, four square, or other soft balls.) The object of the game is to run to the line, grab a ball, and throw it at someone on the other team. Once you have been hit, you are out and must sit right where you have been hit. You may never cross the line, so you must always throw from your side of the playing field. The last person standing wins the game for his or her team!

Debrief: Did anyone deserve to be knocked out? Did you do something that made you deserve to be hit with a ball or was it something that just happened because of the rules of the game?

Have any of you ever had something negative happen to you that you did not deserve? (Take some time and get their stories.)

OPTION 2:

On either a white board or a sheet of butcher paper, make a list of all the ways Christians in your community are either persecuted or treated differently. (This may be anything from being excluded from a certain group of friends to being teased for waiting until marriage to have sex.)

Ask: Does anyone have a story to illustrate how this is so?

DISCOVERY

What if we expanded this to our country? What are some ways Christians face difficulties? (This may include the accusations that Christians are unkind and unloving for taking a stand on moral issues, or the struggle for rights and understanding separation of church and state.)

When writing this list, be certain to leave at least half of the space to add the list of what Paul went through that you will cover later in this section.

Ask: What would you say to someone who tells you they are content with weakness, insults, distresses, persecution, and difficulties? (Give a few minutes for responses.)

Crazy? Out of touch with reality?

Say: This is just what Paul said!

MEMORY VERSE ACTIVITY: Tyvek is a deceptively strong material. It looks like a sheet of paper and yet is next to impossible for the average person to tear apart. Use scissors and cut a strip of tyvek for each person in your group. Provide markers (Sharpie's or any permanent marker) and have each person write the memory verse on the tyvek. Point out that while it may look like a piece of paper, it is strong. Often, in what seems to be the weakest of things comes the greatest strength. In what seems to be our weakest parts, God is allowed to shine through and these become our greatest strengths. You can obtain tyvek either through tyvek envelopes (often the kind Federal Express uses) or if you know someone in construction, tyvek is used on a new house just after framing.

Ask: So what do we really have to learn from Paul? He is the super apostle of the New Testament, isn't he? He was confident, skilled, and led a charmed life, didn't he? Well, not exactly.

Teacher's Note: If your students are entirely unfamiliar with Paul, you may want to offer the 60-second update! Understanding the context of one of the best-known followers of Christ in history, we understand that his life was far from idyllic. He began as one who persecuted believers (Acts 7:58; 8:1; 9:1–2; 1 Corinthians 15:9) and then offer a look at his conversion (Acts 9:1–19). You may want to point out that many of the books we love and frequently read in the New Testament are attributed to Paul as the author. He is no insignificant figure in our Christian heritage.

Break into groups of three. Give each group a sheet of paper and a pen/pencil. Have each group read through 2 Corinthians 11:23–28, telling them to look for as many specific struggles Paul mentions. (There are several way to break this down, but there are at least 13 different struggles.)

After a few minutes, ask the groups to offer up the trials of Paul. List these next to the list of trials your students offered.

v. 23—more labors, more imprisonments

v. 24—5 times, 39 lashes

v. 25—3 times beaten with rods, 1 time stoned, 3 times shipwrecked

v. 26—in danger from rivers, robbers, his countrymen, dangers from Gentiles, dangers in the city and the wilderness, on the sea and from false friends

v. 27—labor and hardship, sleepless nights, hunger and thirst and cold

v. 28—concern for others

LIFE APPLICATION: Check out the two lists side by side. The list made of struggles today is compiled from the struggles of all of us. No single person is experiencing all of these. (Be certain to not belittle any of the struggles today. Some of your students may have in the past or may currently be experiencing horrific circumstances. As adults, we also have the benefit of perspective. A teenager who has been rejected by a friend can feel like the world is collapsing—not quite the same as being beaten with a rod, but be careful to not dismiss what they experience as a hardship. Our role is to offer gently the alternative perspective.)

In particular, point out that in verse 26 Paul mentions being in danger from his countrymen and false friends. Especially in the teenage years, friends shift and a former best friend can become an enemy in the space of a few months. Paul knew what it felt like to be betrayed.

Ask: How can you relate to this struggle?

MAKING IT PERSONAL: Ask: Have you ever been on the other side of this struggle? Have you ever been the one to betray someone?

Ask: To which other of Paul's struggles can you relate? (Depending on your group, you may want to offer a few moments of silence or quiet music for reflection or to ask them to turn to partners and share where they can relate.)

Close in prayer, re-reading 2 Corinthians 12:9–10. Ask the Lord to not only call to mind weaknesses for individuals but the grace to know that it is in those places of weakness that we are made strong through Him.

CONNECTIONS: Mark 4:13–25

SONGS: "Native Tongue" by David Wilcox on *Into The Mystery*

QUOTABLE   QUOTES :

For to me, to live is Christ, and to die is gain.

—Paul, Philippians 1:21

Persecution—Midweek

MEMORY VERSE:
And He has said to me, "My grace is sufficient for you, for power is perfected in weakness." Most gladly, therefore, I will rather boast about my weaknesses, that the power of Christ may dwell in me. Therefore I am well content with weaknesses, with insults, with distresses, with persecutions, with difficulties, for Christ's sake; for when I am weak, then I am strong."—2 Corinthians 12:9–10 (NASB)

SCRIPTURE: Romans 5:1–6; Hebrews 11:13–16

LESSON IN A SENTENCE: Struggles and persecution are a part of the Christian life.

FOCUS

Obtain several stories of Christian martyrs. These can be found in many places. The book *Jesus Freaks: dc Talk and The Voice of the Martyrs* is an excellent place to begin. You can also check out the website www.persecution.com, www.worldvision.com, or check with your denomination for statistics and stories that pertain to your tradition. Try to keep the stories you choose to no more than 1–2 pages in length.

Ask: What does the word martyr mean?

Hand each person present a story of a martyr. Depending on the size of your group, either have your students share the stories in small groups or take turns and have each person present read the story of their martyr.

As each story is read, make a list of the hardships and persecutions the martyrs had to endure.

DISCOVERY

Have half of your group read Romans 5:1–6 and the other half read Hebrews 11:13–16. As they read, ask each group to consider how their scripture relates to the stories of the martyrs they have just read. Have each group present for the entire group what they have discovered.

Ask: How do these two passages relate to each other?

Teacher's Note: The Romans passage looks at struggles producing perseverance, and perseverance producing character, and character producing hope. After their presentation, ask the group if they think hope can occur without perseverance.

The Hebrews passage covers being an alien in this land—that the earth is not where we belong, but there is a heavenly home awaiting us. How can this bring any understanding and/or comfort in light of persecution and struggles.

APPLICATION: Persecution to hope, we do not belong in this world. This is a tough lesson to consider. The application can come on two levels. For those days when your students feel like they don't belong and that following Christ makes them an outcast, they are correct. They don't belong. We are indeed only passing through this world for a season until we are in our real home with God in heaven.

That said, we do have this season here on earth. While we are here, knowing that difficult times will come can ease the sting of surprise. We also have a role on this earth. You have spent time reading through the stories of martyrs. The church around the world is being persecuted. Take some time to pray for Christians around the world.

Depending on your group, you may want to become more informed or involved with the persecuted church. Look up resources from the web sites provided or do a search with "persecuted church" as the key words for more suggestions.

JULY 31, 2005

Is It in You?

By Anna Aven

MEMORY VERSE:
Let your light so shine before men, that they may see your good works and glorify your Father in heaven.—Matthew 5:16

SCRIPTURE: John 8:12; Matthew 5:14–16; 28:18–19; John 9:5

LESSON IN A SENTENCE: We can only be the light of the world when we are saturated with the Light of the world.

THE BIG PICTURE:

Spending your time trying to be the light of the world so that you can live up to the verse that tells you that you are the light of the world just might be the wrong place to start. If your energies are going into trying to be a good light and a good role model and a good witness, then your focus is not where it should be, because you're constantly focused on yourself. However, if your energies are focused on knowing Jesus for the sake of knowing Him and growing closer in your relationship with Him, you can't help but be filled with His light and thus be the light of the world.

IN THIS LESSON STUDENTS SHOULD:

- Realize where the emphasis in their life must be in order to be the light of the world.
- Stop worrying about their witness and start worrying about their walk.

STUFF YOU NEED:

- A Gatorade commercial, if possible (any ad from the "Is it in you?" campaign, television or otherwise, will work)
- PowerPoint, white board, or overhead with the Scriptures John 8:12 and Matthew 5:14 on them.
- Paper hearts (one for each student)
- Pens, pencils, and/or markers

Teacher's Note: This lesson requires a lot of Bible flipping. It would be very helpful to put all the passages on PowerPoint, or some other method of display.

The song, "Jesus, Lover of My Soul (It's All About You)" would make a great reflection song at the end.

FOCUS

What do Jesus and Gatorade have in common?

If possible, tape a Gatorade commercial from the "Is it in you?" campaign. Or, go to http://ad-rag.com, search "Gatorade," pay $2 for a 30-day viewing, and download the videos off the Internet. If you can't do either of those, then do a Power Point slide of a Gatorade bottle with the lesson's title on it. Most of your youth should have seen the ads.

Break up into groups of 3–4 and have them discuss what the Gatorade slogan is supposed to mean. Questions to get them started can include: "What is the significance of having Gatorade in you?" "What is the company trying to get across with this ad?" "What is the significance of the neon colored sweat pouring from the athletes' pores in the commercial?"

The purpose of this exercise is that the point of the ad is if the Gatorade is in you, that's what oozes out of your very pores. Thus, whatever you saturate yourself with will naturally overflow from you.

DISCOVERY

Bring up the slide/whiteboard/overhead with John 8:12 and Matthew 5:14–16 on it. Notice that the Gospels say both that Jesus is the light of the world and that we are the light of the world. Ask the students how it is possible that in both cases it says "the light." Don't make them answer this. Point out that the use of the article "the" implies there is only one light. If it had said "a" light, there could be more than one. What does this mean? Then have them flip over to John 9:5 and ask them if they see the connection. The connection they should get is that Jesus was the light of the world, but now we are the light of the world because He's no longer in the world in human form.

LIFE APPLICATION: Now that you've discovered the connection between the different "light of the world" passages, have your students look at Matthew 28:18–19. Here's where we apply it. Jesus told us that we are now the light of the world. In this passage He says that all authority has been given to Him, therefore, we are to go and make disciples, etc. Note He did not say that all authority has been given to us. He has the authority, yet we are supposed to do the actions. The only way that this is possible is if we know that our only authority comes from Him. We are using His authority. How does this relate to our discussion on the light of the world? He is the light of the world. However, He has chosen to shine that light through us. We are the light of the world when we let Him shine through us. We use His authority to do what He has assigned us to do. We use His light to shine as a witness to the world. It's not really about us at all.

MAKING IT PERSONAL: This leads us back to our Jesus and Gatorade discussion. At the end of that, we concluded that the point of the ads is that whatever you saturate yourself with will naturally overflow from you. Pass the paper hearts and pens out to your students. If your youth room will allow it, have them spread out and find a place where they are more "alone" (without leaving the room, of course). Ask them to draw, write, or make some kind of representation on their paper hearts of what their lives are saturated with. Dim the lights (to enhance privacy, but leave them bright enough that they can see to write) and have your worship team come up and play "Jesus, Lover of My Soul (It's All About You)" or another reflective song as they do this. After about 10-12 minutes, have them turn the heart over, and, based on what they are saturated with, write/draw what they think they are "shining" out to the world.

After another 5–7 minutes (or sooner if they seem restless), stop the worship team, and tell your students that at this point in the service they ought to have a really good idea of what kind of a witness they are based on what they are saturated with. Depending on the age and size of your group, you can: (1) Have them write on the heart one thing they can do this week to change what saturates them; take it home and put it somewhere they will be reminded to do that. Or (2) Have them break up into groups of 2–3 and share with each other what they wrote/drew on their heart and what they want to change this week so that they can hold each other accountable (this works better with older students then with junior highers).

CONNECTIONS: Matthew 4:16 quotes Isaiah 9:2, which says: "The people who walked in darkness have seen a great light; those who dwelt in the land of the shadow of death, upon them a light has shined." See also Isaiah 42:6; Phil 2:15.

SONGS: "Lord, Light the Fire Again": Brian Doerksen
        "Light of the World":Tim Hughes
        "Jesus, Lover of My Soul" (It's All About You): Paul Oakley

Is It in You? — Midweek

MEMORY VERSE:
Let your light so shine before men, that they may see your good works and glorify your Father in heaven.—Matthew 5:16

SCRIPTURE: Mark 1:14–20 (from Sunday: John 8:12; Matthew 5:14–16; 28:18–19; John 9:5)

LESSON IN A SENTENCE: We can only be the light of the world when we are saturated with the Light of the world.

FOCUS

We are called to be the light of the world. That's a pretty tall order. Who thinks that they can live up to it? I don't find myself being as good a light as I would like to be most of the time. But how good I am at being a light always stems directly from how much time I have spent with the Light. Is there a pattern? Definitely. *The rest of this lesson is meant for small group discussion, so break your group up into groups of 4–5 and go from there.*

DISCOVERY

Remind the students of what was discussed on Sunday, particularly about John 9:5 and how while Jesus was in the world, He was the light of the world, but now that He is not in the world, He has called us to be the light of the world. Then read Mark 1:14–20 and 3:14.

Observation. What is the order of things in these passages? The more astute students in your class should observe that Jesus called the disciples and then sent them out.

Interpretation. What is the significance of Jesus calling the disciples to Him before He sends them out? Play with this questions some. Jesus first calls us to Him and then to the work that He has for us, but the first call is always, "Come, follow Me." This would be a good time to interject some teaching and point out that the disciples' ministry didn't really begin until Acts after Pentecost. They spent the first three years after Jesus called them following Jesus around. Now, obviously there's no set time frame for how long you should wait to be in ministry, but there is a definite point to be observed that the first call was to Jesus and Jesus alone. If we don't have the order straight in our lives, then our light won't shine nearly as effectively.

APPLICATION: *Interpretation. Read Mark 1:35.* What is the significance of Jesus going to a solitary place to pray? Jesus was God, and yet He spent time alone. If we are called to follow Jesus, and Jesus Himself makes an effort to go spend time with the Father, how much more should we do the same thing?

Application. We've talked about how the call of Jesus is first to Him, and then to do whatever else we've been called to do. That call to Him is to follow Him. One of the first things we find Jesus doing in Mark is spending time with His Father. What does your life look like at this point? If someone looked at your life, could they tell you are a follower of Jesus? What are you going to change so that you spend more time actually following Jesus?

Walking Rocks

By Anna Aven

MEMORY VERSE:
Now you are the body of Christ, and each one of you is a part of it.
—1 Corinthians 12:27 (NIV)

SCRIPTURE: 1 Peter 2:4–6; 1 Corinthians 12:12–31a

LESSON IN A SENTENCE: If we understand that we are the church, then we must live consistent lives rather then switching between our "school selves," "home selves," and "church selves."

THE BIG PICTURE (OR WHAT YOU'RE TRYING TO GET ACROSS):
Sometime in the last 10 years or so it became "cool" to follow Jesus, but there has been a struggle with being church. There is a whole movement underway to consider just this subject—following Christ connected in community. But what exactly does that mean and what pragmatically does that look like? While being in the presence of a beautiful cathedral can certainly connect us with saints of the past and the architecture alone speaks volumes about the meaning and focus of those who have built, the church is comprised of the people, within or outside of the walls of any building!

IN THIS LESSON STUDENTS SHOULD:

○ Understand that the church is us, not a building.
○ Know they need to be the church, not go to church, and because of that, there should be no difference between their church life and their non-church life because to God there is no difference.
○ Understand that all roles in the body of Christ are important, not only the visible ones.

STUFF YOU NEED:

○ Pictures of houses under construction for PowerPoint, preferably the same house at different stages. Search Google images for houses under construction. I found a series of the same house.

○ A set of blueprints, or a slide that is a picture of blueprints.
○ Lincoln Logs or Legos or craft sticks and glue guns
○ Something for prizes, like candy, but enough for everyone in your youth group

FOCUS

Start with a picture of a house under construction that is just the foundation showing. Ask the students what they think it is. If they answer a house, ask them, "Is it really?" Because it isn't. It's the beginning of a house. In the same way our lives are not a complete picture when people look at them and our church is not a complete picture when people look at it. Ask your students if their church is complete. If they say yes, then ask what they mean by church. If it's the building they're talking about, tell them they're just wrong. Yes, you will have tricked them, but you'll get their attention. This is a good time to bring out the blueprints or picture of blueprints if you have it. Ask them what they see. Talk about how when you start building something, you have to be able to read the blueprints to know for sure where the building is going. To the rest of us, it looks like a heap of building supplies and a lot of blue lines.

At this point in our lives and in our church, only God can really see what it's going to be. Bring up a picture of a house that is framed or somewhat framed (by that I mean the technical term for the wood skeleton of the house, not a framed picture). Now we can start to see something of what the house will become since some of the work has been done, but we still can't see what it will look like in all it's glory. The same goes for us and the church.

DISCOVERY

Read 1 Peter 2:4–6. Ask them what the living stones are. Ask what the spiritual house is, and what the significance of the spiritual house, living stones, and cornerstone together are. (NOTE: for a junior high group, or a group of younger Christians, you may want to make these questions rhetorical, and teach the meanings.) The significance of this passage is that we are the building blocks of a spiritual house that has as its foundation or cornerstone, Jesus Christ. This is what the church is. Not the building you're sitting in if you're in a church, or any building that they perceive as "a church." Thinking that the church is a building is as ridiculous as thinking that the person is one and the same as the clothes they wear. Church buildings are merely containers for the real church.

LIFE APPLICATION: Okay, so if we are the church, and the building isn't, what does that mean about our parts in the church? Ask them what they think that "ministry" is, or what an "important" role in the church is. If you have a white board, or butcher paper handy, have them write this out so that people's answers are remembered. Or type it up on the overhead, etc. Read 1 Corinthians 12:12–31a. If we are the body, then this passage tends to imply that everyone has a part. There are inside parts that don't get seen, and there are outside parts that do get seen. Generally, the outside parts get more attention. I mean, when was the last time you heard someone compliment you on your beautiful liver? Why don't they? They can't see it! Can you survive without your liver? No. So the liver is a beautiful organ, but it never gets complimented. Seriously, if the sections of your body only functioned based on the compliments they got, then only the outside of us would work. And then what? If only the outside worked, we'd just be pretty corpses. And yet, in the body of Christ we often treat the visible roles as if they were the only ones that matter and if we want to "minister," we think it has to be one of those roles. If we try to function like that, then the body of Christ will die just as surely as your physical body would die if the only parts that functioned were the ones that got complimented from time to time.

MAKING IT PERSONAL: Break the students up into groups of 4–5 and pass out your "building supplies" (the Lincoln Logs, Legos, or craft sticks from the supply list). Have them see how good of a house they can build in ten minutes. Have your adult volunteers be the panel of "judges." IMPORTANT! In order for this "competition" to have it's effect, then everyone has to win! Instruct your judges before they judge that they need to find something that's good about EVERY house, regardless of how functional or how pretty it looks. After you've "judged" the competition, pass out the *same amount* of candy to everyone.

Ask them how they felt as they figured out that everyone was winning? Did anyone feel they had done a better job that "deserved" more of a prize then someone else's? Did someone feel that someone else's group did a better job and "deserved" a better prize then they got? This second question will probably be the one they answer because they won't want to admit the first one. Ask why? (as a rhetorical question) Why do we feel that someone else's is "prettier" or "works better" (fill in whatever they actually said) and thus deserves more praise, when our "judges" clearly found value in every house? If God finds value in every house—every person—and wants to use each of our unique gifts to build His spiritual house, or the church, then why do we insist on saying that some are better then others?

Now, that's the application that they'll apply to church, but shake it up a bit more for them at this point by reminding them that the building is not the church—*they* are the church. And since that is true, that means there can be no difference between their personal life and their church life, because to God it's all the same. Ask if there are certain things that you shouldn't do "in church." After they've listed some things, ask if any of those things are okay to do outside of church. Ask what the difference is, now that we understand that we are the church. Play a song of reflection here and ask them to think about what they need to change in their lives in order to appropriately "Be the church."

CONNECTIONS: Isaiah 28:16

Teacher's Note: The "church" in Acts met in people's homes, not in a defined building, and yet they called it the church.

Walking Rocks — Midweek

MEMORY VERSE:
Now you are the body of Christ, and each one of you is a part of it.
—1 Corinthians 12:27 (NIV)

SCRIPTURE: 1 Corinthians 13:1–13; 1 John 4:7–12

LESSON IN A SENTENCE: If we understand that we are the church, then we must live consistent lives rather then switching between our "school selves," "home selves," and "church selves."

IN THIS LESSON STUDENTS SHOULD:

❍ Work on what it means to "be church."

FOCUS AND DISCOVERY

Read through 1 Corinthians 13 with your name in it instead of love, and encourage the students to hear their name in it as you read. Ask how many can live up to this definition of love. Then read 1 John 4:7–12. This passage says that if we know God, we will love. And yet, we are barely living up to the standard of love as we have just read it in 1 Corinthians 13. To make matters worse, it says if we don't love, then we don't know God. Here's a significant reason to take the standard in 1 Corinthians 13 seriously. It is by this measure that we are judged as to whether or not we know God. So, ask yourself, based on the standard in 1 Corinthians 13, do you really know God? Pause. Now that you are thoroughly depressed, let's break up into small groups and discuss what this passage in 1 John says about love.

LIFE APPLICATION: Icebreaker. How do you feel about the statement in verse 8 that whoever does not love does not know God? Is this an impossible standard?

Observation. There's another definition of love in this chapter. Where is it and what is it? Answer: Verse 10. This is love: not that we loved God, but that he loved us and sent his Son as an atoning sacrifice for our sins (NIV).

Interpretation. What new light does this definition of love shed on the standard that we were talking about before? Thoughts: It's true, we can't live up to the standard set in 1 Corinthians 13; however, this is love, not that we could somehow do it on our own, but that God loved us and died for us.

MAKING IT PERSONAL: *Observation.* There is a cause and effect in this passage; what is it? If they don't know this already, explain that they need to look for words like "therefore" or "because" to determine cause and effect. In this case, the word is "since" in the NIV and it is found in verse 11. "Since God so loved us we also ought to love one another.

Interpretation and Application. Here is another definition of love: God died for us. Because of this we are supposed to love one another. Again, we have a high standard. God died for us. How are we supposed to live up to that? Jesus said in John 15:13, "Greater love has no one then this that he lay down his life for his friends" (NIV). How are we to "lay down our lives" for our friends and family? Specifically, what can you do this week to lay down your life for your friends or your family? Have them give examples of little things in life they know they could be more Christ-like in. Then have them list ways that they can follow Jesus, and show they love God by loving others in laying down their lives for them.

AUGUST 14, 2005

Life in the Crosswalk

By Anna Aven

MEMORY VERSE:
Then he said to them all: "If anyone would come after me, he must deny himself and take up his cross daily and follow me."—Luke 9:23 (NIV)

SCRIPTURE: Luke 9:18–25

LESSON IN A SENTENCE: The reason we find it so easy to put down our crosses and take up our lives is that we are not nailed to our crosses.

THE BIG PICTURE (OR WHAT YOU'RE TRYING TO GET ACROSS):

Why is it so easy to put the cross down? It's easier to lay down the cross and take up your life then it is to lay down your life and take up the cross because we're missing the nails. We're talking about a figurative cross and if we have a figurative cross, then there must be figurative nails. The figurative nails are the little every day decisions that are fairly easy to make, and even easier to pass up. But if we continue to make the right little choices, to accept the little nails, they are what keep us on our crosses.

IN THIS LESSON STUDENTS SHOULD:

- Understand why the Cross has become such an important Christian symbol.
- Understand the meaning of carrying their crosses.

STUFF YOU NEED:

- Three-inch galvanized nails, 2 for each student (There are about 80 3–inch nails in a pound).
- Two-inch galvanized nails, 2 for each student (note, there are about 2x as many 2–inch nails in a pound than there are 3–inch nails. That means you need 2 pounds of 3–inch nails for every pound of 2–inch nails).
- Steel wire, 18–20 gauge, about 18 inches for each student

○ A yardstick or pre-measured wire to use as a guide
○ Wire cutters (1 per 10-15 students)
○ A wooden cross, perhaps made from 2x4s, to carry
   around as a prop

FOCUS

Ask the students: How many of you have seen the show "Who Wants to Be a Millionaire?" *Briefly explain the concept of the show and then say*, "I'd like to tell you about a different kind of game show." *Tell this story:*

The contestant walked out onto the stage of the new game show. There were bright lights in his eyes and he could barely see the audience. The prize for winning had not been announced, but the rumors about what it could be were flying. You see, the host of the game show was becoming really well-known and popular among a lot of people. Of course there were some that didn't like him, but most people just figured that they were jealous. Anyway, because this host was so well-known and so popular, the rumor was that whoever won the game show would be selected by the host to accompany him on his next tour. Fame, riches, you name it, all the contestant had to do was answer two questions correctly, and his fortune would be made! He licked his lips and rubbed his hands together nervously as he took his seat opposite the host of the show. After the usual opening remarks, and introduction to the new show, the host turned to the guest and asked him if he was ready for his first question.

The contestant felt his mouth go dry. Not trusting his voice, he nodded his head. "Okay," said the host, "here it is." "Who does everyone think that I am?"

The contestant breathed a sigh of relief. This was easy. Sure there were conflicting opinions, but he'd heard them all. He quickly made a list of what everyone was saying about the host. "Okay then," the host replied. "But what about you? Who do you think that I am?" Again, this wasn't so hard. The contestant knew who the host was. So, he told him. Two questions. Two right answers. The contestant couldn't believe that it had been so easy. What was the prize? His heart was thumping in anticipation. He had been right! He knew his stuff! Surely some great prize awaited him! "For your prize," the host said, "you will be able to accompany me on my tour." "I knew it!" the contestant thought, "I've got it made now!"

But the host wasn't finished. Reaching behind a curtain on the set, he pulled out a broom and a janitor's cap. As he handed them to the contestant, he said, "It will be your job to keep the trailers that we travel in clean. Congratulations on knowing the right answers!"

Sound hard to believe? There's a story in the Gospels where Peter gets the answers right, and Jesus gives what might seem like a strange answer. Let's look at that story.

DISCOVERY

Read Luke 9:18–25.

So, Peter figures it out. Go, Peter! He knows that Jesus is the Christ of God. This is an important identification. Christ is a title. It means Messiah, or Anointed One. You see, the Christ was promised to Israel a long time before Jesus showed up. As the nation of Israel went through a bunch of tough times, they started forming an idea of what this Christ person would look like. See Israel had gotten carried off from their land. And in the middle of all of this hardship, being captured, having their country destroyed—you know, little things like that—they got the idea that this Messiah or Christ or rescuer person was going to come and get rid of all of their enemies and be this awesome king. Basically, they expected the Christ to kick butt. So, if Jesus was the Christ, then hanging with Him would be really good for your reputation once He did kick the Roman's behinds and start ruling everything.

Point out how the disciples didn't really get it at first when Jesus tried to tell them who He was. We find the disciples arguing about who is going to be the greatest. (See verses 46–50, but you don't have to read them.) Can you imagine that? Jesus has told them he's going to be killed—told them twice! It's like they were standing there going, "I'm gonna be greater." "What are you kidding me? I'm going to be greater. I got more people to follow Jesus then you did this week. I'm clearly the best."

Back to Peter's prize for figuring out the right answer. Jesus tells him that he can come with Him on this journey, but that he must take up his cross and follow Him. What! A cross? Come on, Jesus. Do you know what a cross is? It's what they kill people on. It's what the Romans kill people on. Why on earth do you want me to carry one of those around?

LIFE APPLICATION: Why on earth? Let's break this down and apply it to us. I want to leave you three commands that Jesus tells us from this passage. Listen carefully, ready? (*Teacher: say with emphasis*) (1) Take up your cross daily. (2) Take up your cross daily. (3) Take up your cross daily.

"Take up your cross daily." If you know who Jesus is and you choose to follow Him, then you need to live in the Cross-walk. That means laying down your life and picking up your cross! A cross is an instrument of death. We've made crosses into an art form. Some people wear them as a kind of "good luck" charm. How weird is that? A death instrument as a good luck charm. THE cross was not pretty. It was not something that people then would have ever thought we would turn into jewelry. The cross was bloody. The cross was messy. The cross was painful—excruciatingly painful—painful beyond anything that you can imagine. (*Pick up nail*) Can you imagine this nail being driven into your flesh? Can you imagine the whole weight of your body hanging from just three nails? And this is Peter's "prize" for getting the questions right. (*Pick up cross from side*) I confess, I don't like carrying a cross around. For starters, it's really obvious a lot of the time! I mean, this is one way to stand out, carrying this cross with you everywhere. Draws a lot of stares. Sometimes a lot of laughs. You know, the kind where they're not laughing with you. I don't have to carry this around. I can put it down. See? But then, Jesus didn't have to go to the cross either. He did it because He knew what was on the other side of the cross was a lot better than what would happen if He didn't. See, He'd have lost all of us. And that would have made Him so sad that He went to the cross to save us.

And what about me and you? We don't have to carry the cross. But if we don't, we miss out on what God has for us. Sometimes we want to put the cross down and do other stuff. It's boring to stay in the cross-walk. Sometimes it's a lot easier to run across the street wherever you happen to be, right? I mean, haven't we all done it? Sometimes it takes walking the long way around to cross in the crosswalk. So, what do we do? We run across the street.

We do this with God too. We want a shortcut. We want excitement. After all, dodging traffic can be a lot more exciting then going in the crosswalk. But it's also a lot more dangerous. You can get killed. The same thing happens in life. We put down our crosses and play around outside of God's plan for us, and we can either wind up dead or injured.

Staying in the crosswalk usually takes effort. It's not usually close enough or exactly where you want to go at the moment. But it's the safest route. Carrying the cross means staying in God's plan. But it takes effort. It takes work.

The second point is "Take up your cross daily." This walking with God thing is something that we have to work on every day. When we get up in the morning we don't go out the door without getting dressed, we don't go out the door without our books for school, and our homework, hopefully. But a lot of times we do go out the door without our crosses. Why is it so easy to put the cross down? It's easier to lay down the cross and take up your life than it is to lay down your life and take up the cross. This is because we're missing the nails. Nails are little, but they are what keep us there. See, the nails in our lives are the little decisions that we make every day. The ones that are not easy right away. That's a nail. It's not staying to hear that joke, or going to see that movie, or spreading gossip about that one person when you know it would make you more popular, and after all, it's such a small thing. When you choose to do the right thing, it's a nail. How attached are you to your cross? How set are you in your walk with God? The answer to those questions is answered by how many nails a day you take.

The third point is "Take up your cross daily." You've got to make this walk with God yours. It's not enough to go to church, or go to cell, though those things are important. It's what you do when you're alone. What you do when no one is watching. What you do from Monday until Friday. Do you have a cross? Do you really walk with God, or do you just say you do?

Teacher's Note: In the "Making It Personal" part is where the rest of the supplies are needed. It's helpful to have several people to help you with this: adult volunteers, if your group is young, or just student volunteers if you have a high school group. The point of this project is to make a cross out of nails as a reminder that that is what keeps you on your cross. Set up several stations before the service with wire cutters, wire, and both sizes of nails. It's also helpful if you as the leader make several crosses before the lesson to show them what it looks like.

MAKING IT PERSONAL: Divide your group into however many stations you have set up and give these instructions: (1) Tell them not to start until you say so. (2) Take two 3–inch and two 2–inch nails each. (3) Take 18 inches of wire each. (4) Put the two 3–inch nails side-by-side with their points going opposite directions so that the points are against the head of the other nail. (5) Wrap the wire down the nail and criss-cross it as you come back up to the point where you will put the cross-piece. (6) Take the 2–inch nails and lay them side-by-side with the points going opposite directions. (7) Lay them as the cross-piece across the 3–inch nails. (8) Continue wrapping the wire down one "arm" of the cross. (9) Wrap back up the one arm, and continue across to the other side and back to the upright portion of your cross. (10) Finish wrapping the very top of the cross, tuck the wire under one of the strands, and snip the excess. (*This sounds complicated, but the effect is really cool. I did this with my group, and they still remember this lesson! Just play with it so you as the leader have it figured out before the lesson.*) Have your worship team play and sing "The Wonderful Cross" as they do this activity.

Then tell them: You just made a cross out of nails. It might seem really hard to take your cross, to walk with God everyday. But if you start by taking the nails that come your way every day, the little decisions, you'll end up with a cross. Remember that when you look at this little cross. Walking with God is not about one big decision to pick up a cross: the big decision is salvation. Actually walking with him means taking the nails—the little decisions—every minute, every hour, every day, every week, every month, every year. The nails add up. And if you take the nails every day, you will be carrying your cross, you will be walking with God in the "crosswalk"—the very center of His will and plan for you, which will amaze you beyond anything that you could imagine.

CONNECTIONS: Isaiah 28:16

SONGS: "The Wonderful Cross": Chris Tomlin's version

Life in the Crosswalk — Midweek

MEMORY VERSE:
Then he said to them all: "If anyone would come after me, he must deny himself and take up his cross daily and follow me." —Luke 9:23 (NIV)

SCRIPTURE: 1 John 3:16–24

LESSON IN A SENTENCE: The reason we find it so easy to put down our crosses and take up our lives is that we are not nailed to our crosses.

IN THIS LESSON STUDENTS SHOULD:

- ○ Understand the meaning of carrying their crosses.
- ○ Apply that meaning to their lives.

FOCUS AND DISCOVERY

On Sunday, we made little crosses from nails to remind us that it's by accepting the little nails that come to us on a daily basis that we stay nailed to our crosses. That's a lot of figurative speech, so let's look at a passage that will help us come to a practical understanding of this concept. Look at 1 John 3:16–24. *The rest of this lesson is meant for small group discussion, so break your group up into groups of 4–5 and go from there.*

LIFE APPLICATION: *Observation.* What word(s) is/are repeated the most in this passage? This works the best in the NIV because everywhere it says "know" it also says "how." In the NKJV, it only says, "know" and it doesn't say it as often, but it does say "by this" several nearby.

Interpretation. What is the significance of this repetition? What's so important that John wanted us to pay attention to it so he repeated it? The idea here is that this is the definition of what it means to love someone else.

Observation. John gives two definitions here. What are they? Verse 16: " This is how we know what love is." Verse 19: "This is how we know we belong to the truth."

MAKING IT PERSONAL: *Interpretation.* What is the significance of the statement "For God is greater then our hearts, and he knows everything"? Look also at the context (verse before and after). Regardless of what standard we've convinced ourselves is okay, God knows our hearts. He's put a built-in monitor of whether what we are doing is right or not, and we need to learn to pay attention to conviction in our spirits. Depending on the spiritual maturity of your group, you may want to diverge for a moment and discuss the difference between conviction and condemnation.

Application. Does your heart condemn you before God, or do you have confidence before him? Why or why not? If love is laying down your life for your brother or sister, what will you do this week to lay down your life?

AUGUST 21, 2005

Broken Promises

By Anna Aven

MEMORY VERSE:
He has showed you, O man, what is good. And what does the LORD require of you? To act justly and to love mercy and to walk humbly with your God. —Micah 6:8 (NIV)

SCRIPTURE: Matthew 9:9–13; 12:7; Hosea 6:8; Micah 6:6–8; 1 Corinthians 11:23–26

LESSON IN A SENTENCE: Because Jesus died to seal a covenant in His blood, we can return to Him even though we are incapable of keeping the covenant in and of ourselves.

THE BIG PICTURE:

An important symbol in the Christian faith is that of communion. Communion represents the covenant or promise that Jesus made to us—a covenant that cannot be broken. He made this covenant and fulfilled all the parts because we are not capable of living up to this covenant. We all make promises and break them; we all fail. The beauty of communion is in remembering that God understands that about us so intimately that He made a plan so that we could come back to Him, so that our promises can be renewed and our fellowship restored. That's the personal beauty in remembering Jesus' sacrifice with this sacrament.

IN THIS LESSON STUDENTS SHOULD:

○ Come to an understanding of how God measures our devotion to him: inside then outside.
○ Realize that how we measure what makes a "good Christian" is the reverse: outside then inside.
○ Realize that though we can never keep the perfect covenant, God made a way for us to be able to keep it— through Jesus' death on the cross.

STUFF YOU NEED:

- Communion set-up (even if this isn't your normal week to do communion, do it this time anyway). Important! You need a set-up that allows people to walk up to the table rather then serving it to them. Read lesson for context.
- Two pillar candles for communion table (or whatever candles you want, see Service Options)
- Paper and pencils for each student
- Trash can or some other wastebasket by the communion table
- A cross somewhere near the communion table

Teacher's Note: This service has a different dynamic to it that's very solemn and private. If it's feasible to do the back and forth rhythm between speaking, singing, contemplation, speaking, and singing, it works really well, though it takes some advance preparation and coordination.

FOCUS

God and AIM. Chances are high that your students use some internet messaging service, so this concept makes a great opening to discuss the inside/out versus outside/in approach to walking with God that we're going to be talking about. Say something like this: If you've ever used AOL Instant Messenger (AIM) or MSN messenger and so on, it is interesting to notice that sometimes we like using AIM better then phone or face-to-face conversations because without the emoticons, it's nearly impossible for the other person to get what you're feeling over AIM. You can put a smiley face when you're sad, or type "LOL" when you're crying. What the other person sees doesn't necessarily have anything to do with what you are actually feeling. It's kind of weird, but true.

Sometimes in our Christian walk, we think we can get away with this with God. Some of you might think that's a little strange, but it true. I know it's true because I've done it myself. (Leave them hanging at this point and move on to the Scripture.)

DISCOVERY

Tell them that you noticed this week that Jesus quotes the same passage from the Old Testament twice in Matthew, once in chapter 9 and once in chapter 12. Say something like: Now, I don't know about you, but when Jesus says something once, I really do try to pay attention, cause after all, this is Jesus, right? So, if He says it, it must be important. But, you know, I'm a little hard-headed, so sometimes I need to hear things twice. And He says this same quote twice. It got my attention. Let's look at the first time He says it: Matthew 9:9–13.

Okay, so the quote from the Old Testament is the part where it says, "I desire mercy not sacrifice." Jesus says, go learn what this means. So, I guess we'd better go learn what this means. What is He quoting? Thanks to the footnote in my Bible, I know that it's from one of the Minor Prophets. (Depending on the age of your group, you may want to explain what the Minor Prophets are.) The reference is Hosea 6:6. (It's up to you whether you want to flip there or not. You can explain the context without going to the passage.) And if you read Hosea 6 right before and right after this verse, the context is God talking to the nation of Israel about how they'd broken their covenant—or their promise—to God. BUT, even though they had broken the covenant or promise, they were still doing the outward stuff—still making sacrifices and offering burnt offerings. You might ask then (don't actually ask this as a question: say it), if they were still doing the things that they were supposed to do, then how had they broken their promise? The answer is in the verse that Jesus quotes: "I desire mercy and not sacrifice." See, sacrifice was the outward part, the part people could see, but mercy comes from the heart. You have to be able to love to have mercy. Mercy is when you don't get what you do deserve. Showing mercy then means not treating others as they might deserve, but instead acting in love toward them. What is God emphasizing here? He's emphasizing the inward and not the outward.

LIFE APPLICATION: We can do the outward without the inward. We can come to church faithfully, appear to be worshipping God, say all the right things, but inwardly we don't care, or we're doing it for the wrong reasons. We can maintain the outward, what other people see, when our hearts are not in tune with God at all. Now, deep down inside, if we really think about it, we probably know we're not fooling God. But we're wrapped up in the outward show, and we are after all worried about what other people think of us. It's "cool" sometimes to be "spiritual" at church. Or, at least, to come regularly, and even participate in worship a little, and be doing the things that we think a "good

Christian" ought to be doing. But then we don't really live like it. Or even if no one else knows, we don't live like it when we're by ourselves.

What does God want from us? There is a passage that goes along with the one we already looked at, from another minor prophet: Micah 6:6–8. This basically asks how we can impress God. What do we have to bring him that will impress Him or make Him happy? The answer is "Nothing," if our hearts are not His. He wants the inward stuff first. Do justice, love mercy, and walk humbly with your God.

MAKING IT PERSONAL: So now what? How does this apply to us? Ask your students if any of them have ever made promises to God. It should be unanimous. I think we all have made promises to God. We get in trouble and we do the, "God if you'll just get me out of this I'll…" fill in the blank. We've all done that. We bargain with God as though something we do can impress Him into helping us. But it doesn't work. There's nothing we can do to "earn" God's help.

The other problem with those kinds of promises is that we often break them. Most of the time our deals with God either don't last very long, or are non-existent. When He does answer, we explain away the answer so that we don't have to live up to our end of the deal. Sometimes we just stop doing it, and feel guilty at first, and then we just stop thinking about it altogether because we don't want to fix it.

At this point in the message say to your students: I want to pause for a moment and take some time to think through the promises to God that we've broken. Bring your band back on stage and pass out paper and pencil. Invite the students to spread out and write something on the paper that symbolizes promises to God that they've broken. Explain that no one is going to read this, but if they wish, they can make initials or draw or whatever. Have the band play "Heart of Worship." Bring the house lights to 50 percent and leave them there for the rest of the service. Don't rush this time.

Keep the keyboard or guitar playing softly in the background as you come back to lead the communion time. Say: All right, if you'll just turn toward me from wherever you are right now. I don't know how some of you feel exactly, but I have a pretty good guess that if you came up with even one thing to write down that you're feeling pretty crummy right now. I know. I've done the same kind of thing, and had to go before God and deal with broken promises, and deal with knowing that I've broken His heart.

Fortunately for us, the story doesn't end here. It doesn't end with broken promises. God loves us so much that He keeps coming after us. We created a big barrier between Him and us because of our sin. We got ourselves in such a mess that we could never ever get ourselves out. He would have been totally within His rights to wipe us off the planet. But instead of that, He died.

We take communion. And sometimes, maybe a lot of times we take it for granted. We do it just because it's one of those "Christian" things that we're supposed to do. But if you read what Jesus said when He first did communion with His disciples, you'll see that it has everything to do with new promises. If we broke the old promises, the old covenants, that we made with God, and oh, have we ever! Listen to what He says now, right before He went to the cross so that He could have a relationship with you. Read 1 Corinthians 11:23–26. A new covenant. A new promise. That's what He offered to us by dying. And as we take communion today, we are telling Him that we remember what He did, and because of Him, the fact that we've broken our promises before can be forgiven. So as we eat of this bread and drink this cup, we can rejoice that even though we failed, He hasn't. And He wants us to come back to Him. He died to give you a second chance. And we all need second chances.

So, I want you all to come up here in a minute, and bring those broken promises with you. As you come to the table, I want you to look here at the cross, and drop those broken promises into this trash can and be totally free from feeling guilty about them ever again. But know that you are only free of them because of this cross, because of the body that was broken for you and the blood that was spilled for you. So that you might be free.

When I say come up here, I want you to come. Give instructions for communion and have them come forward, walk past the trash can and drop their paper in, and then take the bread and juice back to their seat to take it AFTER they've had time with God to make their hearts right. Have the band start playing softly in the background, and again, don't rush this; it's powerful. Tell them: As you take the communion back to your seat, take as long as you need. Confess any other sin to Him that you haven't written out here. Thank Him for what He did. Then when you feel the time is right, take the communion. After a while, we'll sing a final song, but there's no rush. Then when it feels right, signal the worship leader to lead them in a song of rejoicing such as "Blessed Be Your Name."

SONGS: "Invitation Fountain," Michael J. Pritzl, Album: *If You Say Go*, Vineyard Music

"Heart of Worship," Matt Redman, Album: *Heart of Worship*, Worship Together

"Blessed Be the Name of the Lord," Matt Redman, Album: *Where Angels Fear to Tread*, Worship Together

SERVICE OPTIONS: If your youth room has a platform and band, try taking out some of the chairs in the front and bringing the band down off the stage. Move your chairs so that they are a semi-circle, and put a table with your communion set-up and candles in the middle of this arrangement. Put a trashcan or some kind of waste bin at the front by the communion table. At the point in the service that calls for contemplation, bring the house lights down to about 50 percent and leave them there for the rest of the service.

Broken Promises —Midweek

MEMORY VERSE:
He has showed you, O man, what is good. And what does the LORD require of you? To act justly and to love mercy and to walk humbly with your God.—Micah 6:8 (NIV)

SCRIPTURE: Hosea 6:6; Micah 6:6–8; James 2:14–26

LESSON IN A SENTENCE: Because Jesus died to seal a covenant in His blood, we can return to Him even though we are incapable of keeping the covenant in and of ourselves.

FOCUS

On Sunday the concept talked about was how God wants the inside and then the outside. The focus of the discussion was that we often measure what makes a "good Christian" from the outside. On a white board, blackboard or overhead, ask the students to list things that make a "good" Christian. If they start into Sunday's lesson, give them credit, but then ask what they thought made a "good" Christian before Sunday. The rest of this lesson is meant for small group discussion, so break your group up into groups of 4–5 and go from there.

DISCOVERY

Read Hosea 6:6 again and then look at James 2:14–26.

Observation. Where do you see the concept of inside and outside in this section? Faith is inside, works are outside. The outside is the evidence of this inside.

Interpretation. Do you think this emphasis of deeds or works contradicts the passage we just read in Hosea 6:6? Why or why not? The emphasis in Hosea 6:6 is mercy, not sacrifice. You may need to explain that these "inner" concepts that we've been talking about from Hosea and Micah stem from a real love for God, and result in action. This is how it connects to this passage.

APPLICATION: Okay, so now we have that God desires justice, mercy, and humility over sacrifice. But we also have that faith without works is dead. Ask the next two questions together. How do we reconcile the two? Could it be that we have put such an emphasis on the outer that some people attempt to have the outer without the inner because that's what gets them credit when in fact if you have the inner, the outer will flow naturally from that? Where are a couple of places in your life where you know you emphasize the outer because that's what gets you recognition when you know that in fact the inner side is neglected? What will you do to change that?

AUGUST 28, 2005

Substance Abuse

By Amy Jacober

MEMORY VERSE:
But take heed to yourselves, lest your hearts be weighed down with carousing, drunkenness, and cares of this life, and that Day come on you unexpectedly.—Luke 21:34 (NKJV)

SCRIPTURE: Romans 13:1, 12–13; 1 Peter 2:13; 1 Corinthians 6:19–20

LESSON IN A SENTENCE: Substance abuse is bad for the temple of God.

THE BIG PICTURE (OR WHAT YOU'RE TRYING TO GET ACROSS):

TV, radio, and magazine ads are all filled with the latest drug to fix every problem from allergies to migraines (not to mention all of those unmentionables)! Alcohol is even more prominent, with advertisers showing dull parties and bored people who can only seem to find fun in a bottle or a case. Whether illegal drugs or prescription drugs, weight loss supplements or liquor, the adults in our culture have too often modeled and taught teenagers that self-medicating is not only an option but the best option. This can seem to be in sharp contrast to the regulations. While there are ways to get around every rule or law, we do live in a country where there are laws about drinking alcohol for anyone under age and about drugs for any age. Adolescents (and an awful lot of adults for that matter) hate being told "to" or "not to" do anything because it is a law. Shedding light on the damage that can accompany this kind of abuse helps to sort through the reasons for some of these rules. Take this lesson as deep as you think your group needs and can handle. It is written for the most surface of discussion, knowing you can easily tailor it to speak more to authorities or specific substance abuses as your group requires.

IN THIS LESSON STUDENTS SHOULD:

- ○ Define substance abuse (both alcohol and drugs, over-the-counter/prescription/illegal).
- ○ Understand that the damage that can occur impacts more than their bodies.
- ○ Realize obedience to God includes obedience to the laws of the land.

STUFF YOU NEED:

If choosing option 1:
- ○ A bat
- ○ Prizes for winning team

If choosing option 2:
- ○ Copies of sketch for players (ideally rehearsed ahead of time)
- ○ 3 x 5 cards
- ○ Pens/pencils

FOCUS

OPTION 1:

Dizzy Izzy! Grab a bat or bat-sized wooden dowel rod. Split your group into two teams. Have the teams gather on one end of an area or VERY open room at least 30 feet long. Have the teams race against each other, with one person at a time running to the bat, placing their forehead on the bat, and running in circles at least 6–10 times. (You may want a spotter holding the bat and counting to be certain they indeed go around 6 times!) Run back and tag the next player on your team and sit down. The first group to have the entire team sitting wins!

Note: While most students will simply be dizzy, there is the possibility of hurting themselves or others. Be certain to have adults spotting to keep the "dizzy" student from crashing into others or the ground.

Debrief, talking about how even being off just a little can dramatically impact our judgment and movement. While this is funny in this setting, being out of control in any way can actually be quite dangerous!

OPTION 2:

Derek's Solution

By Sarah Ware

The scene begins with Lisa and Derek walking together to center stage. It's dark and the two of them have just been kicked out of Lisa's junior prom. The audience can see the two as they walk upstage and faintly hears them fighting. As they reach center stage, Lisa begins the scene, continuing her argument with her boyfriend.

Running Time: 2 min.

Players (2):1 Male—Derek is Lisa's older boyfriend, who began experimenting with drugs right after he graduated high school 2 years ago. Derek cares about his girlfriend, Lisa, but not enough to quit using drugs.

1 Female—Lisa is a junior in high school and a very good student. Although she cares about her boyfriend, Derek, Lisa is tired of dealing with her boyfriend's drug habit.

Prop: Prop lighter, fake cigarette

Lisa:	What is your problem?!
Derek:	What do you mean? I was just trying to have a good time.
Lisa:	A *good* time?! Derek! You just got us kicked out of junior prom!
Derek:	It's no big deal. They just kicked us out. You're not going to get in any trouble, Lisa. Don't worry. Your record will still be spotless after this. (Derek crosses in front of Lisa upstage right while reaching into his pocket for a cigarette. He has his back to her.)
Lisa:	This is not about my school record.
Derek:	Whatever. (Derek continues to fumble with his cigarette and finally lights it.)
Lisa:	Whatever? Derek, this was supposed to be *my* night. (Derek takes a hit from his cigarette. Long pause.) If you didn't want to take me, why didn't you just say so?
Derek:	(Derek turns to answer Lisa and steps towards her.) Who said anything about not wanting to take you? Of course I wanted to take you.
Lisa:	Well, obviously not, since you felt the need to get high at the dance. You know, I'm so tired of . . . (Derek interrupts her)
Derek:	(Interrupting Lisa) HEY! I didn't ask to take you to the prom! You asked me to take you, so I did. Don't get started on me, Lisa! I hear enough of that already.
Lisa:	You're right. You're right! I shouldn't have asked you to take me. I should have known better. I made the mistake of thinking that my own boyfriend would want to take me to the prom. I thought you could go one night, Derek—one night, without a smoke or a drink.
Derek:	Well, I guess that you thought wrong. I have a drug problem, Lisa! There! I said it! Is that what you wanted to hear,

huh?! Does that embarrass you? What do you want me to do, Lisa? HUH? I admit it! (Shouting) HEY EVERYBODY! LISA'S BOYFRIEND IS MESSED UP! HE HAS A DRUG PROBLEM!

Lisa: You don't get it. Drugs have never been your problem, Derek. Drugs are your solution. (She exits stage right)

(Derek takes the cigarette that he's been smoking out of his mouth and smashes it on the ground. Scene ends as the lights fade out on Derek standing center stage.)

DISCOVERY

Ask: How many of you like being told what to do? What is the most ridiculous rule you have been told to follow?

We have all had times when the rules just seemed crazy or ridiculous.

Break into groups of 2–3. Ask each group to come up with at least two rules they would like to change at school. Write these on separate 3 x 5 cards. Once each group has at least 2, trade cards with another group. Once traded, have the group look at the rule written and talk about why it might have been made a rule in the first place or why it is actually a good rule. (Many of your students will agree that the rule should be changed. This is not the point. Try to get them to see the bigger picture of where the rule may have begun in the first place.)

Have each group read Romans 13:1 and 1 Peter 2:13.

From where does authority come?

How are we to respond to authority?

For whose sake are we responding this way?

Why do you think God wants for us to submit to the governing authorities over us?

LIFE APPLICATION: Ask: Do you think it would be OK for someone to come and trash the church? Would you care if you saw a friend drawing on a desk at school? What about drawing something on the side of the church? Why? Is the church any more sacred than any other building?

For a lot of us, the church is symbolic of where God is.

Read 1 Corinthians 6:19–20 in small groups. Have each group answer the following four questions.

Is the church building where God is?

Have you ever thought of yourself as a temple?

If this is true, where is God?

What have you done that has trashed your temple?

If you used Option 2—Refer back to the sketch. Would Derek have liked to be told what to do?

Say: We're going to tie these two concepts together, that of submitting to authorities and you being the temple of the Holy Spirit. For anyone underage, drinking shouldn't be an issue, but we all know it is. In fact, we're going to talk about being drunk and/or abusing drugs of any kind. Scripture doesn't talk about steroids or X but it is clear about the principles.

Ask: Do any of you know of anyone who has abused alcohol or drugs?

Do you think this is an issue we should even be talking about at church?

Read Romans 13:12–13.

Verse 13 specifically mentions drunkenness. Verse 12 calls that a deed of darkness. Why do you think this is? What other things would fit into being a "deed of darkness"?

Is it more important to stay away from substance abuse because it is against the law or because it is harmful for you?

MAKING IT PERSONAL: Each person will have a different weakness. Some will never be tempted by alcohol but are addicted to steroids. Others will smoke at a party or socially, only to find they can't stop.

There are rules and laws in place. While we often don't like to be told what to do, many of these rules are to protect us.

Think of what you do or are tempted to do that would pollute your temple. Create a plan to keep yourself from being in situations where you are tempted. Pray and ask God for strength to not give in to this temptation. If you are comfortable, share this prayer with someone else and ask for accountability in this area.

EXTRA! EXTRA!: There is a great temptation to tell teenagers that the Bible says no one may ever drink. That verse is simply not there. This does not mean at all that we do not have strong biblical support to keep ourselves pure and healthy, not only for ourselves but by the command of God. When I was just starting out in ministry I was on summer staff for a camp. As often happens, the students asked the questions about drinking. We searched Scripture and had a long discussion about what honors God and what does not. Later that day, a counselor came to me furious! She asked why I had not said that as Christians we are forbidden to drink. I repeated what we as a group had read and concluded: that never is being drunk OK, and that we are to follow the law of the land, and as this country says that no one under age may drink at all, the issue should be settled for teenagers. I asked what scripture she used, as I would love to know where it was and would happily apologize to my group and offer the correction. She snapped back that they don't use scriptures for this point; they just tell their students the Bible forbids it, and that I had undone their hard work.

An interesting point is that the next day one of her students came to me with several questions about Jesus. She wanted to know, if her leaders had lied to her about what the Bible says about drinking, what else had they lied about?

SONGS: "Whatever It Takes" by Nate Sallie on the album *Inside Out*

QUOTABLE   QUOTES:

A life of peace, purity, and refinement leads to a calm and untroubled old age.

—Cicero

EXTRA! EXTRA!: See You At The Pole is just one month away (September 21)! Don't forget to find out times for your local school and encourage your students to participate.

Substance Abuse —Midweek

MEMORY VERSE:
But take heed to yourselves, lest your hearts be weighed down with carousing, drunkenness, and cares of this life, and that Day come on you unexpectedly.—Luke 21:34 (NKJV)

SCRIPTURE: 2 Corinthians 6:16–7:1

LESSON IN A SENTENCE: Substance abuse is bad for the temple of God.

FOCUS

Hand each student a piece of lined paper and a pen or pencil. Tell them they have 2 minutes to write down every kind of drug they know. At the end of two minutes have all pencils put down. Go around the room and have each person read one from their list and compile the list on a whiteboard that everyone can see. Keep going around the room, not repeating until every drug is listed. (For some of you, it may be quite alarming how much your students know! This does not necessarily mean they are doing any of these, rather that they live in a world where they are saturated with availability and information.)

Ask: Did you ever dream as a group that you could come up with so many?

Where have you learned the most or heard the most about drugs?

You may want to keep an eye out in the local or national paper for any recent stories surrounding issues of drug use/abuse.

DISCOVERY

Say: We talked last time about submitting to authorities and that drug and alcohol abuse is against the law in this country.

Why do you think it is still such a huge problem?

Do you even see it as a problem? Why or why not?

Read 2 Corinthians 6:16—7:1.

On the back of their list, have each student re-write this passage in their own words.

Take turns reading what each student has written. If your group is large, ask a few volunteers to read.

If God has said we are His dwellingplace and He calls us sons and daughters, why is it that the temptations of substance abuse are just as present for Christians as for nonbelievers?

APPLICATION: *Re-read 2 Corinthians 7:1.*

Ask: How do we go about cleansing ourselves from all defilement of flesh and spirit?

Are there any substances you would not consider to be defiling your flesh and spirit? (Many students do not consider prescription drugs or diet pills to be wrong at any time, not being able to make the distinction that when used under the care of a doctor, these can be helpful. Outside the care of a doctor, these can become harmful if not deadly.)

God clearly does not desire that we mess up His temple, His dwellingplace. In fact, Scripture uses a strong word for this very concept: defilement. Putting into your body what ought not be there is not only wrong in the eyes of the law, and harmful to your health, but the defilement addresses the spiritual side, stating that you are also damaging your own spiritual health and relationship with God.

As a group—

Discuss ways you can be certain to keep your own temple clean.

Discuss ways you can take a stand and encourage others to do the same without being harsh and judgmental.

Pray for those in your church, school, and community who are struggling with some manner of addiction or substance abuse. (Be certain to remind your students to not use names! This is not intended as a gossip session!)

SEPTEMBER 4, 2005

Mercy Me!

By Amy Jacober

MEMORY VERSE:
For judgment is without mercy to the one who has shown no mercy. Mercy triumphs over judgment.—James 2:13 (NKJV)

SCRIPTURE: Matthew 5:1–12, focus on v. 7

LESSON IN A SENTENCE: Those who show mercy cannot be self-seeking!

THE BIG PICTURE (OR WHAT YOU'RE TRYING TO GET ACROSS):

Mercy isn't exactly the characteristic most people want to be known for today. It is most often misunderstood and viewed as passé at best and weak at worst. And yet, God states, on more than one occasion, that we are to be merciful. Being merciful is not a one-time thing. It is a characteristic, a word describing part of who are we as believers. Our actions flow out of who we are. If we are merciful by character or nature, we will offer mercy in our actions. While this sounds nice and sweet, it is anything but. It is not for mild-mannered wimps! It is gut-wrenching, difficult work pushing against the easy ways the world offers. Revenge, getting even, hurting others to stand up for ourselves is much more common than offering forgiveness or pardon.

IN THIS LESSON STUDENTS SHOULD:

- Be able to define mercy.
- Identify places in their own lives where they can offer mercy.
- Realize that they have already been offered the greatest mercy available.

STUFF YOU NEED:

If you choose option 1:
- Bubble gum (enough for at least one piece per person.)
- Sugar free gum (at least two packs, for a prize)

If you choose option 2:
- Fireballs (or any really hot cinnamon candy)
- A penny for each student

FOCUS

OPTION 1:

Give each person in your group a piece of gum. (The sugary bubblegum kind works best!) Have each person find a partner. The object of this game is to see which team can stretch their gum the furthest! Have each person chew their gum, put the pieces together and begin to pull! Give a pack of sugarless gum to each person on the winning team!

Ask: Have you ever felt stretched to the point of breaking? How did you find mercy or relief?

OPTION 2:

How much can you stand? This is a relatively harmless game that can leave your students begging for mercy! At the beginning of playing this game, give each person a penny and a fireball (any really hot cinnamon jawbreaker-type candy will do).

Have each student find a partner. Have students stand back to back. Each person puts a fireball in their mouth and a penny between their lip and chin. Once the penny is in place, they cannot use their hands. On the count of three, the players turn and face each other. The first one to drop their penny is out and sits down. The winner moves to a new partner. Somewhere between the laughing (which makes the penny drop) and the fireball (which can cause a few watery eyes not to mention a bit of drool), keep playing until there is a final couple and a winner!

DISCOVERY

Ask: What does it take to be really successful or to make it in the eyes of the world? Money, power, the right connections—ask for a story or explanation to go with each.

Write these answers on one side of a whiteboard.

Once you are finished getting new answers, write the following on the opposite side.

Poor in spirit, mourning, meek, righteous, merciful, pure in heart, peacemaker, and persecuted.

Ask: How do these characteristics compare?

Ahead of time have two people prepared to read Matthew 5:1–12 from *The Message*.

When Jesus saw His ministry drawing huge crowds, He climbed a hillside.

Those who were apprenticed to Him, the committed, climbed with Him.

Arriving at a quiet place, He sat down and taught His climbing companions.

This is what He said:

"You're blessed when you're at the end of your rope. With less of you there is more of God and his rule.

You're blessed when you feel you've lost what is most dear to you. Only then can you be embraced by the One most dear to you.

You're blessed when you're content with just who you are—no more, no less. That's the moment you find yourself the proud owners of everything that can't be bought.

You're blessed when you've worked up a good appetite for God. He's food and drink in the best meal you'll ever eat.

You're blessed when you care. At the moment of being "care-full," you find yourselves cared for.

You're blessed when you get your inside world—your mind and heart—put right. Then you can see God in the outside world.

You're blessed when you can show people how to cooperate instead of compete or fight. That's when you discover who you really are, and your place in God's family.

You're blessed when your commitment to God provokes persecution. The persecution drives you even deeper into God's kingdom.

Not only that—count yourselves blessed every time people put you down or throw you out or speak lies about you to discredit me. What it means is that the truth is too close for comfort and they are uncomfortable. You can be glad when that happens—give a cheer, even!—for though they don't like it, I do! And all heaven applauds. And know that you are in good company. My prophets and witnesses have always gotten into this kind of trouble.

Say: You've just heard one interpretation of Matthew 5:1–12. In groups of 3–4, re-write this same passage in your own words. After 5–10 minutes, ask for groups to volunteer to read what they have written.

Teacher's Note: While the focus of this lesson is to be on mercy, it is found within the Beatitudes. Beatitude comes from a Latin word meaning "happy" or "blessed." Mercy fits within the context of the eight Beatitudes. It is the mercy, the forgiveness offered when one has indeed been wronged.

LIFE APPLICATION: Say: While we could talk about any one of these, for this time, we are going to focus on verse 7. Blessed are the merciful.

Ask: Have any of you ever been wronged by someone else? If yes, what's the story?

After each story, ask how they responded.

Ask: Have any of you ever wronged someone else? If yes, what's the story?

What response did you get?

We have all been in both positions. At times we have been so hurt and treated so badly that the other person deserves whatever punishment they get! We have also all been in the place of really hurting someone else and absolutely deserving to be punished. God does not work on this kind of scale. His justice is true, but He offers mercy all of the time and calls for us to do the same. (While this discussion runs counter to our culture, there are a few areas where it can be particularly problematic. If you have students in your group who are in abusive situations currently or have been in the past, be certain to emphasize that while we are called to mercy and forgiveness, this does not mean staying in or having to accept abuse.)

In the Beatitudes Jesus says that the merciful will receive mercy. It is in the middle of a bunch of verses that talk about sin (hurting someone else), repentance (being sorry for hurting someone else and turning from this), and then a call for mercy, a call for forgiveness.

According to this scripture, when someone does something against us, what are we to do?

MAKING IT PERSONAL: Say: Think of one person you need to forgive.

Ask: What would it take to forgive this person? How would it change their life? How would it change yours?

Often, grudges, anger, and hate do more damage to the one refusing to forgive than the one not being forgiven. For many of us, we are in arguments and not forgiving people who don't even think of us anymore. We hold onto anger and it eats away at our souls, while that person at whom we are so angry gets to walk away unaffected. While we all need mercy at times, most often the mercy we give others is for our own benefit.

CONNECTIONS: God offers mercy to us every day. His ultimate offering of mercy was in the gift of salvation. Romans 6:23 reminds us that our sin should bring death, but in God's mercy we are offered eternal life!

SONGS: "Rain Down" by Delirious? On the album *World Service*

Q U O T A B L E   Q U O T E S :

Mercy is only to the undeserving. But such we all are made in the sight of God. . . . Nothing can make injustice just but mercy.

—Robert Frost

Mercy Me! —Midweek

MEMORY VERSE:
For judgment is without mercy to the one who has shown no mercy. Mercy triumphs over judgment. —James 2:13 (NKJV)

SCRIPTURE: Proverbs 11:17; Matthew 25:34–36

LESSON IN A SENTENCE: Those who show mercy cannot be self-seeking!

FOCUS

Get in a circle. Depending on your group, your students may be more comfortable going male-female-male-female, etc. Turn to be back to front. Be certain you have enough room to stick out your arms. Give a backrub to the person in front of you. After 3 minutes or so, have everyone in the circle turn to face the other way and give a second back-rub.

It's an amazing thing when you are in a circle. This only works if everyone is willing to give. And for each person willing to give, someone else receives.

Say: There are two words in Scripture and the Christian life that are often used and rarely understood: grace and mercy. For decades ministers have been passing down that grace is what is given and there is nothing we can do to earn it. Mercy describes what is withheld even when we do deserve it. For example, you may not have done your chores, but your family takes you to dinner for your birthday instead. That's grace. Or, you may have failed a test but your teacher decides to give an extra-credit assignment to you so that you don't fail the class. That's mercy.

DISCOVERY

Read Proverbs 11:17.

Ask: How can someone be both merciful and taking care of his or her own soul?

Is it possible to not be merciful (to stand up for yourself, hold on to anger, or seek revenge) and have it not be good for your soul?

Read Matthew 25:34–36.

Ask: What can this teach us about mercy?

Ask: How does helping someone in need and forgiving someone who has hurt you both show examples of the same thing—mercy?

APPLICATION: Every day there are people who have greater needs than our own. It may seem like we have it bad, but there is always someone who has it worse. Often the most difficult people to deal with, however, are those close to home.

Ask: Can you think of anywhere in your life or your community that you know of someone who is need? Brainstorm as a group of a few places where you can identify needs in your community. Come up with a plan to address those needs and offer mercy at the beginning of this new school year.

You may want to consider that offering mercy, according to Scripture, is good for your own soul! While this is not to be the motivation, it's a nice little bonus for doing something good!

Teacher's Note: Mercy is an incredibly complicated but often-used word. It certainly carries with it the sense of forgiveness. But it is more than this. It carries with it the sense of extending mercy, of offering something to someone they do not deserve—in fact the opposite of what the world says they deserve. Mercy gives food to the hungry and a kind word to the hard-hearted. It smiles at the meanest kid at school and offers kindness to those who make fun of you. It is confusing and can be a more difficult task than any other struggle brought your way, because it seems to go opposite to our natural response. Encourage your students to look for ways to extend mercy in their everyday lives. They will need your help in thinking through these issues. It would be a good idea to spend some time thinking of a few examples before you arrive for your time together.

Remembrance

By Amy Jacober

MEMORY VERSE:
Remember now your Creator in the days of your youth, before the difficult days come, and the years draw near when you say "I have no pleasure in them"—Ecclesiastes 12:1 (NKJV)

SCRIPTURE: Exodus 17:8–15

LESSON IN A SENTENCE: Memorials are a way to honor the past and look to the future.

THE BIG PICTURE (OR WHAT YOU'RE TRYING TO GET ACROSS):

Memory is a funny thing. It can be a blessing and a curse. We often remember things either much worse or much better than they were in reality. It's amazing how much better so many of our stories become with a little time!! And then there are those events, the life-defining moments for better or worse, when all time seemed to stand still. These events are so significant that life simply cannot be counted the same after they have taken place. Dealing with them, retelling the stories of where we were and what we were doing, is a part of the fabric of our collective history. They often involve strong emotions that transcend any one person or perspective. It has now been just a few short years since 9–11. We, as a people are not the same as before—we remember. Scripture is full of events within the history of the people that called for remembrance. Many of these were marked with a tangible memorial, not all that different from what we have in locations throughout the country, on the mall in Washington D.C. or being constructed at ground zero in New York City. There is a time for all things, not to dwell or wallow in misery, but to pay attention, to honor those who have gone before us, and to learn from and draw strength from the events we hold in common.

IN THIS LESSON STUDENTS SHOULD:

○ Learn of biblical events worthy of remembrance.
○ Reflect on our own recent history and remember.
○ Learn that God wants for us to remember His work in our lives to draw strength in future struggles.

STUFF YOU NEED:

If you choose option 1:
- ◯ Butcher paper
- ◯ Markers

If you choose option 2:
- ◯ Copies of pictures from the last year in youth group that are disposable

---

FOCUS

OPTION 1:

Before students arrive, have a wall or at least a large section of a wall covered with butcher paper. Write 2–3 things from the summer that have been significant for you as a group—a van with a flat tire, a baptism at the lake or ocean, shaving the youth minister's head, whatever! As each student arrives, hand him or her a marker and ask each person to make at least one contribution of a saying, an event, something worth remembering from the summer.

Say: Looking back over all of the things that have happened, the good and the bad, we have a lot to remember. For most of us, with the exception of a few events, these memories will fade as time passes. Every once in awhile, something so significant happens that it will be with you for life. Hopefully, if you became a follower of Jesus this summer, you will remember that commitment for life! Sometimes these kinds of events are good, sometimes they are painful. They are, however, always markers in life.

OPTION 2:

Gather pictures from the past year and the events you have held. Be certain these are the double prints and not the only copies of precious pictures you want to keep!

The number of pictures needed will be determined by the number of students in your group. At least one picture for each student, perhaps two. Cut each picture into 4–5 pieces. Mix all of the pieces in a bag. Give each student 4–8 pieces of pictures. The goal is to put the pieces back together like many little puzzles! (Tip—Do not stack your pictures and cut more than one at the same time in order to save a few minutes. Even if you are in a hurry, be certain each picture has been cut in a unique way or the puzzle building can take longer than you ever wanted!)

Stories of past events will naturally come as each picture is put together.

Say: These pictures tell only a few of the events from our past year. In fact, some of them are hard to make out now that they have been cut! Our memories are like this. Events may seem to have made an impact, but with time they become distant and worn, sometimes changing over time. There are, however, events that cannot be changed with a few cuts or forgotten with time. These become the markers in life.

DISCOVERY

The setting is the wilderness after the people have been delivered from Egypt. Four hundred years of slavery and bondage have been broken! This victory alone would seem to be enough to sustain the people for life! Unfortunately it did not take them long to complain that the cafeteria back in Egypt had a much better selection. Once again, Moses asked on behalf of the people and God provided. And along comes another attack, only this time it is not of the Israelites' own making; the Amalekites, a nomadic people, attacked them from behind!

Read Exodus 17:8–15.

Say: There are many things we can take from this passage. For today, we are going to focus on verse 15.

Have students get in groups of 3–4.

Ask: What is an altar/what is its purpose? Why do you think Moses built an altar at this time?

Moses named this altar *the Lord is my banner*. Do you have any idea why this name would have been chosen?

ANCIENT PRACTICE: For many of us the only time we think of banners are the one's hanging in the sanctuary as decoration. In fact, many minds have wandered in services wondering, how did we ever decide to hang banners in so many churches? Is it less expensive than paintings? Are they easier to hang and change out? In reality, banners have a long history and biblical precedent.

Banners are markers; they are flags or streamers attached to a standard. Often these are for military purposes, which would help to explain the choice of name Moses gave to this altar. Banners have had three standard uses: to identify a group, to make a public claim to an area, and for celebration!

Teacher's Note: The Amalekites were a nomadic people about whom we know relatively little. They are the descendants of Amalek, the grandson of Esau (Genesis 36:12). While this is the first battle about which we know, the animosity between Israel and the Amalekites continues up through the eight century B.C. (1 Chronicles 4:43).

LIFE APPLICATION: In your groups, think of at least one example for each of the three uses of a banner mentioned in the ancient practice. (Your students may need a little prompting: to identify a group—tour groups often use flags or umbrellas held high so all members may know where the leader of their particular group is, or before particular groups in a parade there will be one or two people in the front with a banner to identify the group to follow. To stake a claim—when the astronauts from the U.S.A. landed on the moon, a very famous picture is that of placing the American flag into the surface. For celebration—flags are waved at games, on the Fourth of July, and streamers are found at New Year's Eve.)

Ask: Given these three very distinct meanings, how does this change the significance of naming the altar *the Lord is my banner*?

Say: Today is a sober day in the lives of who we are as people from the United States of America. It has been just a few years since the tragedy of 9–11. Some of us lost family and friends.

Just like the Israelites, we were attacked. And just like the Israelites, that one day of tragedy set off years of struggle. For whatever reason, though, God instructed Moses to write this event in a book as a memorial. Moses chose to build an altar, not in celebration of a great victory, but as a reminder of a difficult time that began a new difficult season for his people.

Ask: How is our situation today similar? How is it different?
What kind of memorial should we have?

MAKING IT PERSONAL: When we think of holidays, most of our minds race to Christmas, Easter, Thanksgiving, or some other such day. These are happy days—days filled with celebrations of good things! The word holiday is often taken for granted. It is a holy day, a day set aside to be different from all the rest. In the modern Jewish tradition, there is a holiday to remember the holocaust. This is day both to celebrate the lives of those who survived and the end to a horrible tragedy, as well as a very somber day to remember the horrific reality of a chapter in history. It is a day to remember in hope that it will not be repeated.

There are few things we as Americans genuinely and universally hold in common. The sorrow of 9–11 is one of them.

Ask: What do you do, if anything, to remember this day? Take a few moments and discuss what this means for you as a group; what this means for us as Christians.

Close in prayer for the families and friends of those killed in the attacks, for the strife both in this country and throughout the world as the fighting continues. Pray for peace that only God can bring.

CONNECTIONS: Deuteronomy 25:17–18 offers more insight into the attack on the Israelites from the Amalekites and a further admonition to remember!

SONGS: "He Reigns" by Newsboys on the album *Adoration*

QUOTABLE   QUOTES :

Grief and tragedy and hatred are only for a time. Goodness, remembrance and love have no end.
—George W. Bush

Remembrance —Midweek

MEMORY VERSE:
Remember now your Creator in the days of your youth, before the difficult days come, and the years draw near when you say "I have no pleasure in them"—Ecclesiastes 12:1 (NKJV)

SCRIPTURE: Joshua 4

LESSON IN A SENTENCE: Memorials are a way to honor the past and look to the future.

FOCUS

Concentration is a game that requires attention and memory. Give a deck of cards for every five people. Shuffle the cards and place them all face down. Each person takes a turn flipping over two cards trying to find a match of number (or face) and color. For example, a 3 of diamonds and a 3 of hearts are a match. If the cards do not match at first, they are flipped back over and the next person goes. You must pay attention to learn where the cards have been placed in order to make the matches. This may take a little while to get going for the first match but once the first few are found, the game will move quickly.

Say: Just like you had to use your memory to be able to play this game, memory plays a key role in many passages in Scripture.

DISCOVERY

In your groups, read Joshua 4 (yes, the whole chapter).
Ask each group to answer the following three questions:
What happened?
What did Joshua want the people to remember?
What did they do to help themselves remember?

Teacher's Note: Joshua's very name means *Yahweh is salvation.*

APPLICATION: Have each person go outside and find a rock. (If your church has no yard or area with rocks nearby you will want to bring some to the meeting, enough for one for each person.)

Think of one time when you know that God has provided for you. With a marker write a word or draw a picture on your rock that reminds you of that time. Encourage each student to take their rock and place it on a dresser or a windowsill—somewhere at home where it will be a constant reminder for the days when God seems absent, that He indeed is faithful as He has been faithful in the past.

Mission

By Amy Jacober

MEMORY VERSE:

Declare His glory among the nations, His wonders among all peoples.

—Psalm 96:3 (NKJV)

SCRIPTURE: Mark 16:1–15

LESSON IN A SENTENCE: The gospel is intended for everyone, everywhere, and we have a responsibility in sharing it.

THE BIG PICTURE (OR WHAT YOU'RE TRYING TO GET ACROSS):

Do you know of anyone who sincerely prefers bad news over good news? We have good news to share! In fact, believers don't just have it to share, we are commanded in Scripture to share it with everyone from our next door neighbor to the people around the world. One of the difficulties for many is the mistake between sharing the gospel in word and deed, allowing the Holy Spirit to do His work, and turning our good news into the harsh judgmental rulings of a Christian world-view. We are *not* the ones who do the saving. That's God's job! God has been busy reconciling the world to Himself since the Fall. It is our privilege to be allowed to join God in this undertaking. With privilege comes great responsibility. It is indeed our responsibility to not hide our faith but to carry the gospel, even to the ends of the earth.

IN THIS LESSON STUDENTS SHOULD:

- ○ Understand sharing the gospel is not an option for believers.
- ○ Relate to Mary as she shared the gospel and was not believed.
- ○ Identify and practice ways to share the gospel.

STUFF YOU NEED:

If you choose option 1:
- ○ Lists of five random words

STUFF YOU NEED:

If you choose the Memory Verse Activity:
- ◯ World map
- ◯ Cardstock for blank bookmarks
- ◯ Markers

FOCUS

OPTION 1:

Not quite reality TV! It's time for the next great group to rise to the top of the charts—or at least your youth group. Break into groups of no more than 5. Give each group a list of five words. These lists are best if the words are totally unrelated, i.e. giraffe, palm tree, soda, tractor, and radio. Give each group a different list of five words. Once they have their words, give each group 10-15 minutes to create a song! Let them know that at the end they will be performing for each other. The more creative the better!

Say: In a world that often doesn't know how to speak of God apart from exclamations and curse words, our words in sharing Christ can sound as silly as many of these songs!

OPTION 2:

A twist on the old telephone game! Ask for at least three volunteers. Have all but one volunteer leave the room. Instruct the volunteer to choose an activity to act out: skiing, basketball, the more active the better. Once the person knows what their activity is, inform the group and invite one of the volunteers back in the room. Don't forget to tell the group to be silent! The first person acts out their activity for the second. Without speaking or confirming, invite the next volunteer back in the room. The second volunteer acts out what he or she thinks the activity is for the third volunteer. Continue this until all volunteers are back in the room. Remember the key is they can never speak to confirm what they think the activity is! Your group will laugh as the volunteers try to understand one another and mix up the signals!

Say: Just as these charades can be misinterpreted, our words are often lost when we don't know best how to share Christ in a language all can understand.

DISCOVERY

Have your students get in pairs. Have each pair read through Mark 16:1–15.

Ask them to pay particular attention to the characters included in this passage.

Once they have read it for themselves, invite each student to find a place in the room where they can get comfortable. Once everyone is settled, ask what characters they identified (Mary Magdalene, Mary the mother of James, Salome, an angel, Peter, one of the disciples, Jesus). Instruct each person to choose one of the people in the story and to listen to the entire passage from that perspective. For example, what would it have been like to be Mary Magdalene? To be the one who was so sorrowful, to find the tomb empty, to see Jesus, to have others not believe you? Have one of your leaders re-read through this passage out loud.

You may choose to either read through the entire passage and ask at the end, "What was it like from the perspective of each character?" or read through the passage one verse at a time, asking for input and perspective regarding each step of the account.

LIFE APPLICATION: Ask: With which character did you most identify? Why?

Spend a few moments allowing your students to reflect on this question. If it is a younger (more concrete thinking) group or simply a typically quiet group, you may want to offer your own insight first.

Ask: If you could name one way we are to respond in light of this passage, what would it be? (Re-reading verse 15 may help!)

There are many people in the world who have taken this verse literally as a call in their lives. In most churches we call them missionaries or church planters. (This is a great time to offer information about denominational missionaries, missionary programs, or opportunities for teenagers.)

On a whiteboard, make a list of all the possible "jobs" you can have as a missionary that would allow you to go to all the world. (This may take a few creative nudges on your part. All missionaries do not travel door to door with a Bible in hand; they are plumbers and art teachers, medical teams and farmers, children's workers and nutritionists. Missionaries can take the form of almost any occupation as we are called to go into the world and share Christ.)

MAKING IT PERSONAL: Ask: Do you think it is appropriate to try and tell every person, everywhere about Jesus? How does your answer match up with Scripture? What would this mean for you?

Think of one way you can begin to apply this scripture to your life right now. Share this with one other person and spend a few moments praying for each other.

CONNECTIONS: Matthew 28:17–20 is probably the most well-known of passages when speaking about missions. It is the Great Commission! We have been set apart so that we may be sent out. If there was ever any doubt whether we were to simply live in a way that honors God privately or to live in a way that honors God both privately and publicly, this indeed clarifies it for us as followers of Jesus.

MEMORY VERSE ACTIVITY

As students arrive, have a map of the world on the wall with the memory verse written above it. Ask each student to choose one country where they have always wanted to visit and one country from the map of which they have never heard.

Hand out blank bookmarks (cutting cardstock on 1″ strips works well!). Have each person write the memory verse on one side of the bookmark and the names of their two countries on the other side. Take a few moments to pray for each country named. (If your group is mature and accustomed to intercessory prayer, spend a few more moments praying around the world as you look over the map and pray for the peoples in countries far and near.)

For the Follow-up Lesson:

Ask students to bring any current magazines they have at home to the group the next time you meet. See September 21 lesson for details.

SONGS: "Take MyHand" by The Kry on the album *You*

QUOTABLE   QUOTES:

We are certain there is forgiveness, because there is a gospel, and the very essence of the gospel lies in the proclamation of the pardon of sin.

—Charles H. Spurgeon

EXTRA! EXTRA!: Don't forget See You At The Pole is this week! For more information see www.syatp.org

Mission —Midweek

MEMORY VERSE:
Declare His glory among the nations, His wonders among all peoples.
—Psalm 96:3 (NKJV)

SCRIPTURE: Acts 1:6–8

LESSON IN A SENTENCE: The gospel is intended for everyone, everywhere, and we have a responsibility in sharing it.

FOCUS

What is that message?

You will want to bring a few magazines yourself but hopefully your students will have brought plenty. Pass around magazines for a few minutes. After they have glanced through them, ask your students to be looking for the messages that are written both blatantly and in-between the lines. Another way of saying this: If you were going to describe what daily life is like and these were your only source of information, what would you say it is like to live in the U.S.A.?

Say: For many places in the world, fashion magazines, a handful of TV shows, and movies are their textbooks for life in the U.S.A. We are seen as fast-paced, wealthy, educated, playful, excessive, selfish, sexually driven, extremely thin, materialistic, youthful people with constant parties and a handful of unfortunates who actually have to work—and even a few who have to work non-glamorous jobs! This is far from the reality of our daily lives. Whether we like it or not, we are already sending messages all over this country and to the ends of the world. Now the question is, what message is being sent?

DISCOVERY

Ask: What does it mean to be a witness?

Is it easier to be a witness alone or with others in a group?

Read Acts 1:6–8.

Ask: How does this passage change your understanding of the word witness if at all?

While there is much that is rich in just a few verses, the three main points for our focus are: (1) The Holy Spirit brings power; we are not doing this alone; (2) we are all witnesses; (3) we are to be witnesses in our own backyard and all around the world!

Different groups will have a need to focus on different areas. Choose one of these three or a combination thereof as a focus for discussion.

Teacher's Note: Verse 8 offers quite a bit of insight not only for what we are to do as Christians, where we are to witness, but also how we are to live. We are not to live on our own strength, hoping to one day be able to live like Christ. God sends the Holy Spirit to give the power to us that we could not produce on our own. A common excuse for not becoming a Christian is the fear that the Christian life can never really be lived. In our own human strength, that is true! It is not by might nor by power but by the Spirit that we are able to walk daily with God.

APPLICATION:
Re-read verse 8.

This verse states that we are to witness in Jerusalem, Judea, Samaria, and to the ends of the world. If you have maps in your Bibles, look at the maps and find each of the locations mentioned (this is often under a heading something like Palestine in the time of Christ). Jerusalem is a city, Judea an area including Jerusalem close-by, and Samaria out even a little further. The ends of the world—well, that one is self-explanatory.

In pairs, re-write this verse in language for today and for where you are living. Share these with the group.

What keeps you from sharing in your own town? County? State? Country? And world?

Before your time together, get the names of a few missionaries on the field both in the U.S. and around the world. As best as you can, offer a description of the person and of the work he or she is doing. Give a notecard to each student and spend a few moments writing a note of encouragement, a prayer, or scripture for that person. Remind your students that for now, while they are in school their "Jerusalem" is all around them. One day, they may go to the ends of the world, but for now they may participate by lifting up our missionaries in prayer.

THE CHURCH AND PARA-CHURCH

By Rev. J. Clifford Anderson
VP FOR YOUNG LIFE

The first line of a song in the musical *Oklahoma* says, "The farmer and the cowman should be friends." The message of the song is that in order to tame the wilderness territory about to become a state, all Oklahomans need to focus on common goals, not the issues that separate them. My point in this article is to encourage us as followers of Christ to sing a similar song—"The church and para-church should be friends"—not destined to be a hit, but true nevertheless. This is especially true as we look at youth ministry. Our common goal is to share the gospel of Jesus Christ with all young people and help them grow in their faith. The task sounds simple, but the world of the adolescent is often just as wild as the territory of Oklahoma was before becoming a state.

Though there are certainly many expressions of church, yet we all have a decent working knowledge of it. The same is not true regarding an understanding of the meaning of para-church. Just what is this thing called "para-church"?

The term literally means "alongside" the church, and usually includes some form of specialized ministry. There have been specialized ministries of the church since the apostles first organized a group of men to focus on caring for the needs of the diverse group of widows in the early church (Acts 6). These have been called Orders, Missionary Societies, Diaconate Ministries, and many other names over the centuries. Their common characteristics included calling to this specialized ministry, specific training, community life, and a connection to the church. According to Dr. Darrell Guder of Princeton Seminary, the first use of the term "para-church" occurred at a World Council of Churches meeting in the late 1960s as a descriptive phrase for non-parochial ministries.[1]

As Evangelicals became organized and committed to common vision, doctrine, and mission, para-church organizations grew and multiplied in the 1940s and 50s. A few of these include Campus Crusade for Christ, Young Life, Youth For Christ, The Navigators, and the U.S. version of InterVarsity Christian Fellowship. As these organizations grew and became effective, they took on all the characteristics of specialized ministries through the ages, but their connection to the church became more and more tenuous. What went wrong?

After World War II, the church in this country, like every other institution, had to deal with the emerging baby boomer generation. The church had virtually no structure in place to minister to this very new and different generation. The established programs of Sunday school, youth groups identified with denominations, and catechism classes did not capture the attention of these kids. Para-church groups established whole new paradigms. They met in kids' homes. The leaders spent time with young people on campus and at events instead of traditional church meetings. They crossed denominational lines and reached out to disinterested and unchurched young people. They operated camps that resembled teen and college-age resorts, rather than spartan-like camping in tents or small cabins. Their focus was on Jesus and calling youth to a lifelong commitment to Him. Relationships between the young people and leaders was their hallmark.

Today it's a different story. Most church youth groups have adult leaders who build relationships and do contact work with the young people on their turf. In fact many churches are equally as effective, if not more so, than their para-church counterparts. Few churches magnify denominational names anymore. Youth groups often identify themselves in ways that are adolescent seeker-friendly rather than bound to the old labels.

In many ways the church no longer needs the para-church. However, let's recall that this article is aimed at friendly cooperation. Is there really a legitimate reason for cooperation and partnership? I believe the answer is "Yes."

The period we call "adolescence" is defined by virtually every expert as starting earlier and lasting longer than ever before. Most agree that the parameters now are between 13 and 25.

The values of young people today are molded as much by MTV as school, home, church, or any other traditional group. All of us as parents and youth ministers are limited, but not adequate. We have expertise and skills, but adolescence today is marked by very different characteristics. We all know that kids must develop their own identity and separate from their parents. This is the process called individuation and naturally involves the questioning of all values, including those of home and church. Instead of panicking, all of us in the church must come together to reach young people, perhaps like never before.

It's fascinating to note that these same young people have demonstrated a real interest in spirituality. We see this in movies, songs, writings of all sorts, symbols, etc. It's not always the best kind of interest, but it's there, nevertheless. While they may be turned off by parents or others in the church or a specific group, they generally want to relate to other caring adults.

This is why followers of Jesus must maximize our efforts to reach more young people with the gospel, call them to a lifelong commitment to Jesus, and help them grow in their faith. We simply must cooperate, combine our efforts, communicate with each other, and pray together for the young. This process will include confrontation and stating of differences and concerns. It must also involve all of us recognizing that no one church or para-church organization can do the job alone.

The church is Christ's body on this earth, but the church from the beginning has had pastors, leaders, and many volunteers, all working together in different ministries to bring glory to God. I believe it's time for church and para-church to be friends and co-workers in God's kingdom.

---

[1]. Darrell Guder, Lecture given at Vanderbilt University, Sept. 23, 1994 and quoting Dr. Robert Paul.

SEPTEMBER 25, 2005

You've Got a Friend

By Amy Jacober

MEMORY VERSE:
No longer do I call you servants, for a servant does not know what his master is doing; but I have called you friends, for all things that I heard from My Father I have made known to you.—John 15:15 (NKJV)

SCRIPTURE: Mark 2:1–12

LESSON IN A SENTENCE: True friendship takes time and trust.

THE BIG PICTURE (OR WHAT YOU'RE TRYING TO GET ACROSS):
Many students today are surrounded by peers, laughing and always busy. Few students can name true friends they can trust. Sure, they may have a group, but those often change every six months or so. Every once in awhile, if they are lucky, they will stumble on a true, unconditional lifelong friend. Sadly, many of our students don't even get far enough to have acquaintances. Adolescents by definition are self-focused. Friendship requires that the spotlight, at least some of the time, be moved from your own head to that of another. Time and trust—these are the things of which friendships are born. Jesus wants to be that kind of friend, the One who is there when the rest of the world turns and walks away. He also wants to model that friendship, knowing that we are a communal people not meant to be alone. Just as Jesus wants to be our friend, He wants for us to build authentic friendships with one another.

IN THIS LESSON STUDENTS SHOULD:

- Know that God does not desire a distant impersonal relationship.
- Identify ways they can be true friends to others.
- Hear that we all feel lonely sometimes.

STUFF YOU NEED:

If you choose option 1:
- Deck(s) of cards

If you choose option 2:
- ○ Tarp or plastic garbage bags
- ○ Ice cream
- ○ Bowls
- ○ Spoons

FOCUS

OPTION 1:

Table-less cards! Pass out at least one whole deck of cards as students walk in. (If you have a large group, use more than one deck. If you have a small group pass out more than one card to each person.) Call out combinations and they have to try to come up with that combination as quickly as possible, i.e. red pairs, a run of four, etc. Play several rounds as long as they are still having fun—typically no more than 5 rounds.

Say: It would be nice if friendships could be formed this quickly and easily. Someone calls out a situation, you work on a project at school together, or end up on the same team or with the same interests, and you are friends! Reality is that for true friendship to take place, it takes time.

OPTION 2:

A little messier than most and certainly a test of true friendship! Ask for six volunteers (three pairs). Once the pairs are established, let them know they get to eat ice cream! You'll want to put down a tarp or use large plastic garbage bags cut open to protect the floor. Have each pair lie down on the plastic, top of head to top of head. Hand each person a bowl of ice cream. While lying down and without ever getting up, each person must empty his or her bowl by feeding it to his or her friend! This activity brings a whole lot of mess and a whole lot of laughs!

After there is a winner, congratulate the teams!

Say: While this may seem truly silly and pointless (and well let's face it, for the most part it is) there is one thing to be learned. You just never can tell what being friends with someone will get you into!

DISCOVERY

Break into at least three groups.

Tell them you are going to hold an investigation to find out the truth of what happened in Mark 2:1–12. Each group is going to re-write the account.

For one group, have them re-write it from the perspective of the paralytic.

For the second group have them re-write it from the perspective of the friends of the paralytic.

For the third group have them re-write it from the perspective of the scribes.

Have each group present their findings to a chosen panel (either your leaders, guest adults, or a few chosen students). After all three accounts have been given, be certain to ask questions of where they seem to contradict.

Ask: From what you have just read and heard, how would you define a friend?

Teacher's Note: This story takes place in Capernaum. Capernaum is a working town; it is not a cosmopolitan city like Ephesus nor famous for the birth of Jesus. It was a simple, working, fishing town on the shores of the Sea of Galilee. It became the center of many of Jesus' activities shortly after His ministry became public.

LIFE APPLICATION: Think of the craziest things you have gotten into with your friends! Share at least one story of a time when you found yourself where you never thought you would be all because your friend got you into some mess!

Ask: How do you know he or she was a friend? How do we know anyone is a friend?

Are you careful about the friends you choose, or do you pretty much go along with whomever happens to be around?

Ask: What are the characteristics you think make for the best friends?

Write these on a whiteboard.

Say: The paralytic had some rather amazing friends! Scripture never mentions that the paralytic asked for help. His friends knew the need, saw the opportunity, and without regard for the consequences went ahead and cut a hole in the roof of some person's house just to get their friend near Jesus!

Verse 5 is a wonderful testimony to God creating us in community. It does not say when Jesus saw the faith of the paralytic or when Jesus asked the paralytic if he believed he would be healed. Rather, verse 5 says, "When Jesus saw *their* faith, He said to the paralytic, 'Son, your sins are forgiven you.'" God is the one who changes our lives. We don't have to have enough faith to earn His blessing. Jesus was moved by the faith of his friends so much so that He chose to forgive the paralytic his sins and in just a few moments to heal him of the paralysis.

Ask: How do the friends you have display their faith? How do the friends you have offer their friendship even when you are unable to offer back in the same way?

MAKING IT PERSONAL: Say: At some point or another, most of us have had friends go above and beyond for us. There are, however, many people in this world who have not experienced this very often if at all.

Ask: What could you do this week that would demonstrate your friendship to someone even if they cannot offer back the same thing? Pray that God would open your eyes to opportunities and give you the strength and courage to follow through on those opportunities this week.

CONNECTIONS: Matthew 9:1–8 offers this same incident from a slightly different perspective. Either way, it was the faith of the friends that moved Jesus to heal the paralytic. This is a powerful testimony to the kind of friends with which we need to be surrounding ourselves.

SONGS: "My Heart Goes Out" by Warren Barfield on the album *Warren Barfield*
"More than You'll Ever Know" by Watermark on the album *All Things New*

QUOTABLE   QUOTES :

The real test of friendship is: can you literally do nothing without the other person? Can you enjoy those moments of life that are utterly simple?
—Eugene Kennedy

You've Got a Friend —Midweek

MEMORY VERSE:
No longer do I call you servants, for a servant does not know what his master is doing; but I have called you friends, for all things that I heard from My Father I have made known to you.—John 15:15 (NKJV)

SCRIPTURE: Proverbs 18:24; Ecclesiastes 4:9–10

LESSON IN A SENTENCE: True friendship takes time and trust.

FOCUS

Walk through a series of trust falls. If you have never done these before, stay with the simple on the ground fall. Have people get in pairs with others their own approximate size (this needn't be exact!) Have one person stand behind the other person. Be certain that the "catcher" has one foot slightly in front of the other for leverage and their hands up with palms toward the person falling. The "faller" needs to have his hands clasped in front of him to avoid arms flailing and hurting the catcher. Begin with just a few inches of falling. Have the "catcher" step back by just a few inches. Repeat this until the distance becomes uncomfortable for the "faller." Switch roles.

Another option is to have the partners face one another and have two points of contact as they try to lean against each other and create the biggest distance between them. For example, two people facing each other touch the palms of their hands. Each takes a step back still touching palms. Continue taking steps back while leaning until they are no longer able to balance.

Say: These are relatively easy activities to do. Even still, they took trust and a little time to get them just right.

DISCOVERY

Friendship is like this. It takes time and trust.

Have half of the group look at Proverbs 18:24.

Have this group consider the following questions: Can a friendship take place if only one person is friendly? What does it mean to have a friend stick closer than a brother? What would it be like to experience this?

Have the remaining half of the group look at Ecclesiastes 4:9–10.

Have this group consider the following questions: What does verse 9 have to say about friendships? Why is it considered better to be with someone than alone?

Teacher's Note: Ecclesiastes is widely accepted to have been authored by Solomon. Solomon was a wise and wealthy man who knew only too well that the things of this world fade. The general theme in this book is the pursuit of happiness. It is shown over and over again to not be something you can attain on your own. Of course the message is that happiness is futile apart from God, but there are many other secondary messages along the way. One of them is that we were never meant to try to live this life alone. Companions and friends have been a part of God's design from the beginning.

APPLICATION: Depending on your group, you may either want to talk about these out loud or to offer these questions as points to ponder. If you do the latter, put some music in the background and pass out paper and pens. Ask each question giving each person a few moments to think and then write their response. (Assure them they needn't show anyone their response if they don't want.)

Ask: Is it easy or difficult for you to be in a friendship? Clarify—a real friendship, the kind that moves beyond being an acquaintance or simply superficial.

Is it more difficult for you to be a friend to someone or to receive friendship?

How do you think this impacts how your relationship with God plays out?

Read this week's memory verse aloud, John 15:15.

There was a time when a distance was held between us and God. Jesus bridged that distance and says He calls us friend. Friendship is no small matter. It is not to be taken lightly or for granted. It is a precious gift from God and the pattern set by Jesus Himself.

OCTOBER 2, 2005

Who Is God?

By Sharon Koh

MEMORY VERSE:
Taste and see that the LORD is good; blessed is the man who takes refuge in him. Fear the LORD, you his saints, for those who fear him lack nothing. —Psalm 34:8, 9 (NIV)

SCRIPTURE:
> Shepherd—Psalm 23; Ezekiel 34:11–16; John 10:14–18;
> King—Psalm 24:7–10; Daniel 4:2, 3
> Nurturing parent—Psalm 131
> Rescuer—Psalm 82:3,4
> Warrior—Psalm 18:14,15
> Creator—Psalm 74:12–17

LESSON IN A SENTENCE: No one biblical metaphor for God gives us a sufficient picture of who God is. Thus, a multi-faceted image is necessary.

THE BIG PICTURE:
God is beyond our finite human comprehension. Our minds are simply not able to grasp His identity. So, the Bible offers us many different metaphors for who God is. Each one of these allows us to build up a multi-faceted image that gives us insight into His divine character. It is in the weaving together of these many images that we are able to gain a little bit of understanding about who God is. The consistent things we can say about God amidst all these images is that God is good. He is always good.

IN THIS LESSON STUDENTS SHOULD:

- Gain an appreciation for just how complex God is.
- Recognize that, like a diamond with many different sides, God is like a beautifully sparkling diamond with many different parts to His character.
- Appreciate how the selected Psalms reflect these different parts of His character.

STUFF YOU NEED:

◌ A case of tennis balls (or any item of which you have
many of the same item, small enough to be handled and
passed around)

FOCUS

This game is a game about object identity. Participants stand in a circle. The first person grabs one of the items and says, "This is a _____" (fill in the blank with any word such as "ball, pen, comb, etc"). The word used in the blank has nothing to do with what the item actually is (because they are all the same thing, right?) The initiator hands the item to the person next to them as he identifies it, and the receiver replies, "A what?" This goes on two times before the receiver exclaims, "Oh, a _____!" Then, this continues around the circle with new balls being introduced each round. The complexity of the game is keeping one's mind on what is being handed to them while passing on the previous item. Everyone in the circle's chant will sound like this:

"This is a ball."
"A what?"
"A ball."
"A what?"
"A ball."
"Oh, a ball!"

DISCOVERY

The game above is entertaining because it is confusing. Everyone is chanting about the objects in their hands, but they are all holding on to the same object. After a brief introductory comment on how all the same objects (tennis balls) had different identities in the game, the point can then be made that God has many different sides. His character is very complex, and each image we get in the Bible really is only one side of God's character.

After this point is made and student seem to understand and accept it, the scripture references in Psalms can be assigned to different students, asking them to identify what the image for God in their passage is.

LIFE APPLICATION: There are many different images that the Bible offers us to think about God with. Some of them are very comforting:

God is our shepherd, God nurtures us, God rescues us, etc. Some of them evoke some fear if carefully considered: God is a warrior (for justice and righteousness), God is a king, God is Creator, etc. Clearly, there are more images in Scripture than this study allows us to explore. However, if anything, this study portrays just how infinite the sides of God are and how we honestly can spend our whole lives trying to know more about God while seeking to know Him better. If there is one consistent thing that can be said about all the different sides of God, it is that God is always good. God is a good God.

MAKING IT PERSONAL: What are some of the biblical images of God that are easier for you to picture God as? (Friend, Creator, Loving parent?) Which images are difficult for you to imagine? (King, Shepherd, Judge?) When you think about God, are you in awe of His holiness? Or, do you feel "buddy-buddy"?

It is important to keep a balance in our view of God. Yes, He is close and desires intimacy like closeness between a married couple. However, He is far too great and too awesome to be treated as an equal. Perhaps the best "image" the Bible offers as insight into who God is can be found in the living, walking, breathing person of Jesus Christ. His physical existence on earth helps us to bring our abstract ideas of God into a more concrete place.

When you think about God, remember that God is always good.

Who Is God? —Midweek

MEMORY VERSE:
"As the heavens are higher than the earth, so are my ways higher than your ways and my thoughts than your thoughts." —Isaiah 55:9 (NIV)

SCRIPTURE: Psalm 121 and Psalm 139

LESSON IN A SENTENCE: In the midst of acknowledging that God is a very complex God with many different characteristics, it is important to remember that He cares deeply about us and can be trusted.

FOCUS

Ask students what allows them to trust anybody in their lives. (Trustworthiness? Faithfulness? Loyalty? Wisdom? Goodness?) As they begin to list characteristics in the people around them that allow them to trust these people, take note of how many of these characteristics can be attributed to God as well. Then, ask them to note which ones of these trustworthy characteristics God possesses.

Next, ask students to list the people in their lives who know them the best. Ask how they know these people know them. Ask if feeling known makes them feel special and loved.

DISCOVERY

The wonderful thing about God is that He is so immensely complex that it is literally impossible to wrap our finite minds around the concept of who he is. So, it never gets boring to learn about God. There is always something more that we can discover about Him, and this causes us to be more and more fascinated with Him with each day that passes.

If it were just left up to this, the infiniteness of a holy God can be intimidating and incredibly scary. What could a perfectly holy God do to creatures that are sinful and imperfect?

Yet, there are two main reasons that we can trust God: (1) He is all-powerful and completely in control of all things; (2) He knows us intimately and loves us for and despite all of who we are (Psalm 139). Thus, if a God who can do anything and loves us deeply is in control of our lives, He can be trusted—more than anyone else. So, we can look to Him for comfort.

APPLICATION: Ask students what kinds of factors prevent them from trusting God completely to run their lives? Brainstorm with them as to how these obstacles can be overcome. Take some time to pray and acknowledge God's goodness and trustworthiness.

THE STEP YOU'VE SKIPPED

By Debbie Karpinski-Novero
DESIGNER

We are NOT lacking in ideas!

If you have ever been a part of a church, you know members are constantly excited about their ideas: how the service should have this, a great activity the youth can do to learn, how to reach the community, etc. Good ideas are all over the place. Another thing you have probably noticed, but perhaps have been fearful to acknowledge, is that the outcomes of these great ideas frequently fall short. They are rarely as good in reality as they seemed when the lightbulb first went off.

The purpose of this article is to provide a backbone for developing all of these good ideas into great realities! Idea Development? How many times have you skipped this step? Many don't even know it exists. As a professional designer, I have had the opportunity to design and develop ideas at Walt Disney Imagineering for theme parks around the world. This experience, along with many others as a designer, has helped me formulate the following process for idea development. At Disney there is a phase of design called "concept" where weeks, sometimes months, are spent developing an idea, prior to putting anything into place.

Here is my favorite tip: if you really want to make an idea good, you need to research what has been done before. This does not take away the originality of an idea, as many times pride would have us think. By looking at what others have done, we are often provided a springboard from which to launch our ideas. Imagine you are Magic Johnson, standing on a concrete sidewalk. Mustering up all of your energy, you jump as high as you can. You probably made it three feet off the ground—ASTOUNDING. Now imagine you are standing on a trampoline, this time as yourself, not Magic, mustering up all your energy, you jump. Careful, you might go through the roof! Think of research as a creative trampoline. You don't have to be a creative genius to take your ideas to new heights. Besides, it's no grand secret that youth ministry has taken creative borrowing to new heights!

The moment when that light bulb goes off is not the moment you start to implement your flash of brilliance. At this point, it is still a flash. First, you must understand your *purpose*. Not knowing your purpose is like being stranded in the middle of the ocean not knowing which way to head for the nearest land. Purpose gives you direction. It is a compass pointing you to solid ground.

Next, you must define your *context*. What are the existing circumstances surrounding your project or purpose? What are your material resources? If your idea is afloat in the ocean, look and see if there is a raft nearby, any scattered pieces of wood, a rope to lash them together?

Now, evaluate *human resources*. Who is available to help make your idea happen? Are your arms strong enough to tie the boards together or do you need someone to help you? If you are the only one in the water, you may end up having to hold on to the largest piece of wood and paddle on that.

Once you have defined your context and evaluated your resources, your idea may look different than you had originally expected. Knowing everything available, you have a more realistic picture of the shape your idea is taking. You are ready to take your idea further. What do you do with that piece of rope now, and what about that stick and ripped up sheet you unexpectedly found floating nearby? Rigging the stick up to the board and tying on the sheet as a sail, you find yourself with quite a nifty life raft, though not what you first expected. It is essential to revisit the *brainstorming process* after understanding your purpose, defining your context, and evaluating your resources, in order to determine how realistic it may be.

What next? Now that your idea is developed, it's time to see if it will indeed stay afloat as you get ready to dive into the process of *implementation*. It can be difficult to see what you are doing during this stage. So many things can derail our ideas while we are trying to make them happen. Stress and frustration are simply a part of the process. Often in the midst of these things, we lose track of why we are doing what we are doing, or things can take unexpected turns and become disjointed. It can be like trying to draw a picture in the dark. When the lights come back on it doesn't look so good.

How can you prevent this from happening during the creative process? You need a reliable power source—something concrete that stays on even when the power goes out. I call this a *concept statement* or directive. This is a clear premise that is capable of "creatively" guiding an entire project from concept to completion. At Disney, only when we had sufficiently developed this "concept" was it was time to move on to the implementation phase.

Youth ministers are notorious for dreaming big! Unfortunately those big dreams too often become big time-consuming messes! Slowing down, taking the time to develop the concept, can not only save you time and headaches but will bring about a camp theme, a new game, or a room design that is both amazing and realistic!

OCTOBER 9, 2005

Follower of Christ

By Alicia Claxton

MEMORY VERSE:
This is to my Father's glory, that you bear much fruit, showing yourselves to be my disciples. —John 15:8 (NIV)

SCRIPTURE: Various scriptures from the New Testament will be used in this lesson

LESSON IN A SENTENCE: Those who choose to follow Christ are called to an extreme life of eternal significance.

THE BIG PICTURE:

Many people who claim to be Christians never take seriously the life that Christ calls His followers to live. The Lord's will for His disciples is that they live in such a way that the world is impacted by their obedience, their passion, their motivation, their unity and their faith. Christ Himself taught us how to live this extraordinary life and His words describe both the reward and cost of following Him.

IN THIS LESSON STUDENTS SHOULD:

- ○ Be able to identify characteristics of a follower of Christ.
- ○ Discover the life they have been called to as disciples.
- ○ Be willing to make changes in the way they live in order to honor their Leader.

STUFF YOU NEED:

- ○ Pens
- ○ Blindfolds (Focus – Option 1)
- ○ Sports equipment (Focus – Option 2)
- ○ Butcher paper

FOCUS

Depending on group size, choose option 1 or option 2. Be sure to watch your time and not get too carried away with this part of the lesson.

OPTION 1 (SMALL TO MEDIUM-SIZED GROUP)

X-treme Follow the Leader: This activity can be done indoors or outdoors. Before the session, map out an obstacle course and write down the objectives for each part of the course (i.e. walk over the picnic table, under the rope, around the parked car and through the back door). For this activity, everyone will be blindfolded at the beginning; then you will choose a leader. Once chosen, the leader can take his/her blindfold off but they cannot reveal their identity to the rest of the group. Tell students that they will be going on a journey and that they have a guide to lead them. Their guide can communicate with them through signals/noises but cannot use words. The leader will then begin the task of trying to get everyone connected in a line and through the obstacle course. You will want a few extra adults to help make sure no one gets hurt along the course. Once the course has been completed or the task is deemed impossible, bring everyone back together to debrief. Ask questions like:

GROUP: "What was it like to follow someone when you didn't know whom you were following?" "How did you feel at the beginning of the activity? During the activity? Once the course was completed?" "What would have made this activity easier?"

LEADER: "What was the most difficult thing about being the leader in this activity?" "Did you feel like they followed your directions well?" "Would you lead them differently if you had to do it again?"

Once they have had a chance to talk through the activity, say something like, "In this activity you had to trust a leader you couldn't see and follow directions that weren't always clear. Many people feel that way about their faith journey. In our lesson, we're going to study God's Word and see the directions given to those who choose to follow Christ. Even though we cannot physically see the Lord, we can always trust His leadership." Open in prayer.

OPTION 2 (LARGE GROUP)

Play a couple rounds of "Do As I Say, Not As I Do." In this game, the leader calls out a command such as "Hop on one foot" or "Sing Mary Had a Little Lamb while touching your toes" which players have to follow immediately (the crazier the command, the more fun it will be). The catch is that the leader can do something completely opposite of the command they give in order to throw off the players. As soon as someone fails to do exactly as the leader commands, they are out of the game and must sit down where they are. They can act as judges for those who are left in the game. Have a candy bar as a prize for the winner (s).

After a few minutes of this game, transition to the lesson by saying something like, "It's not as easy as it seems to try to follow a leader who does the opposite of what he/she tells us to do. Thankfully, as followers of Christ, we can be confident that our Leader has gone before us and has left a perfect example for us to follow!"

DISCOVERY

Ask a volunteer to describe what it means to "follow Christ." Who else might we follow if not Christ? Where does that path lead? How can those around us tell which leader we have chosen to follow?

Say, "Just as the memory verse says, people will know whom we follow by the fruit of our lives. And when we chose to follow Christ we should become more like Him over the course of the journey. As we look at God's Word, we will find some important characteristics that give evidence to the world that we are disciples of Christ."

Character Traits of a Disciple:

Obedience to Christ (John 14:15; John 14:21; John 15:9–10)

Passion for Christ (Matthew 5:6; Mark 12:30; Luke 10:38–42)

Motivation to proclaim Christ (Matthew 9:37–38; Mark 16:19–20; Acts 1:8)

Unity in Christ (John 13:12–17; John 15:12–17; John 17:20–23)

Faith like Christ (Mark 11:22–24; Luke 17:6; John 14:12–14)

Write the 5 character traits and corresponding verses on a large sheet of butcher paper. Divide students into 5 groups and assign each group a character trait (if you have a large group then assign each trait to multiple groups). Challenge them to look up the verses listed and discuss the significance of that trait according to Christ. Why is it important and how are their lives affected when they aren't obedient /passionate / motivated /unified / full of faith?

Give students 5–8 minutes to complete the assignment, then bring everyone back together to share their thoughts.

LIFE APPLICATION: "Christ, our Leader, not only gave us clear direction on how we should live but He showed us by example what true character looks like. As we follow Him through the wisdom of His Word and through the power of the Holy Spirit, we too will develop character like that of our Leader."

Ask students to name some examples from God's Word of seemingly ordinary people who lived extraordinary lives by striving to be obedient, passionate, motivated, unified, and full of faith. Next ask students to list a few examples of believers who failed at one time or another in these areas? Where they able to learn from their mistakes?

Say, "Though we are all human and will falter along the journey, He is still able to transform us into His likeness. The more time we spend with Jesus, the more we reflect His image and glory!"

MAKING IT PERSONAL: Give each student an index card and pen. Have them write down the Traits of a Disciple and consider the following questions:

Does obedience to Christ come easily and immediately in my life?

Am I passionate about my relationship with Christ?

Am I motivated to share Christ and be a part of His eternal work in this world?

Do I strive for unity with other believers?

Do I live my life believing that nothing is impossible for the One I serve?

Encourage them to spend a few minutes in prayer asking for the courage to live as a true disciple so the world will know they follow Christ.

After a few minutes of personal prayer time, offer up a closing prayer.

CONNECTIONS: If you have extra time at the end of this session or have students who want to study more about following Christ, encourage them to trace the lives of the 12 disciples and the process of their character development as portrayed in the Gospels.

SONGS: "Lead Me (I'll Follow)" by Rachel Lampa (from the album *KALEIDOSCOPE*)

Follower of Christ —Midweek

MEMORY VERSE:
This is to my Father's glory, that you bear much fruit, showing yourselves to be my disciples. —John 15:8 (NIV)

SCRIPTURE: Romans 10:14–15

LESSON IN A SENTENCE: Those who choose to follow Christ are called to an extreme life of eternal significance.

FOCUS

Use this activity to help prepare your students for the Bible study. Keep an eye on the time as you lead this activity.

Divide group into 10-12 students per team. Before class, write each word of the memory verse including the reference, John 15:8, on separate sheets of paper (note: it's easier to use half sheets). Each team should have one full set of words that make up the memory verse and reference. Place these sheets face down on the floor in front of each team and put a small piece of double sided tape on top of each sheet. Instruct the students to wait for the signal then step on the sheets of paper in front of them and using only their feet put the series of words together to form the correct sentence. The first team to complete the sentence wins. They can sit down in the correct order or they can pass sheets down the line but they cannot use their hands.

When the activity is done, lead into the lesson by asking, "How many of you felt awkward trying to use your feet for this activity? We don't often think about using our feet to present God's Word, but in this lesson we're going to talk about how important our feet are as we follow Christ."

DISCOVERY

"As we follow Christ, we are called to live a life of eternal significance. Our character and life choices should result in more people being introduced to the Savior, Jesus Christ. One of the traits of a true disciple is the motivation to share Christ and to take the Light of the world into the darkness around us. Here's where our feet come in: While our hearts and minds may have good intentions, we must be motivated and ready to go where God leads. We must put our faith into action by stepping out and doing what we've been called to do."

Ask a student to read Romans 10:14–15. What does this scripture say about our responsibility to share the gospel? How does it describe the feet of those who are motivated to share Christ?

Ask a student to read Acts 26:15–18. What is Paul's mission according to verse 18? Before he can accomplish that mission, what must he be willing to do (first part of verse 16)?

Ask a student to read Luke 9:1–6. What did Christ send the twelve disciples to do according to verse 2? What were they to do if the people rejected the gospel according to verse 5? Does the fact that some people will refuse to accept Christ as Savior excuse us from *going* into the world and preaching the gospel?

"Our feet symbolize our motivation to go where He leads, to follow His commands, to take His Word to those who have not heard. Until we are willing to put feet to our faith, we cannot live eternally significant lives."

LIFE APPLICATION: Ask students to list some reasons why it's difficult to step out and share the gospel. Ask them to consider some ways they as a youth group can take the Light of Christ into their community.

PERSONAL APPLICATION: Ask students to look back over Romans 10:14–15. Encourage them to spend a few minutes considering these questions:

Am I motivated to share Christ or do I assume someone else will do it?

Are my feet quick to follow Christ's example or do I try to make my own way?

Can the world tell that I am a follower of Christ?

After a few minutes of reflection, close this time in prayer.

OCTOBER 16, 2005

Is Anybody Out There?

By Sharon Koh

MEMORY VERSE:
The LORD himself goes before you and will be with you; he will never leave you nor forsake you. Do not be afraid; do not be discouraged. —Deuteronomy 31:8 (NIV)

SCRIPTURE: Genesis 37, 39 – 48 (The story of Joseph)

LESSON IN A SENTENCE: Even in our loneliest of moments, God is there.

THE BIG PICTURE:

Many of us have lonely times when we feel like nobody cares about how we are doing or whether we are even alive. Sometimes, these moments are so emotionally dark that we even doubt if God remembers us. This is probably how Joseph felt in prison. His dreams (of Genesis 37) were a distant memory, and his daily life showed no hope of ever being vindicated for a wrong that he was not responsible for. His own brothers had gotten him into this predicament, and it did not seem like there was any hope of ever getting out or being noticed by the outside world. Yet, as the story of Joseph's life unfolds, it becomes evident that God *was* thinking about Joseph. As a matter of fact, God had great plans for Joseph's life and God never left Joseph.

IN THIS LESSON STUDENTS SHOULD:

- ○ Honestly identify the times in their lives when they felt completely alone in the world. Perhaps some of the students are currently going through such a time as this.
- ○ Understand that God is with them in these times as well as in the times when life is going well and feeling "blessed."
- ○ Develop an understanding that God is ever-present in a comforting and loving way, even if it doesn't *feel* like it.

STUFF YOU NEED:

- ○ A facility large enough to play hide-and-go-seek safely

FOCUS

Sardines-in-the-dark: This games works somewhat like hide-and-go-seek except that only one person hides and the rest of the people are "seekers." At the beginning of the game, the person designated to "hide" is sent out to find their hiding place. After they are given a minute or so to hide, the rest of the group looks for them. When they find the person hiding, they hide *with* them. As the game goes on, the group of people hiding grows bigger and bigger, and the number of people wandering around looking for the group gets smaller and smaller. After a few rounds of this game (which is often more fun to play in the dark), an interesting conversation can be sparked about the "scary" and lonely moments of the game (such as when they were hiding by themselves waiting for people to find them or when they realize that they are the last person left still "seeking").

DISCOVERY

After playing sardines-in-the-dark, have the students talk about feelings of loneliness. Allow them to speak of the moments in the game when they felt alone in the dark, and ask them to think of other times in their lives when they have felt alone emotionally and physically. For some of them, this loneliness can still be felt even in the midst of a lot of people. Try to get them to talk about what makes a person feel lonely.

Then, carefully consider the Joseph story in Genesis 37, 39–48, taking special notice of the times when Joseph would have felt the loneliest (e.g. in the cistern, after he had been sold as a slave by his brothers, trying to defend his honor against Potiphar's wife's accusations, in prison, etc.

Was Joseph *actually* alone at these times of his life? How do we know that God was with him all along?

When we feel completely alone, is there anybody out there who cares about us? How can we be sure that God is with us? (See memory verse.)

LIFE APPLICATION: There are many moments in our lives when we feel lonely. Joseph's story includes many moments when he was probably feeling lonely. Some of those moments were when he was actually alone (like in prison). Other times, he might have felt alone even though he was surrounded by people (such as when his brothers did not recognize him because he was such a powerful Egyptian leader and he wept from the emotion of it all). In all of these times, God was with Joseph.

In our loneliest moments, when it feels like nobody else notices and nobody else cares, God is there. He remembers us and feels with us. His empathy comes from caring deeply about whether each one of his precious children knows He is present in their lives. God is always there —in the midst of the hustle and bustle, in the midst of insecurity, in the midst of feeling rejected and unaccepted.

Is there anybody out there who cares? Yes. God cares enough to say, "I will never leave you nor forsake you."

MAKING IT PERSONAL: Have students think of times when they have known loneliness, and then help them to picture that and accept that God was with them in the midst of all of it. Being alone does not necessarily make a person "lonely." Allow the students time to reflect and be comforted by the idea that they never have to be completely alone. There really is Someone out there.

OPTIONS: Since the Bible reading for this lesson is somewhat long, perhaps the students can have the option of reenacting the story of Joseph's life to "spice up" the telling of the details in his life. This way, it is easier for them to identify with lonely times in his life because it will be easier for them to visualize the emotions he was feeling at different points in his life.

Is Anybody Out There? —Midweek

MEMORY VERSE:
The LORD himself goes before you and will be with you; he will never leave you nor forsake you. Do not be afraid; do not be discouraged. —Deuteronomy 31:8 (NIV)

SCRIPTURE: 1 Kings 17:1–24 (Elijah)

LESSON IN A SENTENCE: God is present and provides for us during times in our lives when it *feels* like there is nobody there for us.

FOCUS

Have you ever regretted doing the right thing because it got you into trouble with "powerful" people? Ask students to describe by writing on a piece of paper one time in their lives when this happened and they felt like God was not present. When have they felt abandoned by the Lord in the midst of doing what He asked of them? Then, ask them to fold the piece of paper up and listen to the story of Elijah in 1 Kings 17. This king of Israel was very angry at Elijah, and this was scary because the king had a lot of power over the nation and therefore over Elijah's life. Elijah himself was simply doing what God had asked him to do.

DISCOVERY

Here Elijah experiences two supernatural incidents when God provided for him at a time when he was in trouble with "higher ups" for doing what God told him to do. As the students listen to and read the story in 1 Kings 17, ask them to note the ways that God affirmed what Elijah had done. How did God show His favor and protection upon Elijah's life?

APPLICATION: If students are willing to share, ask them to talk about the difficult situations that they wrote on the pieces of paper. Perhaps they stood up for someone being picked on by a bully and received the redirection of hostilities. Perhaps they insisted on attending a church when their non-Christians parents frowned upon religion. Ask these same students if they saw God affirming them and providing for them in the midst of the situation. Was it supernatural in any way? How do their stories parallel Elijah's in 1 Kings 17?

In conclusion, encourage them to continue to expect God to take care of them when they are doing His will. In the midst of acknowledging this promise of God's, ask students if it strengthens them to stand tall in Jesus' name in the time of adversity. Assure them that God *is* with them even when they feel alone.

Justice for All

By Amy Jacober

MEMORY VERSE:

To do righteousness and justice is more acceptable to the LORD than sacrifice.—Proverbs 21:3 (NKJV)

SCRIPTURE: Exodus 3:1–12

LESSON IN A SENTENCE: We are called to actively seek justice.

THE BIG PICTURE (OR WHAT YOU'RE TRYING TO GET ACROSS):

Issues of justice are at the center of conversations every day. Students talk about the injustice they see on the news or the injustice they experienced in class that week after taking a test that had nothing on it for which they had studied! Interestingly, most teenagers are quite good at noticing global or distant injustice and injustice in their own lives but when it comes to those right near them they are often blind. God promises to take care of us and be our deliverer. God's goal is always reconciliation. In a fragmented and broken world, God helps us to move toward this through His perfect balance of justice and mercy. Likewise, we are to follow His example.

IN THIS LESSON STUDENTS SHOULD:

- Begin to define justice and injustice in biblical terms.
- Distinguish one place in their life where they can seek justice.
- Describe what it looks like to seek justice locally and globally.

STUFF YOU NEED:

- Newspapers and/or news magazines
- *The Prince of Egypt* DVD or video

FOCUS

OPTION 1:

Have your group sit in a circle. Ask for one volunteer who will step outside. While that person is outside, choose one person to be the "leader." That person will become the trendsetter. He or she will choose different movements, i.e., tapping fingers, snapping, or crossing legs. As the "leader" changes position, so must every other person. These movements will begin as soon as the volunteer is back in the room. The object of the game is to try and catch who is the trendsetter. Play for 3–4 rounds.

Say: Have you ever noticed how easy it is to be left out when you don't know where to focus? Still, it does not take long to catch up and blend in. At least if you are given the opportunity to blend in. And it depends on the circumstances. There are some times and places where no matter how hard we try, we simply cannot blend in. What we often forget is that there are others who would love to blend in with us and simply cannot.

OPTION 2:

Show a clip from *The Prince of Egypt*. (While many of your students will have seen this years ago, the animation offers fresh perspectives to the story.) Cue the DVD or video for the scene showing the call of Moses from the burning bush.

DISCOVERY

If you show the video, once the scene is done, have three people ready to read Exodus 3:1–12. (If you don't show the video go straight into this after the game. One person will take the part of narrator, a second the part of Moses, and a third the part of God. (You will want to have chosen these three ahead of time and given them time to practice the reading. Be certain they are all using the same translation of Scripture.)

Finally, ask your students to turn in their own Bibles to Exodus 3:1–12. Ask them to read it for themselves while looking for how God chose to deliver His people.

Ask: From what was God delivering the people of Israel?

How did God choose to deliver the people of Israel?

Teacher's Note: In our world we most often think of justice in relation to the criminal court system or at least in a way that discusses getting back at someone for a wrong done, a crime committed. The Bible has a richer understanding of justice. In the Old Testament it is related to God's righteousness, His *sedaqa*. Laws are not set in place to confine but to protect. They are a reminder that in God's righteousness we are to follow the law as a covenant relationship. Justice is then more about maintaining and restoring relationships than punishing anyone. We are able to "do justice" when we are obedient to God, love others and care for creation. All of these working together help to maintain healthy relationships in covenant with God.

LIFE APPLICATION: Say: We live in a sinful and broken world. There are times where the sins of others make life difficult if not unbearable for the innocent. This was the case when God delivered the Israelites out of Egypt. We often do not discuss that God created the Egyptians as well. Pharoah too was created in the image of God. His choices however were not righteous, they were not just in the biblical sense.

Bring in newspapers and/or news magazines from the past few weeks.

Ask your students to go through these looking for any story that may convey an injustice. You may need to help them move beyond the obvious of war and crimes in the headlines.

Ask: What injustices do you see in this world? With what other injustices are you familiar?

MAKING IT PERSONAL: Say: Thinking about injustice in this world can be overwhelming! While we can't fix everything, we can play a part.

(You will need to do some preparation before this!) Choose from one of several justice-oriented ministries...World Vision, Compassion International, Samaritan's Purse or check with your local denominational office. Each of these offers several ways to be involved, from letter-writing to updates for prayer. These are ministries that cannot continue without the support of other Christians around the country and world.

CONNECTIONS: Proverbs 14:31 offers a concise but clear message on our role in oppression and what it does to our relationship with God.

SONGS: "Glory Defined" by Building 429 on the album *Building 429*
         "All" by Avalon on the album *The Creed*

QUOTABLE   QUOTES :

Justice is not a case of the "haves" giving to the "have nots." This is far too unworthy and shallow an inter-pretation of God's intent for us. We must recognize that all people are our brothers and sisters . . . we are all members of God's family. We would want the best for our family . . . it is our responsibility as part of being God's children to actively make God's Kingdom come on earth.

—Desmond Tutu

Justice for All —Midweek

MEMORY VERSE:
To do righteousness and justice is more acceptable to the LORD than sacrifice.—Proverbs 21:3 (NKJV)

SCRIPTURE: Micah 6:6–8

LESSON IN A SENTENCE: We are called to actively seek justice.

FOCUS

So how hard can it be to drink a glass of water?

Ask for two volunteers to sit across a table from one another and see who can finish their glass of water first. The catch! Each is given not only a large glass of water but a candle and a box of matches. They are only able to drink when their candle is lit. Their only three options are to drink their water, blow out the candle of the other person, or light their own candle.

Say: Our world has us set up to look out for our own good. While it is not bad to take care of yourself, the Bible tells us it is not to be at the expense of others.

DISCOVERY

Read Micah 6:6–8.

The Message puts it this way...

How can I stand up before GOD
    and show proper respect to the high God?
Should I bring an armload of offerings
    topped off with yearling calves?
Would GOD be impressed with thousands of rams,
    with buckets and barrels of olive oil?
Would he be moved if I sacrificed my firstborn child,
    my precious baby, to cancel my sin?
But he's already made it plain how to live, what to do,
    what GOD is looking for in men and women.
It's quite simple: Do what is fair and just to your neighbor,
    be compassionate and loyal in your love,
And don't take yourself too seriously—
    take God seriously.

After reading this version from *The Message*, invite your students to write their own adaptation that is relevant for them in their world.

Teacher's Note: Micah indeed was a prophet. He was for the downtrodden and exploited in a society filled with injustice, corrupt rulers, false prophets, and ungodly priests. In particular it is a book with a repeated message speaking against and calling others to be against those who impose their power on the poor and weak for their own gain.

Micah prophesies not to crush anyone but to point out the judgment that will be a consequence of their actions and ideally to encourage change that would lead to restoration.

APPLICATION: Say: As Christians we often get caught up in what we sacrifice and give up to follow Jesus and forget that God actually calls us to something much higher.

Look back at this week's memory verse. Sacrifice is not enough; we are to do righteousness. It's not about what we don't have or what we give up (a passive approach) but what we do choose to have or what actions we take (an active approach).

Make a list of as many daily things you can consider that would be a way for you to work toward justice. To get things started think of your own examples or try these: Do you buy your clothes from companies that pay fair wages and do not exploit their workers? Do you donate to charities that only work toward the things of God? Do you look for others at your school who may be left out of social circles and invite them to be your friend?

Ask: What one thing can you do (actively) to work for justice or righteousness right here in your own daily life?

OCTOBER 30, 2005

The Powers that Be

By Amy Jacober

MEMORY VERSE:

For we do not wrestle against flesh and blood, but against principalities, against powers, against the rulers of the darkness of this age, against spiritual hosts of wickedness in the heavenly places.—Ephesians 6:12 (NKJV)

SCRIPTURE: Ephesians 4:11–15

LESSON IN A SENTENCE: Our true enemies are not other people.

THE BIG PICTURE (OR WHAT YOU'RE TRYING TO GET ACROSS):

There is much talk around the subject of spirituality today. The problem is, what is meant by spirituality has to be clarified with each new discussion. There is little denying that we are spiritual beings. What this means exactly is a whole other story! Even for some Christians. There is a love affair with prayer and centering and candles but little talk of doctrine or beliefs, let alone Jesus. And then there are those who proudly let the world know at their church they follow the Bible. This of course is wonderful and what we ought to be doing, but for some, it is a badge of honor to put others down in judgment, not simply a description. Christians have been at odds with one another for centuries. We are certainly often at odds with the world around us. We seem to love a fight! And yet, Scripture tells us that this is not a battle against flesh and blood. We too quickly condemn people and allow division amongst ourselves rather than humbling ourselves and praying together, acknowledging there is something greater at work around us!

IN THIS LESSON STUDENTS SHOULD:

○ Learn that false teachings don't always seems false.
○ Recognize that spiritual warfare is real.
○ Find hope in the gifting of the body of Christ for His glory.

STUFF YOU NEED:

If you choose option 1:
  ○ A roll of toilet paper
If you choose option 2:
  ○ Pumpkins
  ○ Old bowling pins
  ○ A tub or large bucket for bobbing
  ○ Water for bobbing
  ○ Items for bobbing (apples, marshmallows etc.)

FOCUS

OPTION 1:

Wind in your sail! So you think you have a lot of hot air in your group? Break your students into teams of 3–4. Give each team a square of toilet paper. The object of the game is to see which team can keep the sheet in the air the longest. They may use their hands only at the very beginning and then must hold their arms behind their backs, finding every other creative way to keep it afloat the longest!

Say: Sometimes our beliefs can be blown around just as easily as the sheet in this game. When we least suspect in and without realizing it, this world is constantly trying to move us off course.

OPTION 2:

OK, these are purely for fun and more in step with the season than the lesson!

Pumpkin Bowling

Stop by a local bowling alley before you meet this time and ask if you can have any old chipped or discarded pins. Ideally get at least 10. If you have a large group, you will want to have more. Bring a few pumpkins, set up the pins, and take turns with a little bowling tournament!

Bobbing for...

While some are bowling, offer an alternative activity as a twist on the old harvest time favorite, bobbing for apples. You may begin with apples but offer alternatives along the way such as marshmallows, candy bars, anything that floats! (You will want to experiment with a few items before your meeting time arrives.)

DISCOVERY

Break into as many groups as you have adult leaders. Be certain there is one adult leader in each group. Read Ephesians 4:11–15.

Ask: What are the roles God has given to some people?

Why are those roles given?

What does it mean to be "carried about with every wind of doctrine"?

What does it mean to speak the truth in love?

With Halloween being tomorrow and the focus of this time being about the battles not with flesh and blood, this is a great time for really having some great discussions with your students. Many of their questions you may not be able to answer. With an adult in each group, however, many of the lies and rumors surrounding the devil and his demons can be set aside. Satan is often portrayed as a scary monster ready to pounce. In some ways this is true, but he is crafty—he fights in subtle ways. He uses others and deceives through false doctrines. Even scarier is that over history, these false doctrines sound true as Scripture is used, but they become half truths distorted for the devil's own desires.

Teacher's Note: Spiritual warfare is a delicate topic in most churches. In the modern western church the Pentecostal tradition is the most comfortable with this topic. The modern church has a history of admitting that there is evil and sinful people fulfill the role of evil but that demons or other spiritual powers may or may not actually exist. There has been a resurgence of dialogue and investigation over the last 30 years, but each tradition and local church tends to land in slightly different places. It would be wise to check with the other leaders in your church and/or association, conference or presbytery for your traditions viewpoint so that you are not speaking out of turn and creating a point of confusion.

LIFE APPLICATION: Say: A common one in the last decade or so is the health and wealth gospel. They use Scripture, they preach with passion, and look clean-cut and very mainstream. When you listen to the words being spoken, however, the doctrine is that God loves us so much he wants for us to be happy—meaning healthy and wealthy. Sounds good up to this point! Scripture does talk about abundant life! But then, if you keep listening, it is said that if your faith is strong enough, you will be wealthy, your bank account literally will increase. It says those with faith will not be ill or have any malady or disability, at least not for long. This message is not only unable to hold up against all of Scripture, but it sends a terrible message for those who have lost a job and are struggling financially. It tells the person with cancer it is their fault they are still sick.

Ask: What do you think of this teaching?

Make a list with the group of every cult or false teaching they can name.

Ask: How do you know these are false doctrines?

Ask: Why is it so easy for false doctrines to lead us astray?

Say: Some things seem harmless and like no big deal! Even these can be dangerous. As soon as you are comfortable thinking something is no big deal, the opportunity for it to be used against you and God is present.

Ask: How do we protect ourselves from being led about by every new wind of doctrine?

MAKING IT PERSONAL: We have all been taken in at some point or another by a false teaching. The difference is that we do not become consumed by this and led away from God. Spend some time in prayer asking God to protect your heart and mind from false teachings.

Pray for those who are already deeply involved in false teachings and living a deceived life. Remember, the enemy is not the person; it is the deceiver himself.

ANCIENT PRACTICE: Prayer relay:

Many churches have prayer ministries. If you have one, you may want to partner with them. If you do not, this is a great opportunity for your student ministry to take the lead on an important time for you and your church. Host a 24-hour prayer covering. Choose a date in the near future and schedule ½ hour slots for prayer. Encourage your students to sign up well ahead of time. You may choose to either hold a joint prayer covering with students and adults in the church sharing a 24-hour time period, or if your group is large enough, have both the students and adults sign up to simultaneously cover the 24-hours in prayer. For each time, sign up with a name and a phone number at which the person may be reached at that time. Shortly before the day arrives, be certain each person has the name and contact information for the person who is to follow them. After the first person prays, she calls the second person to remind him it is his turn. After the second person prays, he calls the third and so on for the entire 24-hour period. Be certain that you touch base with parents for all who will participate and in particular for those who sign up for times late at night or early in the morning.

You may want to create a list of prayer requests and specific needs for those uncertain how to fill 30 minutes with prayer. Print the memory verse at the top of the sheet to remind all that our battles indeed are not against others of this world but against spiritual powers.

CONNECTIONS: Satan is so often thought to be ugly and scary in appearance that we forget to associate him with more subtle evil and deception. In 2 Corinthians 11:14 he is seen as an angel of light. In Matthew 4:6 he misuses Scripture. First Peter 5:8 reminds us that it is the devil who is our adversary.

SONGS: "Gonna Be Alright" by LA Symphony
"Word of God Speak" by MercyMe on the album *Spoken For*

EXTRA! EXTRA!: In the church calendar, this is known as Reformation Sunday. It is the Sunday we remember Martin Luther posting his 95 theses on the church door in Wittenberg. He did this on October 31, 1517. Nearly 500 years ago some of the same kinds of struggles were occurring, battles not against flesh and blood, but against principalities and powers.

The Powers that Be —Midweek

MEMORY VERSE:
For we do not wrestle against flesh and blood, but against principalities, against powers, against the rulers of the darkness of this age, against spiritual hosts of wickedness in the heavenly places.—Ephesians 6:12 (NKJV)

SCRIPTURE: Romans 1:16–17; 1 John 5:4

LESSON IN A SENTENCE: Our true enemies are not other people.

FOCUS
A-r-e Y-o-u R-e-a-d-y?

Wrestling will never be the same. Ask for volunteers for sleeping bag wrestling. Pair up your volunteers and have each get on their knees facing one another. Just before you countdown for the match to begin, let them know one more thing needs to happen. Place a sleeping bag over them. The wrestling won't be as skilled but it will be a whole lot of fun. A winner is declared when one is knocked completely to the floor.

Say: We wrestle against many things all of the time. We wrestle with decisions, we wrestle with anger, and we are wrestling with spiritual powers all of the time and don't even know it. Too often we are like the sleeping bag wrestlers, clumsy and in the dark, not even aware of who truly is our enemy.

DISCOVERY

Read Romans 1:16–17

Ask: What does it mean to be ashamed of the gospel?

Can you think of a time in your life that you were ashamed of the gospel? (Help your students realize this is not the same as being ashamed of being Christian. There are times when the media tells of Christians hurting others; our sin and spoiling the name of Christians has little to nothing to do with the eternal truth of the gospel.)

Read 1 John 5:4

Ask: Who is it that overcomes this world?

How do these two passages relate to one another?

APPLICATION:

Ask: What do we have to overcome in our lives?

Make a list on a whiteboard of all of the struggles and temptations out there (these can be anything from cussing to shoplifting, cheating on papers for school or having to deal with a bully at school). There are temptations and hard situations all around.

Ask: How do you overcome these temptations or trials?

Do you know? Have you thought much about this?

Read Ephesians 6:12, the memory verse for this week. You are not in a battle against flesh and blood. These struggles are about something much greater. Knowing that you are not in a battle against other people and that it is through the power of the gospel that you may live, an attitude adjustment may be in order. You still have responsibility and you may still have to go through some awful things, but there are spiritual forces at work around you. The blessing of it all! God indeed is victorious in the end; He has overcome this world!

NOVEMBER 6, 2005

God Pursues Us

By Amy Jacober

MEMORY VERSE:

[God] wants everyone to be saved and to understand the truth. For there is only one God and one Mediator who can reconcile God and people. He is the man Christ Jesus. —1 Timothy 2:4–5 (NLT)

SCRIPTURE: Hosea 1:2–3; 2:1–23

LESSON IN A SENTENCE: Even in our unfaithfulness, God pursues a relationship with us.

THE BIG PICTURE (OR WHAT YOU'RE TRYING TO GET ACROSS):

We are all sinners. He longs to have a relationship with us! He is not a weak God disinterested in our lives. He is the lover of our souls offering unconditional love and acceptance, if we choose to take it. Whether we have chosen to follow Him or not, we are precious to Him. He relentlessly pursues each person in hopes that they will be won by His love. No person can get cleaned up enough, purified enough to be worthy of God and yet, He loves us anyway. Every person has worth even if they feel like they have already fallen too far.

IN THIS LESSON STUDENTS SHOULD:

- Be able to identify what it means to pursue someone.
- Identify places in their own life where they are unfaithful.
- Begin to deal with their own/feelings/attitudes about being pursued.

STUFF YOU NEED:

- Pens/pencils/markers
- 3 x 5 cards
- Butcher paper
- Small prize for team (i.e. candy)

FOCUS

OPTION 1 (HIGH SCHOOL):

Split into two groups, one female and one male. Ask each group to create a list of their top ten things to do when trying to start a relationship with someone they like. As you collect each list have them sit facing each other. Ask each team to decide the number of guesses they think it will take to match the top ten list of the other team. (I.e. we think it will take us 15 guesses to name all ten on their list!) Each person must take a turn guessing. They may receive input from the team but it is their guess that counts. (Think Family Feud!) The team continues to guess until that team has made three mistakes. Once three mistakes have been made, reveal the rest of the list and switch roles. Give a small prize to the winning team.

Say: Guys and girls have different ideas of what it means to be pursuing a relationship.

Ask: What are the things we do have in common? What do both men and women want in a relationship?

OPTION 2 (JUNIOR HIGH):

Split into groups of 4–5 people (if possible, for this one break into all male and female groups). Give each group a marker and a piece of paper. Ask them to list everything they would do on a perfect day with their friends if money and transportation were not a factor. Have each group share their lists.

Ask: What was different on the two lists? What was similar? Does it change if any of you are talking about hanging out with someone you like for more than a friend?

DISCOVERY

Read Hosea 1:2–3 as a whole group. Explain that Hosea was a prophet, a godly man. Gomer was a slut at best and a prostitute at worst. In this story, we can learn about God's ongoing relationship with humanity.

***Depending on your translation harlot or whore is used. After you stop all of the giggling and jokes, explain that from the Hebrew this means not only to not be faithful to a commitment by being adulterous but also to commit idolatry in any sense.

Hosea 2:1–23 walks through the reactions of one who moves toward an unfaithful spouse. Summarize verses 1–13. In these verses we learn that Gomer was unfaithful, ran after other lovers, assumes all her possessions are gifts from her lovers and does not recognize it was really her own husband providing for her, misuses her possessions to worship Baal (a false master), sells her body for gifts, and dresses herself up with rings and jewelry to attract others.

Teacher's Note: In verse 16 it states that Hosea is asking Gomer to call him Ishi not Baali. Ishi means husband and Balli means master. Hosea is asking her to call him by a name that means she actually knows him personally, that she is not just fulfilling a duty or formality. God also wants for us to be on familiar terms, not disrespectful but much more than being polite in going through the motions.

LIFE APPLICATION: On butcher paper, make a list of all the things we run after, a list of the ways people have been or can be unfaithful to God. Put stars by the ones considered to be the worst.

Read Hosea 3:1 as a whole group.

Say: God tells Hosea to go to his wife again even though she has been unfaithful. This is like God going after Israel again and again. This is also like God continually pursuing us even when we are unfaithful.

Ask: Do you think God should keep pursuing someone even after they have been unfaithful? When do you think God should draw the line?

Is it worse to enter into a relationship and be unfaithful or to be honest in the beginning and never try the relationship in the first place?

Do we have any responsibility to help keep each other faithful to God?

MAKING IT PERSONAL: Do you believe that God pursues you? I mean do you really believe that in spite of all that you do, in spite of your unfaithfulness, your unbelief, your casual use of His Holy name and the times that you run so far that you can no longer even see God, do you think God is still there, longing and wanting to be in a relationship with you?

Ask rhetorically: Are there any things on our list that you recognize in your own life? How does it feel to be pursued despite your unfaithfulness?

Direct each person to take a few moments reflecting on this. Close in prayer asking God to show each of us what response He wants in light of our own lives.

CONNECTIONS: If you are done and still have time or your students are just hungry for more, look for connections in other passages. The lost coin, sheep, and prodigal son are all excellent parallels of God pursuing that which is far away.

SONGS: "It's All about You/Jesus Lover of My Soul" by Charmaigne
        "Security" by Stacie Orrico

EXTRA! EXTRA!: Several years ago Brennan Manning spoke at my church in Phoenix, Arizona. While he was speaking Jon Shillington and Tommy Brinkley (our music ministers) were scribbling notes. By the end of the talk, a new very short but very powerful song was written.

> Abba, Father I belong to You
> Abba, Father I belong to You
> Not because of who I am
> And in spite of what I do
> Abba, Father I belong to You

That little line, "in spite of what I do." We can neither be good enough nor bad enough to change the way God feels towards us!

God Pursues Us! —Midweek

MEMORY VERSE:
[God] wants everyone to be saved and to understand the truth. For there is only one God and one Mediator who can reconcile God and people. He is the man Christ Jesus. —1 Timothy 2:4–5 (NLT)

SCRIPTURE: Luke 15:8–10

LESSON IN A SENTENCE: Even in our unfaithfulness, God pursues a relationship with us.

FOCUS

Many of us leave things behind—books, jackets, coffee cups. Money, however, is rarely left behind. Before your students arrive, hide coins around the room. You may tape them in the corners or on the ceiling, under chairs, etc. Along with the coins, hide one larger bill. Once you have gathered everyone, tell them that you have hidden money all around the room. There are coins and one larger bill. They may keep any money they find. (This does not need to be an expensive activity. I would suggest no more than $5 in coins and hide a $5 bill. Of course group size and your budget may impact this!)

This activity can go in many directions. Depending on the personalities of your students, there may be some who search until the last coin is found, some who will quit once the larger bill has been found, and some who will not find the payoff worth the effort at all (not to mention a whole host of other options!) Spend a little time debriefing what just happened.

Ask: How much do you look when you know you have lost money at home? Does the amount of money missing make a difference in how much you look? How many of you have ever searched when you are missing a penny?

DISCOVERY

As a whole group, read through Luke 15:8–9.

Ask: Do you think it was really worth calling the neighbors over for a celebration?

What would have been a more proportionate response?

Have your students break into pairs and re-read the passage this time with verse 10 included (Luke 15:8–10).

Ask: How does verse 10 shed light on what verses 8–9 really mean?

APPLICATION: Find a quiet song to play in the background.

Ask each person to think of who they think of being valuable enough for God to seek. Ask them to also think of who they think of not being valuable enough for God to seek (everyone has someone either who they know or some stereotype of who they think is out of the boundaries of who God would love.) Tell them not to say the name of either person to anyone around but to just think of why they find them to be valuable or not.

About halfway through the song, ask them to try to see that person through the eyes of God.

Close in prayer reminding each person that even though society values some people more than others, God values all people equally! It doesn't matter what you have done, what you offer to society, how perfect others think you are, how smart you are or how much money you can give. God searches for the lost coin, for the one person who is away from His hand.

Teacher's Note: If you have a group that you know largely struggles with not feeling worthy before God, you may want to adjust the last section and focus more on each person there being valuable before God. It is often easier to see our own faults and forget that we actually have positive qualities. Humility is a virtue. In many Christian circles, humility pushes into false self-degradation and becomes another form of pride. We need to remind our students that each of them is valuable not because they are any better (or worse) than others, rather in that God loves them equally with others.

NOVEMBER 13, 2005

Are You What You Eat?

By Amy Jacober

MEMORY VERSE:
Or do you not know that your body is the temple of the Holy Spirit who is in you, whom you have from God, and you are not your own?
—1 Corinthians 6:19 (NKJV)

SCRIPTURE: 1 Corinthians 6:19–20; Romans 14:14–23

LESSON IN A SENTENCE: Even the food we eat impacts our relationship with God.

THE BIG PICTURE (OR WHAT YOU'RE TRYING TO GET ACROSS):

It has been the unending story for nearly a decade now. People in the U.S., on average are overweight and unhealthy. Diabetes, heart disease, and a host of other maladies have been increasing at alarming rates. All the while there are still thousands who under-eat and exercise, those who binge and purge, and now what is being considered to be the most common of eating disorders, binge eating (without the compensatory action). God has called us to be in relationship with Him and to share the gospel. We have been warned to not make any false idols. Again, this is not to restrict us but for our own good. What may seem to be a harmless false idol quickly becomes a consuming harmful part of our lives. Food, for many, is this false idol. The clothing industry, movies, TV, and magazines all lend their support in claiming that we should be able to eat whatever we want, whenever we want, and look thin, muscular, and healthy. These messages simply do not go together. Just as it is important to take care of the temple of the Holy Spirit regarding sexual activities and drugs and alcohol, we are also called to care for the nutrition needs. Being healthy crosses emotional, physical, and spiritual lines.

IN THIS LESSON STUDENTS SHOULD:

- Know that the body of a believer is the temple of God.
- Talk of what it means to respect and take care of their temple.
- Identify food as a means not an end.

STUFF YOU NEED:

If you choose option 1:
  ○ Tarp or plastic garbage bags
  ○ Donuts
  ○ String
If you choose option 2:
  ○ Copies of the sketch, ideally rehearsed ahead of time

FOCUS

OPTION 1:

Donut on a string

Ask for six volunteers. As the volunteers come to the front, have ready a tarp or plastic garbage bags on the floor and at least three donuts with a 4–foot string tied through the hole. Place your volunteers in partners having half of each pair lie on their back on the floor. The other three volunteers will be given a donut with a string to feed to their partner. The standing partner may use only their teeth to hold the end of the string as they try to feed their partner. The winner is the first to finish the entire donut. (For a messier version of this same game, dip the donut in chocolate sauce just before feeding!)

OPTION 2:

Not Enough

By Sarah Ware

Two students talk about their frustrations with God and their physical appearance.

Running Time: 1–2 min.
Players (2):1 Male = M
1 Female = F
*Female & Male at the same time = M/F

F-   I don't think God hears me when I pray. I pray to Him a lot,…or I used to. Until I realized that He wasn't listening. See,…I'm not pretty like all the other girls at school.

F-   I look in the mirror and I hate what I see.

M-   I'm too short to play basketball and not big enough to play football. I'm too slow and I couldn't even hit a baseball if it was on a tee.

M-   I look in the mirror and I hate what I see.

F-   All the other girls at school have perfect skin, perfect hair, and perfect bodies. It's like, when God made me, he made a

M/F-   Mistake.

M-   My youth pastor says that God doesn't make mistakes, but-

M/F-   I look in the mirror and I hate what I see.

F-   Look at me!

M-   I'm too short.

F-   Too fat

M-   Too slow

F -   Too ugly

M/F-   How can you say that God doesn't make mistakes?

M-   Because I look in the mirror . . .

F-   I look in the mirror . . .

(Starts her line when M is mid-sentence)

M/F-   and I only see me.

M/F-   I look in the mirror and I hate what I see.

DISCOVERY

Before your students arrive, have bowls with snack set around the room. Have half of the bowls be things like baby carrots and grapes and the other half chips and candies or cookies.

Ask: What is the difference between a house and a hotel?

On a whiteboard, make a side by side list to compare and contrast.

(Answers should include that in one you are only there for a short time, the other you really live.)

If you had to choose to have one place ruined...I mean really trashed...would you choose your own home or a hotel?

Read as a group: 1 Corinthians 6:19–20

Ask: Did you know that your body was where God dwelled?

What does it mean to have your body be the temple of the Holy Spirit?

Say: The temple in the Old Testament was where God was. When the Israelites wanted to find Him, they went to a high priest and had someone else enter the holy of holies to be in His presence. When Moses talks of moving the people in the wilderness, he will not go without the presence of God. History tells us of the changes as the physical temple is destroyed and re-built. Jesus ushers in a new understanding. He says that He is the temple, He is the presence of God. Finally, as Jesus ascends into heaven, we learn that God's presence has not abandoned us. Rather He is continuing His act of reconciliation coming to live in each of our lives. The Scripture actually talks of his dwelling or tabernacling in our lives. He is not there for a short stay, rather for the long haul.

Ask: If God is indeed dwelling in us, why is it so easy for us to trash His home?

Teacher's Note: A temple is historically a house or palace for God or in pagan traditions for the gods. Biblically it represented two things to Israel, election and unity—that indeed they had been chosen by God and that all are to be unified. It was Paul who most forcefully set forth the imagery of the body of believers as the temple or dwelling place of God, 2 Corinthians 6:16–7:1.

LIFE APPLICATION: Ask: In what ways do we, in this country, trash the inside of God's dwelling place?

Say: It's easy to think of drugs and alcohol, of smoking and all of the biggies. What about what we eat?

(Be careful to guide this discussion so that it does not slide into a thin versus fat debate. While obesity is an issue at this time in our country, it continues the focus on the outside, on what is seen. There are many thin people who eat poorly and will be creating long term health problems just as there are many larger people working very hard to fight against metabolism and a culture that does not easily promote healthy eating.)

Read Romans 14:14–23.

Ask: What does this say about what and how we should eat?

Ask: Do you think our physical eating habits and how we take care of our bodies really has anything to do with how we are spiritually? If yes, why? If no, why not?

Say: Look around the room. Before any of you arrived we set out bowls with snacks, half healthy and the half not so healthy. Do you notice the difference in what is left at the end? (It is a highly unusual group to have more chips than carrots left!)

Teacher's Note: You may want to do a bit of research at this point on the impact of fast food on teenage diet and health. Current information can easily be found on the internet. Another source from a slightly different angle looks at the issue from a secular society level called *Fast Food Nation*. As you are wrestling through what points to mention, either of these can offer some hard facts to back up taking care of our health as a spiritual act.

MAKING IT PERSONAL: Say: Healthy eating and healthy living is not about how you look on the outside, it is about how you are on the inside. We can all do just fine eating nothing but fast food or snacks for awhile. Eventually though, the nutrition simply is not there and it begins to show in our health and appearance. As the temple of God, as His dwelling place, we need to have the same attitude toward our own health and bodies as we would toward the most ornate of churches. We need to take great care not for how it looks, but for how it honors God.

ANCIENT PRACTICE: Fasting is an ancient practice. While most of us think of fasting from food all together, a fast can be from many things: from TV, from a negative attitude, or from arguing with a sibling. In light of the focus of this lesson, you can also fast from certain foods. Invite your students to choose one thing from which they are going to fast for one month. (This may be soda at lunch, lattes, potato chips—whatever!) Have a sheet of paper on the wall and have each person write their item on the wall with their name. This is not to show off, rather for accountability.

CONNECTIONS: John offers a focus on the body of Christ Himself as the temple, God in human form in John 1:14. While there are many passages and many perspectives, one thing is certain, the temple of God transcends any building or single location.

The Bible is certainly full of connections with eating! I was once told the Bible is a food driven book! From Adam and Eve to the last supper, celebrations and sorrows are surrounded with meals. Daniel 1 offers a closer look at choosing that which is healthy over that which is decadent. While it does not forbid the eating of other items nor is it the main point of this passage, healthy food is clearly at the center of this story.

SONGS: "Beautiful" by Bethany Dillon on her debut album

QUOTABLE QUOTES :

Part of the secret of success in life is to eat what you like and let the food fight it out inside.

—Mark Twain

Are You What You Eat? —Midweek

MEMORY VERSE:
Or do you not know that your body is the temple of the Holy Spirit who is in you, whom you have from God, and you are not your own?
—1 Corinthians 6:19 (NKJV)

SCRIPTURE: Exodus 16, focus on vv. 18–20

LESSON IN A SENTENCE: Even the food we eat impacts our relationship with God.

FOCUS

Musical food?

Similar to musical chairs only this time you have food items to eat. Have the group sit in a circle with one person as the music monitor. Begin passing a food item (baby food is always a good option!) When the music stops, the person with the food has to eat it or they are out. After a few rounds begin passing more than one item. You may want to begin with relatively easy foods like peaches or bananas and move to the chunky chicken surprise by the end!

Say: Most of us will eat if something is put in front of us, whether we are hungry or not. Eating is not about sustenance, it is about a social activity and it fills needs not being met elsewhere. The lack of eating or starving yourself is no better; it is simply the flip side of the same coin.

DISCOVERY

God does provide for us in amazing ways! Somehow we often think we need to help Him just in case He is busy tomorrow.

Read Exodus 16.

Ask your students to re-tell the story of what they have just read.

According to this passage, do you need to eat extra just in case you won't get any next time? What happened when they tried to take extra?

Re-read verses 18–20.

Ask: How would you have felt as the people being told what to do by Moses?

How would you have felt as Moses trying to tell the people what to do?

Teacher's Note: This passage in particular has many layers of application. It can certainly speak into our understanding of God's provision in many ways. If this is a more appropriate tangent for your group, feel free to bring up the general discussion of God's provision. If however you have a group where general health is a concern, this is a great lesson to use in taking only what you need for that day and encouraging lifelong healthy habits!

APPLICATION: While many of us eat for the wrong reasons, there are many in the world unable to eat at all for lack of available food. There needs to be a balance. What you choose to eat is equally as important as how much you eat. You are the temple of the Holy Spirit. When you run low on energy, all of you is impacted.

Ask: In what new ways will you consider eating as a spiritual act? How might this impact your daily life?

SERVICE OPTION:

Ask: In what ways can we take what we have discussed in the last few lessons and respond to them in a tangible day? Brainstorm a way for your group to put one or more of these into action and plan the activity.

(World Vision, Samaritan's Purse or any local food bank would be a good place to start! A few of you may even live near a gleaning network—volunteers glean in fields after the regular harvest and offer the fruits and vegetables to food banks and shelters in the area.)

Here's the Church, Here's the Steeple.

By Amy Jacober

MEMORY VERSE:
And He put all things under His feet, and gave Him to be head over all things to the church, which is His body, the fullness of Him who fills all in all.—Ephesians 1:22–23 (NKJV)

And He put all things in subjection under His feet, and gave Him as head over all things to the church, which is His body, the fulness of Him who fills all in all. —Ephesians 1:22–23 (NASB)

SCRIPTURE: Ephesians 2:19–22

LESSON IN A SENTENCE: The church, established by God, is people, not a building.

THE BIG PICTURE (OR WHAT YOU'RE TRYING TO GET ACROSS):
In recent years Jesus has become "cool" while religion and/or church has been seen as irrelevant. Many of us know the simple childhood rhyme, "Here's the church, here's the steeple, open the door, see all the people." This presents a false picture. The church is not a building filled with people, the church *is* the people. God himself established the church; this was not some creation after the fact of a bunch of people wanting something new. While our hope is in Christ alone, God knew we would need some help while here on earth. He longs for us to be in relationship with Him and with one another. As long as there are people, both those who are followers of Jesus and those who still need to hear the gospel, the church will exist. We may look many different ways, sing new songs, meet in specifically designed buildings, or borrow storefronts on Sunday mornings but we are still, in all our uniqueness, the bride of Christ, entirely established as a people by God Himself.

IN THIS LESSON STUDENTS SHOULD:

- Learn that God, not humans established the church.
- Realize that God desires for all people to have a place in the church.
- Talk honestly and openly about how the church is and is not relevant today.

STUFF YOU NEED:

If you choose option 1:
- ○ Table or flat surface
- ○ Ping pong ball
- ○ Crackers

If you choose option 2:
- ○ Masking tape

FOCUS

OPTION 1:

It seems too easy. Oh wait, it is! Like a rather warped version of tug of war, the object of this game is simply to blow the ping pong ball off the other person's side of the table. Of course that is after you have each person put at least 4–5 saltines in their mouth at a time. Ask for volunteers to go against each other. Be certain you have someone to monitor the crackers that they are not being chewed and swallowed or if they are that more saltines go in! Feel free to do several rounds with a championship at the end.

Say: Unfortunately, this can be a little like what it is when we as Christians get together in the church. With no bad intention, we become a little too focused on the task and forget the people who are around. On really bad days, we end up spewing some not so nice stuff on each other!

OPTION 2:

Tape It Up!

The object of this game is to place a piece of tape as high up on a wall as possible! It seems relatively simple but with some encouragement, your students can go really high! In groups of 6–10, work at placing a tape as high up on a wall as they can. You will need to remind the group that they will need spotters and for safety, they must communicate and pay attention the whole time. Spotters in particular must pay attention, as those on top will be off the ground reaching for the highest spot.

Say: For this activity, every person was needed. Each person is important and no one person could accomplish this alone. This activity is an exercise in cooperation and group effort. First Corinthians 12:22 helps remind us that even those who appear weaker are necessary in the body of Christ. It is not about the task of the group, it is about the people!

DISCOVERY

On a whiteboard, have the word church written in big letters at the top. Ask your students, when the word church is said, what comes to mind? The good *and* the bad. Write all of the words up on the board.

After collecting the words, ask if there is anyone who can define the word church.

Say: Church is one of those strange words that we all use and think we know what it means but in reality most of have a hard time with it. We can talk about it but have a hard time defining it.

Check out Ephesians 2:19–22 for a little insight.

Read Ephesians 2:19
   Ask: Who were strangers but now are fellow citizens?
   Read Ephesians 2:20
   Ask: What does it mean that Jesus Christ is the cornerstone?
   Read Ephesians 2:21
   Ask: What does it mean to have the whole building joined together?

Read Ephesians 2:22
   Ask: Who is built together for the habitation of the Holy Spirit?

LIFE APPLICATION: Based on these scriptures, what makes a church?

If you said the people, you would be correct!!

Four short verses with the whole of what it is to be church! The question then becomes, How are we built together for the habitation of the Holy Spirit?

In other words, how do we move from being a bunch of people who gather in a building to a community of people whose lives are built together around Christ indwelt by the Holy Spirit?

Say: God calls us to follow Him, but not alone. We are supposed to be in community, we are to be in church in the deepest sense of the meaning.

Ask: Do you think this is true? Why or why not?

What does it mean for us in this youth group?

MAKING IT PERSONAL: There is a lot of talk at conferences about Jesus being cool but organized religion not, about following Christ being good but doing so in community is not. Ironically, if one is really going to follow Jesus, He is quite clear that this is to be done in community. It was God's idea to have the church, not any persons!

Ask: What does this mean for you, here and now, understanding that the church is about people, not a building and that it is God's idea?

Spend a few moments sharing what it would look like if the church really were what you understand Jesus to have intended.

CONNECTIONS: While there are many views on the beginning of the church, the most commonly accepted is at the Day of Pentecost in response to Peter's sermon. This also harkens back to Matthew 16:16–17 when Jesus declares that upon this rock (a play on Peter's name—*petros* is the masculine, rock is *petra*, feminine) I will build my church. Peter preaches and this group for the first time in Acts 2:47 is called the church.

SONGS: "Great Light of the World" by Bebo Norman

QUOTABLE   QUOTES :

Going to church doesn't make you a Christian any more than going to a garage makes you an automobile.
—Billy Sunday

Here's the Church, Here's the Steeple —Midweek

MEMORY VERSE:
And He put all things under His feet, and gave Him to be head over all things to the church, which is His body, the fullness of Him who fills all in all.—Ephesians 1:22–23 (NKJV)

And He put all things in subjection under His feet, and gave Him as head over all things to the church, which is His body, the fulness of Him who fills all in all. —Ephesians 1:22–23 (NASB)

SCRIPTURE: 1 Corinthians 1:1–9

LESSON IN A SENTENCE: The church, established by God, is people, not a building.

FOCUS
Magic Shoes

What sounds like an easy task becomes a lesson in cooperation and communication. Mark a space of at least 30 feet across. The object is to get the entire group from one side of the "swamp" to the other. There is one pair of magic shoes that can be worn by anyone in the group. The catch is they can only be worn once and only one way. They cannot be thrown, they must be brought back by an individual.

There are many correct ways to do this. It takes a little concentration and a lot of cooperation.

Ask: What would have made this activity easier? What worked for your group?

Say: The most important element in this activity was that no person was left out. Each person was important and the group could not succeed unless everyone made it!

DISCOVERY

In at least three groups, read 1 Corinthians 1:1–9.

Have each group read through the 9 verses and answer the following questions:

To whom was this written? (v. 2)

Whose church was this? (v. 2)

Who gave grace to them? (vv. 3–4)
Who enriched the Corinthians? (v. 5)
What will they not be lacking? (v. 7)
What will Jesus help them do to the end? (v. 8)
Into what were they called? (v. 9)

APPLICATION: The people of Corinth had come together as a church. More importantly Paul reminds them that they are a church of God— not a human-made organization but a God-ordained group of people brought together in fellowship.

Ask: Who do you think establishes churches today?

Say: Verse 9 tells us that the people were called into the fellowship of Jesus. It is a plural "you;" all believers were called into fellowship.

Ask: Why would God do this?

Is the church today still relevant? Is it relevant for you?

Close in prayer for your local church and for the church as a whole. The church was and is established by God. It is our privilege with each new generation to know what that means in an ever-changing world.

MINISTRY ON PURPOSE

By John Losey
PROCESS CONSULTANT

Do you ever have the feeling you're being watched? You're not paranoid. You are! Whenever you are around students you are being checked out. What's even scarier is that, not only are you being watched all the time, but your students are learning all the time. Not all of them all the time, of course, but you must assume at least one student is gaining an insight, choosing an attitude, or selecting a course of action at any given time. Any moment, from the time they get in the van to go on a group trip, to the fast food meal you share together, has the potential to change a life.

We sweat and agonize over the lessons we want to share. We are very intentional about what we teach, as we should be, but students don't just learn during lesson time. We spend hours of time preparing a lesson that will only be a small percentage of the overall time we spend with students. Most of the time we spend with students is left to chance.

Every moment matters while you're with students. The most powerful lessons learned seldom occur during "lesson time." Not all of these lessons are positive or intended. The lesson may have been on compassion, but if the game you played beforehand emphasized a "win at all cost" competitiveness, they may talk about compassion but they learned that winning is more important. You may not have realized that the kindness you showed the fast food cashier when he messed up your order probably taught your students more then your "brilliant" Bible study on patience. Don't assume that any moment with a student isn't going to be life-changing.

The pressure is on. If students are learning all the time and every moment matters, then you need to take responsibility for what you are teaching. If you are not listening to your own lessons and living out the Bible studies you present, your students may be learning lessons you don't intend for them to learn. You are a model for your students whether you like it or not. Your life and the lives of your staff need to match what you teach. Not only is this important to your own spiritual health but it is crucial for the health of your ministry. Live your life as an intentional model for your student.

Plan your programs on purpose as well. Take advantage of every moment you have with students to reinforce the biblical truths you are trying to pass along. Choose games that may bring up themes you will be teaching later. Plan activities that give students an opportunity to live out the lessons they are learning. Share meals that will open their eyes to different parts of the world so they can pray for them. Choose every part of your program to be intentionally positive or at least neutral. Don't let the impact of your ministry be left to chance. Choose to do ministry on purpose.

How can you take advantage of different moments you share with students? Experiential methods for ministry will help you intentionally use the experience of your students to help them learn and grow. There are several ways you can use experience this way.

Make Moments—Attach meaning to games, activities, or objects. These types of object lessons can touch students deeply because more of their "person" is involved in learning the lesson; their body, emotions, and attitude as well as their mind are involved in the learning. Not only are the lessons deep, but they last. Each time they play that game or encounter that object they will be reminded of the lesson that is attached to it.

Remember Moments—There are moments and memories your students share that can be used to intentionally attach lessons to their lives. This is how parables work. Parables are stories that teach powerful lessons by attaching concepts that may be difficult to understand to an experience that most people share. When Jesus talks about the lilies in the field or the good shepherd He is talking about experiences that were very familiar to the people who were listening. You can create your own parables by telling stories that use the common experience of your students (rather than stories that may be fun and interesting but that are unique to you).

Process Moments—Every day your students face life experiences that have massive potential for life lessons. They bring these teachable moments to us, and too often we are too focused on the lesson we want to give rather than the potential learning God has in store for that student. Too often we see these moments as problems that we can solve for them with a Bible verse and a few words of wisdom. What if, instead, we walked alongside them as they struggle with the lesson, offering thoughtful questions that lead them deeper into their own relationship with God? What if we spent less time trying to prove that the Bible is relevant and just assumed that it is, and then helped students live out its truths? The moments your students are living today are loaded with powerful opportunities to lead them closer to God. Plan to make every one of them count for eternity.

NOVEMBER 27, 2005

Advent: Hope

By Amy Jacober

MEMORY VERSE:
Blessed is the man who trusts in the LORD, and whose hope is the LORD.—Jeremiah 17:7 (NKJV)

Blessed are those who trust in the LORD, whose trust is the LORD.
—Jeremiah 17:7 (NRSV)

SCRIPTURE: Romans 8:18–26

LESSON IN A SENTENCE: The birth of Jesus reminds us of the hope we have.

THE BIG PICTURE (OR WHAT YOU'RE TRYING TO GET ACROSS):
Today is the first Sunday of Advent. (The meaning of this will be explained more fully in the teacher's notes for this lesson.) Whether your tradition follows Advent or not, hope is a universal theme for us as Christians. Teenagers live in a world that is more like a rather violent roller coaster than anything else! There is extreme hope, and then extreme let down. The anticipation of climbs and the impending drop is often more than they think they can bear. Jesus offers something different. While the anticipation of Christmas (and more importantly a reminder of the incarnation) brings a festive season, it also reminds us of the hope that does not come crashing down ending in disappointment. Jesus does not abandon us in the hard times in life. He walks with us, cries with us, and celebrates with us throughout life. In the end, for the believer, we know that we will be in heaven with no more tears in the communion of the saints!

IN THIS LESSON STUDENTS SHOULD:

- ○ Understand that there is always hope.
- ○ Learn that hope is found in God alone.
- ○ Be able to identify where hope is in their lives.

STUFF YOU NEED:

If you choose option 1:
- ⊙ Advent wreath
- ⊙ Advent candles
- ⊙ Matches

FOCUS

OPTION 1:

Begin the next four Sundays with the lighting of the Advent candles. You will need a wreath of some sort with holders for at least four candles around the circle and one in the center. (This can be done with a styrofoam ring and some real or artificial evergreens placed to created a wreath. Use four candles on the outer edge of the ring and a larger, white candle in the center. The four candles may be any color you choose, though by tradition three of them are purple or blue for royalty and one is pink or rose for joy.) Traditionally the Advent wreath is round to remind us of God's eternality, of which there is no beginning and no end. It is also to remind us of His everlasting love and mercy. The evergreen reminds us of hope, the hope we experience in the newness of life in the spring is the hope that is unending in the presence of the evergreens. The candles are to remind us of the light brought into the world through the presence of Jesus. The placement of the candles, four on the outside with a larger white one in the middle is also symbolic. The four outer candles are lit each of four Sundays as we wait for Christmas. They can remind us of the four centuries of waiting between Malachi and the birth of Christ.

Say: Today is the first Sunday of Advent. In the Christian tradition this is the beginning of the time in which we wait as we look forward to the coming of the Lord. (You may want to spend a few minutes explaining the significance and symbolism of the Advent wreath as you prepare to light the first candle.)

Say: The word advent means "coming" or "arrival." This season is spent anticipating the arrival of God. For some of us that is reason to celebrate, for some of us that thought could be a little scary. Each Sunday we will light a candle to remind us of the light of the world on His way. This Sunday is the Sunday of Hope.

Have a volunteer to read Isaiah 9:2,6

Ask: Who do you hope for God to be? Is it Wonderful or Counselor or Mighty God or Everlasting Father or Prince of Peace? Do you believe God could be—that God is—all of these?

Have a volunteer pray for hope to arrive as you begin to look to the birth of Christ. While he or she is praying, light the first candle, the candle of hope!

OPTION 2:

Play a Game of "I Prefer . . ."

Ask your students a series of questions that begin with the phrase "Do you prefer..."

There are many ways to answer, calling out what they prefer, having those who prefer one thing walk to the right side of the room and those who prefer the other thing to walk to the left side of the room or simply by a raise of hands. For example...

Do you prefer chocolate or vanilla ice cream?
Do you prefer ketchup or mustard?
Do you prefer ice skating or roller blading?
Do you prefer being cold or being hot?
Do you prefer anchovies or escargot?

Be creative. It is better to begin with simple ones and move to the more gross or elaborate ones or you will lose them from the beginning. Feel free to let your students make some up as well!

The trick is to end with the following question:

Do you prefer to have hope or to know for certain?

You may need to quiet them down and ask again especially if you have been laughing over all of the choices. Be certain they have heard and lead your group in a discussion of what it means to have hope as opposed to knowing something for certain.

DISCOVERY

Say: We have all hoped for something in our lives. Hope is a gift given when we are simply uncertain if things will work out, if we will get what we want, or if we will know what to do. Hope is at the end of every "if"!

In groups of 3 read Romans 8:18–26.

Have each group summarize the passage in their own words in 3 sentences or less.

Say: Verse 18 talks of the sufferings of this present time.

Ask: What would you include as sufferings today?

What does it mean to be subjected to futility not willingly but in hope (v. 20)?

Say: There are of course troubles in this world and troubles in your lives. They however will pale in comparison to the good that is coming. Hope is that joyful anticipation that something better is on the way.

Re-read verses 24–25

Ask: What is it that we hope for that we do not yet see?

LIFE APPLICATION: Turn to the person next to you and tell him or her one thing for which you hoped that worked out. (Be certain to give enough time for each person to have a turn.) Now tell that same person one thing for which you hoped that did not work out.

Say: It is often only in hindsight that we can see where it may be good to have a prayer, a desire, something for which we hoped to not work out.

Ask: What things can you think of for which you hoped that did not work out that now, years later you are grateful they did not? (Trying out for a school play only to learn that if you had you would have had to miss a family vacation, not getting the first job you wanted only to meet your best friend at your second choice job, etc.)

MAKING IT PERSONAL: Say: Verses 24–25 can seem so unrealistic IF they are all you read. They say hope for what you can't see and do this eagerly with perseverance. For most of us, the longer we have to wait, especially if we are kept in the dark if it will ever come to pass, we wait with anything but joyful expectation! Many have the motto "Expect the worst and be surprised when it actually works out." And then there is verse 26:

Read verse 26 out loud.

Ask: What does verse 26 tell us?

After they have answered, ask: Have you ever considered that the Holy Spirit prays for you? (Even more, that the Holy Spirit intercedes even when we cannot find the words, in our weakness!)

Ask each person to think of one thing for which they are hoping but may not even know how to pray.

Close in prayer asking for God's will in each situation and that each believer would be aware of the work of the Holy Spirit in their lives.

MEMORY VERSE ACTIVITY

Have several strips of cardstock and markers available. Invite students to choose one name of God that seems most relevant to them at this time from Isaiah 9:6 (Wonderful, Counselor, Mighty God, Everlasting Father, or Prince of Peace). On one side of the cardstock write the name of God chosen. On the other side write the memory verse. Tell them to tape this somewhere where they will see it daily (a bathroom mirror is always a good idea!) On the days when you do not see hope, remember that hope is from the Prince of Peace, the Mighty God!

CONNECTIONS: A very different perspective from our current view is that of Amos 5:18–20. In past centuries in both the Eastern and Western church there was an emphasis on penitence and getting oneself right in order to be in the presence of the Lord. As time passed, the Western church shifted from an individual focus of penitence and seeking forgiveness to looking at societal evil and injustices. The problem with both of these is that we often are the ones in sin or contributors to the evil. Amos warns us that while we hope, while we desire the day of the Lord to come, for some it will be almost unbearable as the light can be blinding to those in the dark!

SONGS: "Homesick" by Mercy Me on the album *Undone*

QUOTABLE   QUOTES:

I hope...that mankind will at length, as they call themselves reasonable creatures, have reason and sense enough to settle their differences without cutting throats; for in my opinion there never was a good war, or a bad peace.

—Benjamin Franklin

Hope is the best possession. None are completely wretched but those who are without hope. Few are reduced so low as that.

—William Hazlitt

Hope —Midweek

MEMORY VERSE:
Blessed is the man who trusts in the LORD, and whose hope is the LORD.
—Jeremiah 17:7 (NKJV)

Blessed are those who trust in the LORD, whose trust is the LORD.
—Jeremiah 17:7 (NRSV)

SCRIPTURE: Hebrews 6:17–20

LESSON IN A SENTENCE: The birth of Jesus reminds us of the hope we have.

FOCUS

Play a few rounds of spoons. This can be played with any number of people, though ideally where you may sit in a circle where all are able to reach the middle. You can play with as few as two people and as many as 10–12. Divide your groups up accordingly, keeping in mind you can have two games going at once. Chances are several of your students will already know how to play!

The set up: Place the spoons in the center of the table. You determine the number of spoons by the number of players minus one. Choose a dealer and have him or her deal 4 cards to each player.

The play: Once the players all have their cards, they may look at them. The dealer then begins drawing from the remaining pile one card at a time. If the card is not one the dealer wants to keep, he or she passes it face down to the person to the left. That person may then look at the card and decide if it is wanted. If not, it again is passed to the left. If it is, another card is chosen from his or her hand and that card is passed. This continues until someone collects four of a kind. If the deck is finished and cards make it all the way around the circle, the dealer begins the process again as cards pile up. You are to keep no more than four cards in your hand at any given time.

The object: Once a player has collected four of a kind, he or she takes a spoon. As the other players notice, they too must grab a spoon. As there are not enough spoons for each player, one person is always left out and is eliminated. Play another round, removing one more spoon until there is a final spoons champion remaining.

Ask: Was anyone hoping to lose? Did anyone have to make a conscious choice to hope to win or did you just play? What is the difference between things for which you hope and things you just do?

DISCOVERY

Read Hebrews 6:17–20.

Ask: What is the hope mentioned in verse 19?

What does it mean to have it as an anchor for the soul?

Say: Boats are made to float. Not only that, they are made to float and move on the water. An anchor certainly can and does hold it in place but only for a season and a reason. It is anchored when something else needs to be taking place, getting supplies or fishing. It holds still while it is being prepared for the next journey and periodically stops to accomplish something or for more work along the way. Boats are not made to hold still and look pretty. They are made to be out on water moving.

Ask: What does this kind of word picture say to you about hope being an anchor?

Teacher's Note: Melchizedek was a king and a priest (Genesis 14:17–20). It was from the order of Melchizedek that Christ was associated with the priests.

APPLICATION:

Say: We are entering into the Christmas season. It is the time when we are reminded of the hope Jesus brought with Him as He entered the world.

Hope can sometimes seem distant when we must wait for what we do not know.

Think of one place in your life right now where you think you might be anchored as God is preparing you for something more. What hope has He given you knowing a big move is on the way?

DECEMBER 4, 2005

Advent: Peace

By Amy Jacober

MEMORY VERSE:
These things I have spoken to you, that in Me you may have peace. In the world you will have tribulation; but be of good cheer, I have overcome the world.—John 16:33 (NKJV)

SCRIPTURE: Ephesians 4:25–26; Colossians 3:15

LESSON IN A SENTENCE: Believers are to be about the business of seeking and establishing peace.

THE BIG PICTURE (OR WHAT YOU'RE TRYING TO GET ACROSS):

Most of us are not at peace in general. We do however find peaceful moments. Being up early in the morning before the rest of the house, babbling brooks, walks in the park, the ocean tide, the gentle hum of a city at night—all of these things can conjure up images of peace. Whether it is unrest and fighting and bombings on the news or the fighting and struggles in the halls of school, many of our students find it difficult to believe peace exists, let alone have those peaceful moments. Peace does not just mean an absence of war. It carries with it a sense of rest both inward and outward. Jesus comes to bring peace. Followers of Jesus are called to live a different way. It may seem overwhelming as the world wages war all around us, but we are to be set apart, to live differently.

IN THIS LESSON STUDENTS SHOULD:

- ○ Learn that there is false peace and true peace.
- ○ Recognize that God wants for us to be at peace.
- ○ Identify specific steps they can take toward peace in their daily lives.

STUFF YOU NEED:

If you choose option 1
- ○ Advent wreath
- ○ Advent candles

STUFF YOU NEED:

○ Matches
○ Whiteboard
○ Colored paper
○ Markers

FOCUS

OPTION 1:

Say: Today is the second Sunday of Advent.

Last Sunday we began to turn our thoughts toward Christmas and the birth of Jesus. We began to get ready for His arrival.

Ask: Does anyone remember what the theme of last Sunday was? (Hope)

Say: Hope is eagerly awaiting. We can hardly wait for Christmas to arrive! Not for the presents but for the hope that Jesus brings! While waiting and hoping we realize this is a dark place and often our own hearts are no better than the world. He however is the light of the world!

Say: This Sunday has a different theme.

Reader 1: Let us pursue the things which make for PEACE and the building up of one another.   Romans 14:19 (NASB)

Reader 2: "I will now say, 'May PEACE be within you.'" Psalm 122:8 (NASB)

Say: There are two major ways to consider peace—peace in this world and inner peace. With the coming of Jesus, both are possible!

Have a volunteer pray for peace—peace in this world and peace in the hearts and lives of those sitting with you right now. While he or she is praying, light the first and second candles. The candle of peace joins the candle of hope!

OPTION 2:

Ask: What sounds make you think of peace? Of anything calm relaxing and peaceful? List all of these on the whiteboard.

Say: While we can't always bring in the sound of the ocean or the constant hum of a freeway, we can bring in rain!

Divide your group into three. Tell them you will show an action that will begin with group 1, add group 2, and finally group 3. The actions will change but they are to keep doing each until you signal to finish. The key to this whole thing is to be absolutely silent other than what you instruct!

Begin by having group 1 rub their hands together. Group 2 joins, then group 3.

Go back to group 1, have them stop rubbing their hands together and begin snapping. Group 2 joins and then group 3.

Next comes patting their hands on their legs, patting harder, stomping their feet and then the whole thing in reverse. If they take this seriously, you will have made rain.

Say: Rain is one of those crazy things! It can be one of the most peaceful sounds or one of the most frightening if the storm is accompanied by wind or thunder. Either way, it means change is coming, a vital resource is being replenished, and all things will emerge afresh after it has taken place. Whether it's rain or any other sound in which you find peace, it can bring a sense of refreshment and renewal!

OPTION 3:

Obtain a copy of *Rain* from Nooma videos (see Nooma.org).

Rain clearly depicts the peace and provision God provides even in the midst of the most seemingly overwhelming of storms.

DISCOVERY

Have your students get in pairs and write a definition for the word peace. Remind them they cannot define a word with the word. Have each person write their definitions in large letters on colored paper to put up around the room or under a sign in the room that reads peace.

Ask: Is peace a private or public concern? Should others care if you are in a fight with a friend? What about if you feel unsettled in your own heart? If there are opposing gangs in your community? If there is a war in a neighboring country? If there is a war around the world?

Say: There are almost as many responses to these questions as the number of people who answer. Knowing there are many things we cannot know, let's focus on what we can.

Read Ephesians 4:25–26.

Ask: What is this passage saying to do?

Do you think this is a realistic expectation?

Read Colossians 3:15

Ask: What is this passage saying to do?

Do you think this is a realistic expectation?

Teacher's Note: Don't forget peace in the biblical sense is much more than the absence of strife. Both the Greek (*eirene*) and the Hebrew (*shalom*) carry with them the concepts of well-being, wholeness, restoration, and reconciliation. While the New Testament carries with it a greater emphasis on inner peace, both the Old and New Testaments refer to peace as being reconciled to God and in right relationship with others.

LIFE APPLICATION:

Ask: How do these two passages relate to one another?

Can you work toward peace in the world if you are not at peace in your own heart and immediate relationships?

Create a plan as a group to work toward peace in your own community. This could be anything from an intentional approach to your school campus where you encourage and remind one another to not engage in the gossip and backbiting or where you make a prayer chain for your group in order to pray for one another as struggles in life come. Be as creative as you like, but be certain it is specific to your group.

MAKING IT PERSONAL:

Say: Each of us have areas in our lives that cause us to not be at peace. Decisions that have to be made, relationships that seem to consistently give trouble, or something we must do for which we feel inadequate are all places that can rob us of the peace God desires for each of us.

Re-read Colossians 3:15. It says that the peace of God is to rule in our hearts. It however does not stop there; it also says that we were called to one body. You are not supposed to do this alone.

Choose one thing that is causing you to not be at peace. Share this with the group. Remind the group that Isaiah 9:6 tells us one of the names for God is the Prince of Peace. Call on the Prince of Peace to bring wholeness in each person's life and in the situations they have mentioned in particular.

MEMORY VERSE ACTIVITY

Deuteronomy 14:11–20 gives to us one of the most enduring images of peace, that of a dove with an olive branch. While doves are referred to in many other ways and in many other places in Scripture, this is the passage that has led us to associate the dove with peace. It is in reference to the end of a storm. As they are writing on and decorating their doves, have them think of one storm in their own life they hope to have end soon.

For the memory verse, have the shape of a dove cut out of cardstock or heavier paper, enough for one per student. Give each student a dove and have them write the memory verse on one side. On the other, decorate as for a Christmas tree. Be certain you have string or wire to use for hanging! You may have them either take them home today or hang them around the youth room to be taken home after the holidays.

CONNECTIONS: There are many places in Scripture to connect on the subject of peace. This is the season where we celebrate that the Prince of Peace is to be born. With the birth of Jesus comes the hope for peace. In fact, peace can only be known through Jesus. Many however will try to comfort themselves with a false peace. This indeed will work for awhile, but it will eventually fade away. Jeremiah 6:14 speaks of this false peace so many choose.

SONGS: "Your Touch" by Kutlass on the album *Kutlass*

QUOTABLE QUOTES:

Peace and friendship with all mankind is our wisest policy, and I wish we may be permitted to pursue it.
—Thomas Jefferson

Peace —Midweek

MEMORY VERSE:
These things I have spoken to you, that in Me you may have peace. In the world you will have tribulation; but be of good cheer, I have overcome the world.

—John 16:33 (NKJV)

SCRIPTURE: Ephesians 2:13–22

LESSON IN A SENTENCE: Believers are to be about the business of seeking and establishing peace.

FOCUS

Have a huge piece of butcher paper up on the wall with markers on the table or floor below it.

As your students arrive, ask them to brainstorm past enemies who are now friends. This can be anything from the United States and the former Soviet Union to movie characters to people in your youth group (providing of course that they both know about it and you are not creating gossip!) They may need some help on the more global issues. Take some time and cruise through the newspapers or internet for more recent examples. (Don't be afraid to name some of the big ones from the past century. I recently met with a college-aged young woman who had never heard of the genocide in Rwanda nor of Apartheid. For many, once the crisis is over the memory is gone.)

DISCOVERY

Read Ephesians 2:13–22.

Re-read verses 14–18.

Ask: What does this passage teach us about God?

What does this passage teach us about who we are to be?

What does this passage say about the relationship we are to have with each other? With our enemies in particular?

APPLICATION: Say: There is no mistake, we are all to be united in body, the body of Christ.

Ask: How can so many different people in so many parts of the world with so many different beliefs be united? What is our role as followers of Jesus in this pursuit of peace?

Say: On Sunday, we looked at how peace must first start in our own hearts and then move to the immediate relationships around us. This passage is different. It is looking at the peace that must exist between peoples, the Jews and the Gentiles in particular.

Ask: What ways can we, here and now be a part of seeking peace in the world?

(Your denominational mission agency will have several suggestions. As well as Amnesty International, The Children's Defense Fund, and other web resources.)

Say: Often we think God is missing when there is suffering. It is hard to comprehend His presence in the midst of so much horror. Try reframing this. When we see hurt, when we see suffering, when we struggle to find peace, we see Jesus. Jesus suffered on the cross. In many ways, it is only when we open our eyes to see the suffering around us that we can begin to understand the cross. The good news is that Jesus did not stay on the cross! Suffering is not intended to last forever. Though suffering may last for a night, joy comes in the morning!

Think through some of the current conflicts in the paper or on the news. Spend time in prayer for the peoples in those places of struggle. Pray for peace in the fullest sense of the word.

Teacher's Note: Verse 14 mentions the wall that has been torn down between us. This is in reference to the wall in the temple which separate the Gentiles and the Jews. The penalty for going beyond this wall for a Gentile was death. Jesus, in His death, burial, and resurrection tore down this wall creating unity. The Prince of Peace brought peace in the fullest sense of the word, He brought wholeness and reconciliation.

DECEMBER 11, 2005

Advent: Joy

By Amy Jacober

MEMORY VERSE:
Do not sorrow, for the joy of the LORD is your strength.—Nehemiah 8:10b (NKJV)

SCRIPTURE: Luke 2:8–14

LESSON IN A SENTENCE: Our greatest joy is found in God.

THE BIG PICTURE (OR WHAT YOU'RE TRYING TO GET ACROSS):

As Christmas approaches there seem to be parties and celebrations at every turn! This is a wonderful time of year, especially when you know the real reason for the season! All of life however is not a party. Even in the midst of this most happy of seasons, difficult times can come. End of term papers are due, finals for sports, family commitments, overtime at work—the options are endless. Not to mention that for some, a dependence on the next big thing is what seems to be the only source of joy! Somewhere in all of the festivities and busyness, encourage your students to take a deep breath, savor the moment, and be encouraged by the source of all the attention. God stepped out of heaven, came humbled as a baby to restore our joy. His is no one-time offering, a fleeting moment of happiness. He is the source of joy—in the moment, for life, and for eternity.

IN THIS LESSON STUDENTS SHOULD:

- Learn in detail one more part of the biblical account of the birth of Jesus
- Define joy as being distinct from happiness.
- Understand that God wants for us to have joy.
- Know that joy is found in God.

STUFF YOU NEED:

If you choose option 1
- Advent Wreath
- Advent candles
- Matches

STUFF YOU NEED:

If you choose option 2
- ○ List of Christmas carols
- ○ Helium balloons
- ○ CD for a prize

FOCUS

OPTION 1:

Say: Today is the third Sunday of Advent.

For two weeks now we have been talking of the anticipation of Christmas. Often getting ready for an event can bring just as much joy as the event!

Ask: We have already covered two Sundays. What have the themes been for the last two? (Hope and Peace)

Say: We hope for peace (remember peace is about having a right relationship with God and others). What is it like when we finally move from hoping for peace to experiencing it? What words come to mind?

Say: This Sunday we focus on one result from this state of being right with God.

Reader 1: Nehemiah 8:10

Reader 2: John 15:11

Say: Joy! A tiny word with a lot of power. It moves beyond happiness. It exists regardless of circumstance. It is found only in the depths where neither pain nor pleasure dares to tread. The color of the candles changes this Sunday. On the other three it is purple (or blue) to remind us of royalty. Pink (or rose) is the color for today. This is the traditional color for joy!

Have a volunteer pray thanking God for His gift of joy! Pray for those unable to comprehend or accept this gift remaining tied to the circumstances for their response. While he or she is praying, light the first, second and third candles. The candle of peace joins the candle of hope resulting in joy!

OPTION 2:

The Christmas not-so-much an Idol Contest!

This activity is for no other purpose than to bring lots of laughter to your group! Have a list of Christmas carols on hand and a bunch of helium balloons.

Take volunteers to sing/perform Christmas songs after having inhaled helium from the balloons. (If your group is more reserved be certain to have enlisted a few adults and more extroverted students to begin the time.) If you have enough participants, have the contest go down to finalists. Offer second and third place prizes with the grand prize winner getting a Christian CD!

Say: Contests like this bring lots of laughs! Now we are going to look at what brings joy!

DISCOVERY

Plan with your adult leaders to read the scripture to your students. Reader 1=R1, Reader 2=R2, All=all adults present

R1:   Now there were in the same country shepherds living out in the fields, keeping watch over their flock by night. And behold, an angel of the Lord stood before them, and the glory of the Lord shone around them, and they were greatly afraid. Then the angel said to them

R2:   Do not be afraid, for behold, I bring you good tidings of great joy which will be to all people. For there is born to you this day in the city of David a Savior, who is Christ the Lord. And this will be a sign to you: You will find a Babe wrapped in swaddling cloths, lying in a manger.

R1:   And suddenly there was with the angel a multitude of the heavenly host praising God and saying

All: Glory to God in the highest, and on earth peace, good will toward men!

Write verse 10 on a whiteboard.

Ask: Why would the angel need to tell the shepherds not to be afraid?

For whom are these "good tidings" intended?

Why would this news bring great joy?

LIFE APPLICATION: Ask: What does the world tell us brings joy? You may need to think of commercials or advertisements you have seen recently.

Say: Jesus may be the reason for the season but there is certainly no shortage of suggestions for other things to supplement (unfortunately often to overshadow) that joy.

Ask: What are the hottest gifts this season? (CDs, videogames, trendy items)

Write every item up on the whiteboard.

Say: All of these things may be great but they are just things. They will not last. Joy exists long after any possession can last.

Say: The shepherds were afraid at first.

Ask: How might we live in a way where we are afraid of the joy God wants to give to us?

Say: Often joy seems too good to be true. It may also seem to be something which we do not deserve. It is amazing how many of us run or push others away when authentic love is offered, when good things come our way. We can become so comfortable living in difficult circumstances that when things improve, we can sabotage the change.

Ask: So what is this joy God wants for each of us, for all of us?

Teacher's Note: Joy in both the Old and New Testament refers to something beyond a feeling or fleeting emotion. Joy is a consistent way of being. This doesn't mean hard times don't come nor that a person is never sad—that would be less than human! It means that in spite of the circumstances, there is a grounding in the deep sense of the presence of God. In the Old Testament *simha* (gladness, mirth), *gul* or *gil* (to spring about, be joyful) and *sameah* (to shine or be glad) are some words for joy. In the New Testament *chara* (joy) and *chairo* (to rejoice) are used. Joy was associated with God's salvation, God's Law, and God's Word.

Joy exists not because of ever-changing circumstances. Rather it becomes a way of life. In fact, with its connection to God's salvation, it is life!

Read the words to the first stanza of the hymn "Joy to the World."

Ask: Given this perspective on joy, how can you better understand this song?

(Joy to the world—it is not just wishing happiness or a good time, it is wishing the constant state of being. It is wishing joy, life, salvation, not for a few or many but for all the world!)

MAKING IT PERSONAL: Say: Stating that joy is a state of being regardless of circumstances is often easier said than done. The next time we are together, we will look at having joy in hard times.

The memory verse activity ties into the closing of your time together.

MEMORY VERSE ACTIVITY

Invite each person to find a quiet spot in or near your room. Use Nehemiah 8:10b for your passage. Walk them through the concept of meditation on scripture. Read a passage at least three times, perhaps out loud. Focus on each word and what it might mean in your life. Encourage them to think of what in their life is currently a situation where they need strength. How can joy as it has been defined here today help in this situation?

CONNECTIONS: Joy comes from God. It transcends mere experiences of good or bad. Check out Psalm 16:11; Matthew 5:12; Romans 15:13; and 2 Corinthians 12:9.

SONGS: "This Christmas (Joy to the World)" by Toby Mac on a single

QUOTABLE   QUOTES :

Great joy, especially after a sudden change of circumstances, is apt to be silent, and dwells rather in the heart than on the tongue.

—Henry Fielding

Joy —Midweek

MEMORY VERSE:
Do not sorrow, for the joy of the LORD is your strength.—Nehemiah 8:10b (NKJV)

SCRIPTURE: Psalm 16:11; John 16:24

LESSON IN A SENTENCE: Our greatest joy is found in God.

FOCUS

Spin Doctor!

Often we think our lives have problems. Well, compared to many, it could be a lot worse! Create a list of "worst case scenarios" to hand out to your students. Tell them they have been assigned the task of a spin doctor—to take whatever is written in the story and to find one positive thing that can be seen in it, kind of like looking for the silver lining in every cloud! Depending on the size of your group, you may want to either give each person their own or have them in small groups.

Take turns reading each scenario and the positive point they have found!

Examples of worst case scenarios: Feel free to make up as many as you need. They can be funny as well, but be certain they are indeed truly horrible!

You have contracted a rare disease while on a mission trip. All of you hair has fallen out and you have just been told it will never grow back.

While on an afternoon hike with your Sunday school class, you take a wrong turn and get lost. You brought enough snacks and water for one afternoon. Five days have already passed.

Not only did you get detention for skipping classes, you are grounded for the remainder of the school year.

You are in a car accident and, while no one was killed, you have lost the use of your left arm.

Say: While we hope none of these things ever happens to any of you, even in the worst of situations there can be a silver lining.

DISCOVERY

Split into three groups. Have each group read their passage and answer the following questions. After a few minutes, have someone from each group read the passage aloud and answer the questions for the group.

Group 1 read Psalm 16:11
> What does God show?
> What does He promise to be found in His presence?

Group 2 read Psalm 30:5
> How long does it say weeping lasts?
> When does joy come?

Group 3 read John 16:21–22
> Is a woman always in pain, in labor?
> Does sorrow last forever?

APPLICATION: Ask: How do these three passages seem to have any relation to one another?

Say: When you are having a hard time, when sorrow truly seems to have come, it is hard to picture anything but the darkest and worst of possibilities. In fact, in our moments of greatest sorrow, we become paralyzed with the pain.

Ask: What do these scriptures promise follows the sorrow?

Do you believe joy can be present even in the hardest of times?

Does it ever say that we should not or were not meant to go through sorrow?

Say: Hard times are going to come. We live in a fragmented, broken world. Sin is present and our lives can be difficult. God is clear; this is not intended to be forever!

Ask: Can you think of any times in your past that seemed like the end of the world but now, with time, you have learned to recognize the joy again?

Often our greatest joys come from what were once our greatest sorrows.

Remember that joy is not happiness. It does not depend on the circumstance. It is about something much deeper. It is grounded in God and stems from His wanting to be reconciled with you.

Pray for those you know and around the world who are in the midst of their greatest sorrows. Pray that they may know joy, the true joy that is grounded in God.

DECEMBER 18, 2005

Advent: Love

By Amy Jacober

MEMORY VERSE:
You shall love the LORD your God with all your heart, and with all your soul, and with all your might.—Deuteronomy 6:5 9 (NRSV)

SCRIPTURE: Deuteronomy 6:4–9; Matthew 22:37–40; Mark 12:29–31; Luke 10:26–27

LESSON IN A SENTENCE: God stepped into this world because of His love for His people.

THE BIG PICTURE (OR WHAT YOU'RE TRYING TO GET ACROSS):

Ask you students to define love and you'll get just about as many answers as you have students! We love ice cream and we love a movie, we love our dog and we love our little brother. We fall in love with someone at school—every few months. Love is a term thrown around and used for nearly every positive emotional state or sentiment imaginable. For God love is more than an emotion. He moves it beyond a mere fickle description of sentiment. Both in this holiday season and for all the year, God's love is evident toward us.

IN THIS LESSON STUDENTS SHOULD:

- ○ Understand that love is more than an emotion.
- ○ Know that God loves them.
- ○ Learn that God desires that we respond in love to Him and others.

STUFF YOU NEED:

If you choose option 1
- ○ Advent wreath
- ○ Advent candles
- ○ Matches

STUFF YOU NEED:

If you choose to make cards:
- Names of those for whom you will be making cards
- Construction paper
- Markers
- Glitter stickers
- Glue

FOCUS

OPTION 1:

Say: Today is the fourth and final Sunday of Advent.

Have you ever noticed how as something big gets closer, the waiting gets harder? One week left—the anticipation builds as we remember the Creator of the universe who chose out of His love for us to step out of heaven and walk this earth.

Ask: Three Sundays have passed. Three themes have been covered. What are they?

(Hope, Peace, and Joy)

Say: As we have looked at the hope in God which moves us to consider the peace He desires, joy becomes our state of being. Hope, peace, and joy can all be wrapped into one very powerful concept.

Reader 1: 1 John 3:16

Reader 2: 1 John 4:7–9

Say: God chose to step out of heaven and come as a baby out of His love for us!

Have a volunteer pray asking that we realize the sacrifice love made. Pray that God is understood as love incarnate, far exceeding any emotion. While he or she is praying, light the first, second, third, and fourth candles. The candle of love joins the candle of hope, joy, and peace, helping to explain their presence!

OPTION 2:

Love Song Medley!

Break into groups of no more than five. Tell them they have five minutes to come up with as many songs as they can with the word love in the title. At the end of the five minutes, begin with a group and work your way around the room. Each group must offer one song with the word love in the title. Keep going around the room, having each group offer one without repeating what any other group has said. If a group repeats or gets stuck, they are out! (If it becomes clear using songs with the word love in the title is too difficult, have them choose songs with the word love in a line, and they must quote the line and title of the song.)

Offer a small prize to the winning group—candy, anything heart-shaped, mistletoe (ha ha), etc.

DISCOVERY

Split into four groups.

Group 1 reads Deuteronomy 6:4–9
What does it mean to love God in this way?

Group 2 reads Matthew 22:36–40
What does it mean to love God in this way?
What does it mean to love your neighbor?

Group 3 reads Mark 12:29–31
What does it mean to love God in this way?
What does it mean to love your neighbor?

Group 4 reads Luke 10:25–28
What does it mean to love God in this way?
What does it mean to love your neighbor?

Ask: What is the greatest commandment? The second greatest?

Do you think, if you really took these seriously, that these are reasonable?

Teacher's Note: In the Jewish tradition the passage in Deuteronomy is known as the Shema. It is among the most well-known scriptures and is repeated throughout one's lifetime. For many Jewish homes there is a small holder with a small piece of parchment inserted and attached to the doorpost of the front door. It is known as a mezuzah which actually means "doorpost." The scripture written on the mezuzah parchment is Deuteronomy 6:4–9. Deuteronomy 6:4 begins with Hear O Israel, the Lord our God, the Lord is One. The word "hear" transliterated is *shema*. It is so common, the entire mezuzah passage is often referred to in shorthand as the shema. The command in Deuteronomy 6:9 is practiced literally in obedience as a reminder of God's law and the people to whom they belong.

LIFE APPLICATION: On a whiteboard up front, create four columns: heart, mind, strength/might, soul.

Go through each columns and ask real life tangible ways where we can love God with all our heart, with all our mind, etc. Write each of these under the proper heading.

Ask: Does God request that we do our best knowing we are human?

Say: No! Jesus says not only are these commandments but these are it! If you had to get rid of all of the other commandments (and in Jewish tradition there are 613 laws or mitzvot!) these 2 would cover what is necessary. This giving *all* may seem extreme but in reality it removes the legalism and requires living out of who we were created to be.

Ask: Based on all that we have said up to this point, is love just an emotion?

If it is more than an emotion, what does that mean?

Say: Love is what remains long after the emotions have slipped away! God doesn't ask us to love Him only when we feel like it. He commands that we love Him with all that we are so that when our feelings fail, our mind can remind us to love Him, or when our strength fails, our hearts can still love.

Ask: What gets in our way of loving God with all we are?

What gets in our way of loving others with all we are?

MAKING IT PERSONAL: Say: Next week we celebrate that God Himself stepped out of heaven out of His love for us. We have just talked about how we are to love Him.

Ask: Do you believe you are loved by God? (Depending on your group, this may need to be a rhetorical question. If so, give a few moments for them to really think about their response.)

Do you live your life as one who is loved? If yes, how? If no, why not?

Close in prayer thanking God for His love, the very essence of who He is expressed toward each of us. Ask God that all may experience and know His love.

ANCIENT PRACTICE: Different traditions use the practice of greeting one another with a holy kiss in different ways. Most often, it is a way to greet, not connected to a time of chatting or hello. The time for chatting is reserved to the time prior or just after a service. This kiss reminds us of the love of Christ and the love we have for one another. First Peter 5:14 gives the biblical foundation for this practice.

MEMORY VERSE ACTIVITY

Brainstorm with your group ways to keep this memory verse before your eyes and in your thoughts. After all, Jesus declared this to be the greatest of commandments, it is worth our time. Consider having it written and placed somewhere in plain view for you.

This is also a great verse to learn by sign language. If you have someone available to teach your group, this is a great way to learn and remember this scripture.

CONNECTIONS: A clear connection between love and Christmas is in the song "Love Came Down at Christmas." Check your hymnals! If you don't have the capability for music, recite the words and discuss them line by line.

SONGS: "Show Your Love" by Jars of Clay on the album *Who We Are Instead*

Q U O T A B L E   Q U O T E S :

Love does not dominate; it cultivates.
                                              —Johann Wolfgang von Goethe

Love means to love that which is unlovable; or it is no virtue at all.
                                              —Gilbert K. Chesterton

Love —Midweek

MEMORY VERSE:
You shall love the LORD your God with all your heart, and with all your soul, and with all your might.—Deuteronomy 6:5 (NRSV)

SCRIPTURE: 1 John 4:7–9

LESSON IN A SENTENCE: God stepped into this world because of His love for His people.

FOCUS

A loving act can be offering notes of encouragement or simply acknowledgment! Adopt one or two classes of adults in your church as a youth group. Bring in construction paper, markers, glitter, stickers — whatever you can find! Explain to your group that you are going to collectively respond in love to the love God has given to you. Make cards for each member of those classes. (If you are really ambitious, you can check out a local nursing home as well and ask for the names of residents with family unable to visit or those who are truly left alone in this world.)

Encourage your students to write a note in their own words telling the recipient God is love and has come into the world for them!

Be certain you have a plan for delivering the cards in a timely manner!

DISCOVERY

Read 1 John 4:7–9

Ask: God loved us so much that He did what?

What is to be our reaction in relation to God's love?

Say: We can understand God by His love for us and we can understand love only because of God. It seems a bit confusing and can at times leave a few on the outside. Once you have experienced this true love, once you have experienced God, you know the two are inseparable.

Our love for Him is made possible only in that He first loved us.

Teacher's Note: This can be a tremendously difficult concept to really convey to students, but God is love. He does not fall in love (implying there was a time He was out of love). He IS love. He doesn't have to try to be loving nor try to maintain a loving way. It is simply

His essence. This means that all of His actions are loving—what He rules, what He chooses, what He allows, and what He judges are all loving. The hard part is when we don't understand His perspective (and most often we don't and won't!) He IS love and in the end, who He is manifests in what He does. Why else would He have chosen not to come and live on this earth, rather He chose to come humbled as a baby to die.

APPLICATION:

Ask: How does God loving us impact our loving anyone else?

Ask: How does Christmas relate to God loving us so that He was willing to come and die on a cross?

Jesus didn't come to live on earth and accidentally ended up dying on the cross. God knew exactly what would happen. He came knowing that His very presence would cause Himself pain and suffering not because he enjoy it but because He loved us so much it was worth it to Him!

Ask: Have you ever heard the phrase "love hurts"? What does this mean?

Say: Parents have to make decisions all of the time that inconvenience them or hurt them for the benefit of their children. One person breaks up with another not because they don't care but because they do and they know staying together will be bad for the person they love. It happens all of the time. When it happens to us, we most often do not recognize it. In fact, we often don't believe it!

Think of a time when you knew the right thing to do either would not benefit you at all or even more, that it would hurt you. What does it take to love someone so much that you are willing to get hurt yourself?

Close in prayer thanking God for His love. Thank Him for being willing to come to earth in human form, knowing that He would suffer pain and He was still willing to come! Christmas is just around the corner. We have been hoping and anticipating His arrival, longing for His peace, celebrating with joy, and offering back the very love He first offered to us.

DECEMBER 25, 2005

Christmas Glory

By Amy Jacober

MEMORY VERSE:
Arise, shine; for your light has come! And the glory of the LORD is risen upon you.—Isaiah 60:1 (NKJV)

SCRIPTURE: Luke 2:11–14; Isaiah 7:14, 9:6

LESSON IN A SENTENCE: Christmas is about God coming to the world.

THE BIG PICTURE (OR WHAT YOU'RE TRYING TO GET ACROSS):

Christmas brings with it images of a manger, a young family, and most certainly a baby. Interestingly, while God chose to come as a baby, that was not the main point. God chose to come. He chose to step out of heaven and humble Himself on this earth. It was in fulfillment of prophecy and in anticipation of reconciliation. There were several in His time who were aware of the importance of this event. They not only heard and understood, but it moved them to act. Today, Christmas is a time for us to remember, celebrate, and reflect on what God has done for us—but also to be reminded and renewed that we too have a role in this relationship. Christmas is about hope, peace, joy, and love. It is about God incarnate, the Christ.

IN THIS LESSON STUDENTS SHOULD:

- Define the word incarnation.
- Identify prophecies from the Old Testament fulfilled in the birth of Christ.
- Learn that Christmas is about more than a baby being born. It is about God coming to earth.

STUFF YOU NEED:

If you choose option 1
- Advent wreath
- Advent candles
- Matches

STUFF YOU NEED:

If you choose option 2
- ◯ An elaborately wrapped box with toilet paper inside

For memory verse activity
- ◯ Small candles (enough for each person in your group)
- ◯ Strips of paper with Isaiah 60:1 printed on it
- ◯ String to tie the strip of paper to a candle

FOCUS

OPTION 1:

Say: Christmas is here! It is no longer about the anticipation or the coming—it is here! The excitement is often confused with the world's view, the focus on gifts and family and special meals. The real focus however is that of Jesus Himself. God stepped out of heaven to come as a baby.

Ask: We have observed Advent for four Sundays. Four themes have been covered. What are they?

(Hope, Peace, Joy, and Love)

Say: Anticipation has built with each passing week beginning in hope, moving through peace, celebrating in joy, and reflecting on love. Today, the anticipation ends as we no longer talk about love but realize that love Himself came to the world.

Have a few volunteers read:

Reader 1: Isaiah 60:1

Reader 2: John 1:14

Say: The glory of God is indeed upon us this morning! May we not be blinded as the light comes to darkness. May our hearts realize the most precious gift of the day.

Have a volunteer pray praising God. Thank Him for the incredible sacrifice of leaving heaven just for us. While he or she is praying, light the first, second, third, fourth Advent candles and the center larger Christ candle. At the end of the prayer, point out to your students that the center candle has been lit. Christ is the light of the world!

OPTION 2:

Secret Santa
By Sarah Ware

A Secret Santa drawing takes an odd turn when somebody in the high school group draws the name "Jesus."

Running Time: 4–5 min.

Players (2–6): Nate—a high school student who isn't sure if he wants to be a Christian or not, but most of his friends are, so he's beginning to check it out for himself. Nate doesn't think he has anything to offer Jesus.

Mia—a high school student who has recently become a Christian. Although she wants to share Christ with her friend Nate, she often gets her stories mixed up and uses words he doesn't understand.

Friends—all of the people who participate in the Secret Santa drawing. This group of students may range from 1–4 people.

Props: 1 hat

1 piece of paper for each person participating in the Secret Santa drawing

(Mia, Eric, and their friends crowd into a circle onstage. Everyone's excited and anxiously talking to one another.)

Mia:	Okay! You know the rules. After you draw a name from the hat, fold it up and don't show anyone. I mean it! I want mine to be a surprise this year.
Nate:	Wait! How does this work again, Mia?
Mia:	We all put our names in this hat. Then we each draw one slip of paper. Then we all go out and buy a Christmas gift for the person whose name we draw. Get it?
Nate:	Yeah, I get it, but why are we doing this?
Mia:	So we don't have to buy everyone in the group a Christmas gift. Okay? Oh! And don't tell anyone what name you have. It's called Secret Santa for a reason.
Nate:	All right.
(Everyone draws names, scattering in different directions as they learn the identity of the one for whom they are to be a Secret Santa. Nate is left standing alone center stage. Mia is standing off to the side, talking with one of her friends.)	
Nate:	Okay—no one's looking. . . . (Nate looks at his slip of paper with astonishment. Frantically he looks around.) This has gotta be a joke! MIA! Hey Mia! Um . . . could you come here for a minute?
Mia:	Sure. (Mia says goodbye to her friend.)
Nate:	Is this some kind of joke?
Mia:	What?
Nate:	THIS! (He goes to show her the name on his paper, but she closes her eyes.)

Mia:	NO! I won't look! That's cheating, Nate!
Nate:	No! This has got to be a joke, or a mistake! Look! JESUS!
Mia:	(Gasp!) Don't you dare use the Lord's name in vain!
Nate:	NO! No, look! You don't understand—my Secret Santa name is Jesus!

(Mia looks and reads the name on Nate's slip of paper.)

Mia:	Oh! You did get JESUS! Huh—imagine that!
Nate:	"Huh?!" Are you serious?!
Mia:	Rules are rules, Nate. We drew names, and you got Jesus. Now you have to buy Jesus a Christmas gift.
Nate:	I can't buy Jesus a Christmas gift!
Mia:	NATE! Shhhhh! He'll hear you. (She points up.) This is supposed to be a secret.
Nate:	I can't do this.
Mia:	Why not?
Nate:	Well, I don't even know Jesus, . . . and (Mia interrupts him)
Mia:	Oh! That's okay! I'll tell you about Him! Jesus is the incarnation.
Nate:	(Really confused) He's in whose car?
Mia:	The incarnation.
Nate:	What does that . . . ?
Mia:	You know—He was the word and the word become flesh.
Nate:	Flesh?
Mia:	Yeah. He became flesh . . . um . . . we eat His body and drink His blood because . . . (Nate interrupts)
Nate:	Drink His blood? What?! Why?
Mia:	Because He was the incarnation. Christians do it to remember Jesus. You can do it too if . . .
Nate:	DUDE! I don't even like sharing drinks with my friends, and you want me to be drinkin' somebody else's BLOOD?
Mia:	Well, sure . . .
Nate:	Even if Jesus is in . . . um . . . the nation of cars . . . I mean . . . Oh, nevermind!
Mia:	Look, whether you know Jesus or not, you have to give Him a gift. It's the rules.
Nate:	What kind of a gift do you give Jesus?
Mia:	Your heart, of course!
Nate:	My heart? Thanks, but I think I'm going to be needing mine.

Mia: I'm serious, Nate.

Nate: I'm being serious too, Mia. I have nothing to give Jesus.
           NOTHING.

(Long pause)

Mia: Exactly.

DISCOVERY

Read Isaiah 7:14 and 9:6.

Ask: What light do these two passages shed on Christmas?

Say: We have been saying for several weeks now that Christmas was about God stepping out of heaven and coming to the earth. The word for this is the incarnation—a big fancy term that reminds us that Jesus was indeed God in human form.

Read Luke 2:1–20.

Before you begin reading, remind your students this is more than just a familiar story. It is the story of the incarnation. As this story is read, listen for one thing you have never heard before. Listen for a new perspective that may have particular meaning at this time in your life.

(Many of your students will have heard the story of Christmas before, even those who do not often attend church. The struggle can be in the story not becoming mundane. We can all become callous in handling the holy!)

You may need to read this several times.

Teacher's Note: The very name of Christmas is itself a reminder of the holiness embedded in the "holy"day. Christmas comes from Christ's mass, the celebration of Christ or celebration of the Messiah. In the birth of Jesus, we recognize the Savior of the world come to earth.

LIFE APPLICATION: Ask: What stood out to you this time? (Your students may need help thinking in this new way.) Did the details of the prophecies stand out? Was it the miracle of circumstances to have a census at this specific time? Was it the realization that Jesus did not have a place to fit in at the beginning of His life, just as they sometimes do not feel like they fit in?

Re-read verses 11–14.

Again, re-read verse 11.

For today in the city of David there has been born for you a Savior, who is Christ the Lord.   Luke 2:11 (NASB)

Say: Today we celebrate the birth of Jesus, the birth of a Savior.

Ask: What did it take for Jesus to be the Savior?

Have you ever considered that the baby we celebrate today came to be crucified?

Ask: How could this shift our perspective at Christmas time? How could this shift our practices on this holiday?

MAKING IT PERSONAL: Say: God chose to come. He chose out of His love for you. He left the comforts of heaven, entered this world knowing that in a few short years He would be crucified.

Ask: What does this mean for you personally?

Say: Christmas is full of traditions, of family and happiness. It is full of joy and hope and peace and love! While understanding the reality of the birth of God, we cannot escape His crucifixion. More importantly, His resurrection! It was because He is love that He came.

MEMORY VERSE ACTIVITY

Before your time together, print the memory verse on a strip of paper. Tie this paper to a candle that you will give each person at the close of your lesson together.

CONNECTIONS: The incarnation is not just a theological term. It is supported in many places in Scripture, including: John 1:14; Romans 1:3–4; Romans 8:3; Galatians 4:4; Philippians 2:6–8; 1 Timothy 3:16; 1 John 4:2; and 2 John 7.

SONGS: "New Song" by Ginny Owens on the album *Beautiful*

QUOTABLE   QUOTES :

I will honor Christmas in my heart, and try to keep it all the year.

—Charles Dickens

We consider Christmas as the encounter, the great encounter, the historical encounter, the decisive encounter, between God and mankind. He who has faith knows this truly; let him rejoice.

—Pope Paul VI

Christmas Glory —Midweek

MEMORY VERSE:
Arise, shine; for your light has come! And the glory of the LORD is risen upon you.—Isaiah 60:1 (NKJV)

SCRIPTURE: Luke 2:15–20

LESSON IN A SENTENCE: Christmas is about God coming to the world.

FOCUS

As your students arrive, prepare the following: Have several bowls filled with water placed on tables, with chairs for your students around the table. In the center of the table have the bowl, a pepper shaker, a cotton swab, and a small puddle of liquid dish soap on a plate.

Ask: Have you ever experienced something where you simply had no choice but to react?

Tell each group to sprinkle a lot of pepper on the surface of the water in the bowl. Ask: What happens? (At most, a few flakes fall below the surface.)

Now, take the cotton swab and roll it in the dish soap. Use this to barely touch the surface of the water.

Ask: What happens? (The pepper will have two reactions. Part of it will fall to the bottom of the bowl, part of it will spread to the sides of the bowl. None of it holds still.)

DISCOVERY

Say: Christmas was this week. The waiting is over. We have celebrated the coming of God to this world.

Read Luke 2:8–20.

Ask: What did the shepherds do as soon as they heard about the birth of Jesus?

APPLICATION: Say: Just like the pepper had an immediate reaction to the dish soap, there is an immediate reaction when one encounters Christ. Some run far, some draw close. There is no way to encounter Jesus and not leave changed.

Ask: Could you imagine hearing about the birth of a baby and being told He was to be the Savior of the world? How would you react if you were told this today?

Say: While we may not encounter God in the flesh, we can encounter (and many of us do encounter) God daily.

Ask: Christmas has just occurred. Christ has come. What will you do different this year as a result of encountering the living God?

Close thanking God for His birth, for His love, for His sacrifice. This is indeed still a season to celebrate and rejoice!

Christian Music Resources

www.acaza.com—Offers current news on Christian artists.

www.ccmcom.com—Provides up-to-date news on today's hottest contemporary Christian musicians.

www.christianitytoday.com/music/—Reviews new Christian music and provides interviews with the artists.

www.cmcentral.com—Christian Music Central offers visitors the chance to view editorials on music and artists, shows album and artist reviews, lists tour dates, and offers MP3 downloads.

www.christianradio.com—Christian Radio gives a list of over 2,000 Christian radio stations as well as over 500 Christian artists.

www.christianrock.net—Christian Rock is a 24–hour radio show broadcast on the internet. Christian Rock has two sister stations:

http://www.christianhardrock.net/

http://www.christian-hiphop.net/

www.worshiptogether.com—Provides a great overview of what is hot is Christian music by offering top ten lists, free downloads, and more.

www.youthfire.com/music/compare.html—Youth Fire is a great website to refer to when looking for Christian music that is comparable to what is played daily on mainstream radio.

Curriculum Resources

www.augsburgfortress.org

www.Cokesbury.com

www.cookministries.com

www.grouppublishing.com

www.helwys.com

www.lifeway.com

www.standardpub.com

www.studentlife.net

www.thomasnelson.com

www.tyndale.com

www.upperroom.org

www.urbanministries.com

www.zondervan.com

Games

www.egadideas.com —Offers a directory of indoor and outdoor games for your youth group to play.

wwwfunattic.com—A site dedicated to games of all sorts, for all age groups.

ferryhalim.com/orisinal —A whole host of silly internet games.

www.thesource4ym.com—Provides a huge collection games for youth groups ranging from mixers to swimming pool games.

www.youthministry.com—Offers games that are just for fun, for large and small groups, noncompetitive, and that illustrate a point.

Human/Social Resources

www.adopting.org—Adopt is a website designer to offer assistance, information, and support for adoption.

www.aspenyouth.com—This is a website that provides information about Aspen Youth Ranches which provide education, treatment, and rehabilitation to at-risk youth.

www.breakawayoutreach.com—Breakaway Youth is a ministry that reaches troubled youth through juvenile justice ministries, sports, and multimedia productions.

www.cpsdv.org/index.html—Formerly the Center for the Prevention of Sexual and Domestic Violence, now the FaithTrust Institute. This organization seeks to educate and prevent sexual and domestic violence and is the only one of its kind in the country looking at this from a faith perspective.

www.goshen.net/directory/Teens/—Provides numerous links for youth pastors and youth who are struggling with crisis issues such as suicide, drugs and alcohol, and much more.

www.rainn.org—Rainn is the website to a confidential 24–hour rape hotline.

www.vpp.com/teenhelp—VPP provides a national toll-free hotline designed to assist parents, childcare professionals, and others in finding resources for the treatment of struggling youth.

Magazines

www.briomag.com—Brio is a magazine that is made for teenage girls that wishes to teach, entertain, and challenge girls while encouraging them to grow in a closer relationship with Christ.

www.gp4teens.com—Guideposts for Teens is similar to the original Guideposts magazine for adults. Guideposts for Teens tackles real issues such as sex, dating, faith, and spirituality.

www.pluggedinonline.com—Plugged In is designed to help parents, youth leaders, ministers and teens to both understand and impact the culture that they live in. Plugged In offers reviews and discussions regarding entertainment and its effects on youth and families.

www.relevantmagazine.com—A magazine for considering God and progressive culture.

Missions and Service

www.amnesty.org—A worldwide group seeking to end human rights violations.

www.amor.org—A missions agency specializing in trips to northern Mexico.

www.apu.edu/iom/mexout Mexico Outreach.—A ministry based out of Azusa Pacific University taking high school and young adult groups into northern Mexico for service.

www.agrm.org—Association of Gospel Rescue Missions. An associational website that links to local missions. Missions typically provide shelter, kitchens, community development, and community centers.

www.asphome.org—Appalachia Service Project, a ministry that takes other groups on week-long mission trips to Kentucky and Tennessee to repair homes for the poor.

www.bread.org—Bread for the World. A lobbying group to Congress which provides study materials for high schoolers.

www.compassion.com—Compassion International. World Relief organization with programs that can educate and involve junior and senior high students.

www.gospelcom.net/csm—Center for Student Missions. A ministry offering customized mission trips to large cities for junior and senior high students.

www.childrensdefense.org—Children's Defense Fund. They offer materials on the needs of American children, in particular the poor, for use in churches.

www.esa-online.org—Evangelicals for Social Action. Publishers of a wide array of Bible-based materials on social justice.

www.habitat.org—Habitat for Humanity. Provides housing for low-income families with many service opportunities.

www.joniandfriends.org—An excellent (and one of the only) resource for ministry with those with disabilities.

www.jmpf.org—John Perkins Foundation. Social Justice and service.

www.mcc.org—Mennonite Central Committee. The relief and development agency of the Mennonite and Brethren in Christ churches.

www.newadventures.org—Missions organization providing trips for junior and senior high school students.

Pop Culture

www.christianitytoday.com—Provides a good way to identify with Christian youth and their beliefs, by giving current detailed reviews on movies and music, and provides discussion questions.

www.cpyu.org—Center for Parent and Youth Understanding. A comprehensive site with constant updates covering youth culture from many angles.

www.dickstaub.com—Pop culture review from a Christian perspective.

www.hollywoodjesus.com—A Christians source that offers Christian perspectives of today's pop culture. You'll find reviews for today's newest movies, music, and much more.

www.mrfh.cjb.net—(Screen it Entertainment Reviews)—Offers a detailed description of what viewers will see i.e. violence, sex, bad language in current movies, and why the MPAA rated the movie the way they did.

www.rollingstone.com—Update yourself on what youth are watching and hearing in today's secular media. This source reviews movies and particularly secular music, providing CD reviews, photos, and videos of today's pop stars.

www.screenit.com—Screen It offers reviews on all sorts of entertainment.

www.textweek.com—Gives sermon topics stemming from current and past movies.

www.tollbooth.org—An online magazine that provides reviews of Christian music, concerts, and books. Also provides reviews of past movies.

Spiritual Disciplines

www.lectiodevina.org—A site offering articles and explanations into the practice of lectio devina.

www.sfts.edu—San Francisco Theological Seminary has a Lilly endowed program called the Youth Ministry and Spirituality Project. Many insights and resources available.

www.sdiworld.org—The directory of Spiritual Directors International.

www.taize.fr —Taize site for the Taize community in France.

www.labyrinth.co.uk—Connected with Jonny Baker, the most commonly known labyrinth among youth workers.

Worship Resources

www.audiblefaith.com—Audible Faith offers downloadable worship music and sheet music can be ordered from this website in any key.

www.ccli.com—CCLI is a strong communication network that allows the dispensing of comprehensive and valuable informational resources about worship.

www.christianguitar.org—Christian Guitar is a fantastic Christian guitar resource page with over 7,000 tabs. Christian Guitar also offers lessons, PowerPoint slides, and message boards.

www.heartofworship.com—Heart of Worship features Bible insights and other resources for worship and worship leaders.

www.integritymusic.com—Integrity Music offers a number of different worship resources that include information on artists, albums, and much more.

www.maranathamusic.com—Maranatha Music offers a number of resources for worship and worship leaders.

www.pastornet.net.au/inside—Inside Out offers free downloadable contemporary and evangelical worship music for non-commercial use.

www.songs4worship.com—Song 4 Worship offers numerous worship resources including music, community, freebies and more.

www.worshipmusic.com—Worship Music is a Christian music resource with CDs, cassettes, sheet/print music, videos, software, and more for sale.

Youth Activities

www.30hourfamine.org—30 Hour Famine is a movement led by World Vision that fights world hunger with the help of youth and churches all around the world.

www.adventures.org—Adventures in Missions is an interdenominational short-term missions organization that offers programs for youth, college, and adults.

www.bigworld.org—Big World Ventures offers customized short-term mission trips for youth, adults, individuals, groups, church networks, and Christian organizations. This website provides information regarding all trips and destinations.

www.thejeremiahproject.org—The Jeremiah Project offers missions trips that are planned specifically for Jr. High youth.

www.worldvision.org/worldvision/master.nsf—World Vision is an organization that provides relief to third world countries by reaching out to the poor, and staying aware of current worldwide events.

www.ywam.org—YWAM Urban Ministries is an organization that attempts to bring safe and exciting events to communities in need through innovative ministries and living with the people in the community.

www.noahsark.com—Noah's Ark is located in Colorado, offering a uniquely Christian perspective on whitewater rafting, rock climbing, rappelling, and a whole lot more!

Youth Pastor-Emergent

www.emergentvillage.com—Resources and links for missional Christians across generations.

www.emergingchurch.org—Connecting point for intentionally postmodern thinking churches.

www.churchnext.net/index.shtml—Tribal Generation. A loose look at many topics from a Christian perspective.

www.theooze.com—Online magazine that looks to any and all issues bringing them into a conversation within a Christian community.

Youth Pastor Resources

www.biblegateway.com—A collection of several translations of the Bible online.

www.discipleshipresources.org/downloads.asp—Free discipleship downloads from the United Methodist Church.

www.family.org—Provides articles that help parents know how to better deal with their growing children and changing families. Offers advice and wisdom for the ups and downs of family life.

www.highwayvideo.com—Highway video offers culturally relevant videos to be used in ministry and worship.

www.hmconline.org—A resource for urban youth leaders provides information on up-coming training sessions that help youth leaders become more efficient in their ministry with urban youth.

www.parentministry.org—Provides youth workers with articles that help build a stronger family-based ministry, and offers parents helpful articles for understanding their adolescent children.

www.persecution.com—A site offering updates and prayer requests regarding the persecuted church around the world.

www.reach-out.org—A resource for youth leaders that presents, find books, articles, Bible studies, illustrations, ideas for training volunteers, and insight into leading a successful missions trip.

www.uywi.org—A ministry offering trainings for those specifically working in urban settings.

www.yfc.org—Provides current information youth ministries for youth pastors, youth, and parents.

www.younglife.org—Offers information about Young life and its work with today's youth.

www.youthbuilders.com—A resource for parents and youth leaders offering articles, answered questions that help parents and youth leaders better understand how to work with and relate to the youth in their lives.

www.youthpastor.com—Provides youth pastors with articles, games, youth group names,

Recommended reading, topical music resource, and more.

www.youthspecialties.com/links—This website offers thousands of links to websites on leadership, missions, skit ideas, crisis hotlines, and much more.

www.youthworkers.net—A resource that allows youth workers to be able to connect with each other by region. Also provides links to activities that youth nation-wide participate in.

SUBJECT INDEX

SCRIPTURE INDEX

Compare
and
Contrast—

Before there was *Nelson's Annual Youth Ministry Sourcebook* there was *Nelson's Annual Preacher's Sourcebook*. Like its offspring, the *Preacher's Sourcebook* provides weekly worship resources for the church. Its focus, however, is on the preacher's sermon.

In designing the *Youth Ministry Sourcebook*, the editors made a serious effort to coordinate the weekly themes with the *Preacher's Sourcebook* wherever feasible. When these themes coincide, you will experience the happy serendipity of reinforcement between the youth worship and the church's corporate worship. In the 2005 edition of the *Preacher's Sourcebook* you will find the sermon supplemented by appropriate hymns, illustrative material, prayers, and responsive readings. These can provide you with additional resources even if your pastor chooses not to use that week's suggestion for his sermon.

Sometimes the editors felt that the developmental needs of youth cried out for alternative themes to be addressed at certain times of the year. We believe that you, as a worker committed to strengthening the spiritual lives of youth, will understand and support their decisions.

While you are comparing and contrasting the two books, check out the features scattered throughout the *Preacher's Sourcebook* (ISBN 0785252002). Many of them speak to the lives of all kinds of ministers.

1. Minimum System Requirements
   Computer/Processor
      Intel Pentium III or AMD Athlon with CD-ROM Drive
   Operating System
      Windows 98 SE, Window ME, Windows 2000, or
      Windows XP including all Windows Updates
   Memory
      128MB RAM
   Hard Drive Space
      250 MB Minimum
   Screen Resolution
      800x600 or Higher

2. Contact Information
   Technical Support
   Email:nelsoncdtech@thomasnelson.com
   Web: www.nelsonreference.com
   Phone: (615) 902-2440
   Fax: (615) 902-2450

SOFTWARE LICENSE AGREEMENT

CAREFULLY READ THE FOLLOWING TERMS AND CONDITIONS BEFORE USING THIS SOFTWARE. Using this SOFTWARE indicates your acceptance of these terms and conditions. If you are not in agreement, promptly return the SOFTWARE package unused with your receipt and your money will be refunded.

LICENSE

The SOFTWARE may be used on a single machine at a time. This is a copyrighted software program and may not be copied, duplicated, or distributed except for the purpose of backup by the licensed owner.

The SOFTWARE may be copied into any machine-readable or printed form for backup, modification, or normal usage in support of the SOFTWARE on the single machine.

You may transfer the SOFTWARE and license to another party if the other party agrees to accept the terms and conditions of this Agreement. If you transfer the SOFTWARE, you must either transfer all copies, whether in printed or machine-readable form, to the same party or destroy any copies not transferred; this includes all modifications and portions of the SOFTWARE contained or merged into other software and/or software programs.

You may not use, copy, alter, or otherwise modify or transfer the SOFTWARE or database(s) or any add-on product's text except as expressly provided for in this LICENSE.

If you transfer possession of any copy or modifications of the SOFTWARE to another party, except as expressly provided for in the LICENSE, your license thereupon is automatically terminated.

LIMITED SOFTWARE WARRANTY

LIMITED WARRANTY. *Nelson Electronic Publishing* warrants that, for ninety (90) days from the date of receipt, the computer programs contained in the SOFTWARE will perform substantially. Any implied warranties on the SOFTWARE are limited to ninety (90) days. Some jurisdictions do not allow limitations on the duration of an implied warranty, so the above limitation may not apply to you.

CUSTOMER REMEDIES. *Nelson Electronic Publishing's* entire liability and your exclusive remedy shall be, at our option, either (a) return of the price paid or (b) repair or replacement of SOFTWARE that does not meet *Nelson Electronic Publishing's* Limited Warranty and that is returned to us with a copy of your receipt. This Limited Warranty is void if failure of the SOFTWARE has resulted from accident, abuse, or misapplication. Any replacement SOFTWARE will be warranted for the remainder of the original warranty period or thirty (30) days, whichever is longer. Outside the United States, neither these remedies nor any product support services are available without proof of purchase from an authorized non-U.S. source.

NO OTHER WARRANTIES. To the maximum extent permitted by applicable law, *Nelson Electronic Publishing* and its suppliers disclaim all other warranties, either expressed or implied, including, but not limited to, implied warranties of merchantability and fitness for a particular purpose, with regard to the SOFTWARE and the accompanying written materials. This Limited Warranty gives you specific legal rights. You may have others, which vary from state to state.

NO LIABILITY FOR CONSEQUENTIAL DAMAGES. To the maximum extent permitted by applicable law, in no event shall *Nelson Electronic Publishing* or its suppliers be liable for any damages whatsoever (including, without limitations, damages for loss of business profits, business interruption, loss of business information, or any other pecuniary loss) arising out of the use of or inability to use this product, even if *Nelson Electronic Publishing* has been advised of the possibility of such damages. Because some states do not allow the exclusion of liability for consequential or accidental damages, the above limitation may not apply to you.